That Might Be Useful

Books by Naton Leslie

Marconi's Dream

Egress

The Last Best Motif

Salvaged Maxims

Moving to Find Work

Their Shadows Are Dark Daughters

That Might Be Useful

Exploring America's Secondhand Culture

Naton Leslie

The Lyons Press
Guilford, Connecticut
An imprint of The Globe Pequot Press

The Lyons Press is an imprint of The Globe Pequot Press.

10 9 8 7 6 5 4 3 2 1

Printed in United States of America

Library of Congress Cataloging-in-Publication Data

Leslie, Naton.
   That might be useful : exploring America's secondhand culture / Naton Leslie.
      p. cm.
   ISBN 1-59228-705-0 (trade cloth)
   1. Flea markets—United States. 2. Secondhand trade—United States.
I. Title.
HF5482.15.L47 2005
306.3'4—dc22

                                                    2005002294

Contents

Introduction

❧

The Many Lives of Discards

BUILT FOR COAL MINERS A CENTURY BEFORE, the house I was renting in Athens, Ohio, had a long lineage of tenants, and the cellar was crammed with stuff people had left behind. One day I saw a small oak chest of drawers under some boxes against the back wall. I needed one, so I called my landlord to ask if I could use it. She gave it to me. When I moved to the Cincinnati area, about three hours away, I took the chest with me. I liked its square, unadorned lines, and when I refinished it the wood turned lustrous. I also found a set of casters to replace the ones its legs had needed, so the three-drawer chest stood at its proper height. Next I moved it to upstate New York, where I used it for another seven years.

In 1997 I sold a house in New York I had bought, repaired, and filled with furniture, all secondhand. The chest of drawers, after a decade of service and moving about, needed more work. The top had split, a victim of temperature changes, and the drawer bottoms had bowed out. I could have fixed it, but I needed a bigger chest, so I set it in the front yard when I held a yard sale. I'd find another chest of drawers easily enough.

Early that morning a man in a long brown van pulled up and walked straight to the chest. I had priced it at $55; it was well made, with solid wood and dovetail-joined drawers. "You can't get more than $45 for that," he said, an angry edge to his voice, pointing to its split top. He looked like he had been awake since dawn, with darkly circled eyes and coffee-stained, rumpled clothes. He was an early bird; I had been told such characters would be the first at my sale, looking to pick up the choice items.

I should have held out for the full price. It was too soon in the sale to dicker, but I didn't care; I simply didn't want to fix or move the chest again. I took his money, and he carried the chest to the side door of his van. The interior was already chock-a-block with furniture, and I wondered if he had bought all of it that morning. He loaded the chest, banged the sliding van door shut, and rumbled away.

Two weeks later I visited a friend who refinished and sold used and antique furniture to see if he had a chest I might buy. He did. He had the one I had sold in my front yard. He had bought it at the big antique show in Brimfield, Massachusetts, and the guy who sold it to him was a "picker," someone who finds and resells antiques at a small profit. When he described the man, I recognized him as the guy who had bought it from me.

I had assumed the man had been a full-fledged antique dealer; I had never heard of pickers. My friend had paid $65 for the chest. The picker had known he couldn't pay the $55 I had asked and even cover the cost of the gasoline it took to find it and take it to Massachusetts. I noticed he had fixed the top, neatly clamping and gluing the split closed.

When my friend told me a month later he had fixed the drawer bottoms and sold the chest for $110 to an antique dealer from New Jersey, something about the nature of the used merchandise trade became clear to me. The piece slowly had been repaired, had increased in price, and now had reached its highest value; the dealer would probably price it at $225. After a while, if it didn't sell, he would take it to an auction and at least get his $110 back, and probably make a small profit for his trouble. In the process it had moved through five states, and it would keep moving. How far had it traveled before landing in the basement of the house in Ohio? As long as someone was ready to sell it, and another buy it, as long as fixing whatever ailed it increased its worth, the chest would never lose its intrinsic value as a good, solid piece of secondhand oak furniture.

As a result of never having much money, and in rejection of what I saw as rampant materialism, I decided years ago to buy only secondhand goods when I needed something. This is not always possible, of course, as buying used is time-consuming and finding what you need is less than certain. However, I have found a wealth of other benefits beyond mere thrift. In the secondhand culture I have discovered the joys of a genuine American market, unfettered buying and selling, which most first-level retailing has lost.

While retailers have moved out of downtowns and into malls, and then out of malls and into big-box stores like Wal-Mart and Target, secondhand commerce has remained in communities, locally owned and operated, and off the radar screen of giant corporations. Aggressive chain stores might undercut the prices of owner-operated groceries or pharmacies, driving them out of business, but not even Sam Walton's minions have discovered how to corral and mass-market the swelling abundance of used goods. Likewise, no one can successfully quantify this commerce in big numbers like billions per year or percentage of gross national product. Sales tax records from antique stores and auctions might give some measure, but the many thousands of daily transactions made under the table, through yard sales, flea markets, and other less visible settings, are unquantifiable. Secondhand commerce is ungovernable and thankfully so.

Buying secondhand is a personal affair. Entranceway greeters notwithstanding, new retailing is faceless; for the most part, customers serve themselves, aided by overhead signs and well-organized merchandise. Soon, if the trend toward a cashless society continues, we will not even get a "thank you" when paying our money. Clerkless debit-card lines are appearing, and the personal touch is going the way of the bank teller or gas pump attendant. Buying used goods, in contrast, is a gregarious enterprise. From haggling to appraising the flaws and virtues of an item for sale, used buying and selling is more akin to the traditional bazaar; it's no wonder flea markets or swap meets thrive in areas with large numbers of new immigrants from cultures that still have vibrant and personal marketplaces.

Whether in the antique trade or holding a once-a-year yard sale, most of the sellers I have met agree that meeting people is part of the attraction. Few besides the management care if you come back to big retail stores. I have never seen the same clerk twice in my infrequent forays there, and I've yet to make their acquaintances, despite name tags. Try this sometime. The next time you are buying groceries, read the clerk's name tag and after the cursory "Thank you," say "You're welcome, [Amanda or Russell]." He or she will probably look at you—for the first time—with an expression telegraphing that you have cracked some secret code, breached some invisible wall. In contrast, I know dozens of antique dealers, junk sellers, and flea marketeers, and I count some as friends. Many used goods merchants will not only learn your name but your phone number, too, the better to contact you if they have found something they think you might want.

The popularity of yard sales, flea markets, and antique and collectibles stores is not a new phenomenon. It is a cultural rediscovery. Reusing, recycling, and redistributing surplus goods has long been a central practice of most societies. Gleaning the fields, the practice of harvesting what others have overlooked, is at least as old as the Old Testament story of Ruth meeting her husband Boaz while gleaning behind the reapers during the wheat and barley harvest in Bethlehem, a story scholars think dates to 3,500 years ago. Likewise, archaeologists have found recycled and used merchandise as part of the cargoes of ancient ships lost in the Mediterranean. Throughout the ages metalworkers have been the ultimate reusers, and some of the most coveted pieces among antique tool collectors are those made by blacksmiths that show the iron had been part of another tool, such as a file. Likewise, though not as chronicled as the new mercantile class, used goods dealers undoubtedly plied the streets of Amsterdam and Venice, hawking wares discarded by Renaissance nobles and burghers. Lacking the glamour of spice or silk, used merchandise has sustained generations of common folk who did not get first pick from the next East India Company ship.

Leaving part of the harvest in the field for the gleaners was even required by Judaic law, and such redistribution and reuse is common in many other countries. In France, for instance, the *bricoleur* is a do-it-yourselfer, but also an improviser, especially with unlikely materials. The concept is so common, a popular chain of hardware stores is named *Le Bricoleur*. In America, farmers and others in rural or frontier areas have long been bricoleurs, and in my own family, with roots in Appalachian culture, surrounding yourself with heaps of castoffs and scrap materials was a way of life. My grandfather straightened bent nails and hoarded used lumber, while my father liked to accumulate miscellaneous hardware so he might improvise, fixing something without spending money on materials or hiring a professional. Many traditional American crafts are rooted in reuse, such as quilting or making rag rugs, which all of the women in my family made; in fact, exceptional beauty has been created in these media *because* the materials were castoffs. Likewise, passing down even common household goods from generation to generation was routine. No auctioneer was needed unless kin did not step forward to claim it all. Before we were a new-consumer culture, we were a hand-me-down culture.

Americans, I have discovered, are not naturally wasteful. We are by nature scavengers rather than monied consumers. Following trends and fashions has been turned only lately into a corporate cash cow—a phenomenon of the past hundred years. Throughout the 1900s we craved, or were told we needed, the new model car, the new computer, the newest style of clothing, the most coveted toy. We have wanted it all, often because the technological advances of the last century have meant the newest product would incrementally improve our lives. Despite these bells and whistles, the most efficient buying trigger has been the fad. Wall Street and its advance guard, Madison Avenue, have spent billions identifying or creating fads, and then on devising ways to capitalize on them. Genuine advancements in science or technology aside, fickle public taste is the greatest source of market income.

Retailers have noticed the appeal of the used merchandise market and have made some inroads in the collectibles market. Although they obviously can't mass-market old merchandise, they can artificially create collectibles. The Beanie Babies craze was one of the most lucrative and ingenious marketing strategies of the 1990s. "Retiring" individual animals in their product line, Ty Warner watched as months-old stuffed animals were selling among collectors for hundreds of dollars. In 1997, the biggest year of the craze, Beanies bought at the beginning of the year, and then retired after a few weeks, were selling for up to $5,000 at year's end, a 1,000 percent increase! This, of course, drove up the demand for the next design, with the anticipation that these would also increase in value over such a short time span.

This phenomenon had many of the features of the collectibles trade: limited supply, increasing prices, a variety of specimens of a kind of thing, and discriminations based on condition and rarity. However, Ty Warner had managed to compress the time frame to a ridiculously brief length through their preset retirement schedule. Collectors waited like brides for the next release, when vendors would paste makeshift signs on their storefronts announcing BEANIES ARE HERE! Collecting is an irrational enterprise, a need based on nothing but need itself, and is exactly the kind of response new retailers crave. Called "mystique marketing," such selling campaigns rarely work so well.

When Ty Warner quit making Beanies, I assume the company knew the fad had run its course, that the man behind the curtain would soon be exposed, a revelation that would have been as devastating as when the tulip market collapsed during the craze in the 1600s for what we now know were diseased and deformed blossoms. While entire fortunes were lost by tulip bulb speculators, much less economic disaster followed the Beanie bust; the worst I have seen are collectors balefully trying to sell tables full of the cutesy toys at yard sales and flea markets. Perhaps some-day they will become true collectibles, when enough have been thrown away that they are rare, like the original teddy bear. Now, though, Beanie Babies are nothing but nearly worthless bits of fluff.

Those are the exceptions to the separation between new and used merchandising. Mostly, people who sell new have stuck with promoting a new-is-better aesthetic. It was easy to advocate such a maxim after World War II, when the population was emerging from a decade and a half of depression and war rationing into an economic boom. An antique dealer told me that people's taste in antiques skips a generation, that people are attracted to what their grandparents had owned. A love of antiques entirely skipped the generation that grew up in the 1930s and 1940s; they had been living with their grandparents' stuff for their whole lives, and they desperately wanted new stuff. And the marketplace happily supplied them.

This was my parents' generation, and perhaps my buying used is sim-ply a generational rejection of their values. However, I never bought into the new-is-better culture, even as a child when I was fully respondent to its pitches. My mother, for instance, when commenting on some pur-chase with obvious shortcomings in quality, would always say, "Well, at least it's new," as though its lack of age was an irrefutable quality, one that explained away all other flaws. My father made the same pronounce-ments, usually about cars, which for him were leading symbols of status, a renewable status as you could make another great leap upward every three or so years. This status is quantifiable. Buy a new car for $30,000, drive it for 5,000 miles, and the same car, virtually unchanged, is now worth $25,000. That immediate depreciation—that $5,000—is the price tag of status.

If asked to explain their love of the newest, my parents would grasp at straws; the corporate world had succeeded in persuading them to need something without a concrete reason. Finally, though, my mother would say, "It's new, so it's clean and neat." The coupling of these attributes is not accidental. Advertising for new products in the 1950s stressed both cleanliness and order. Recall, for instance, the gleaming, geometric kitchens or the streamlined cars and furniture, all bearing the stamp of science, the promise of progress. "New" meant we were advancing, and nothing has ever appealed to Americans more than the forward march of their own cultural momentum. Likewise, cleanliness and order suggest higher powers at work. Cleanliness is next to godliness, as the old adage would have it, and order is divine, especially when contrasted with the chaos of world economic disaster or war. Buying a new refrigerator or lawn mower was a morally intact gesture. It was simply the "right" thing to do.

Not content to have so righteously motivated consumers, postwar product designers realized other factors would have to come into play if people were going to keep buying/discarding/buying. Planned obsolescence was the next reason to buy new. Now something was not only out of fashion, it was nearly worn out. At first we didn't notice, but slowly appliances and cars were made with thinner-gauge steel, rusting more easily; furniture was made with wood screws that would eventually strip, instead of age-old joinery; and where a double stitch was required in clothing, a single stitch now sufficed. "Nothing lasts like it once did," was the consumer refrain, but people kept cheerfully buying anyway, again and again.

However, obsolescence began to fuel the growing fascination with old goods as, by comparison, they revealed their qualities. Even my mother began to gather a few antiques, remarking upon the "real" wood of the old lamp stand or rocking chair she got from her mother or mother-in-law or the elegance of old dishes. To this day, though, my mother has never purchased an antique; she prefers to get them in the traditional, hand-me-down fashion. However, she refers to these things as "heirlooms," a label that erases, in her mind, the stigma of owning used goods. She has never abandoned her allegiance to the new.

By the time we realized that planned obsolescence was degrading everything we were buying in the 1960s, the culture had become so hardwired to consumerism that we didn't care if we had been duped. Wanting the new had been so unquestioned that, even now, proposing more things should be recycled or reused is seen as a left-leaning, environmentalist idea. Our national economic health demands that we spend money. High capitalism, the only game in the global village, needs such constant purchasing as fuel for expansion.

New Coke aside, many new products do offer improvements. However, such a disconnect exists between "new" and "improved" that federal regulations now prescribe when a manufacturer can use the words in advertising. If we want something, generally that thing is bigger (Something automatically equated with "improved"). We crave the ever-more-bloated sport utility vehicle, the more opulent house. This is another Gilded Age, but one silvered by our inattention to real quality, real value. While new houses might imitate older Victorian manors, they are, like the furniture that generally fills them, all appearance. The substance, the fine wood and cut stone of a classic mid-nineteenth-century house, would be too expensive even for our affluent society. We are the richest country on Earth, but in many ways this wealth has created nothing more than a Potemkin village, a village of facades.

Still, we eschew last season's goods with a moral certitude. We know better now; we are superior to those old fads. The evolution of taste is considered to be an improvement, which is a perception as flawed as assuming any evolution is aimed toward a positive goal. What we ignore is how our tastes are influenced by marketeers. Learning what youths want and then convincing them to want it more, is the essence of "cool"; millions of dollars are spent in pursuit of the most up-to-date definition of this quicksilver concept. In truth, "cool" is a compromise between advertiser and consumer. The advertiser might declare a trend, but the buyer has to agree to follow it. We have, as the poet William Blake declared, "mind-forged manacles."

In light of this mass manipulation, I have found the secondhand consumer culture refreshingly free. Although the culture of reuse includes the familiar realm of used cars and book dealers, I have not included them here, because they are probably the most regulated and predictable parts of the trade. Instead I have looked at those peddling and buying everything else, an entire reactive subculture that waits for what no longer captures our present-tense attention or fills our mercurial needs. These people occupy the highest and lowest class distinctions, from the antique collector who buys only the finest, handmade seventeenth- and eighteenth-century furniture at upscale auctions, to the humble, clever scavenger, cruising the streets in a battered pickup on trash-collection day.

Despite the wide social strata separating them, and the vast difference in wealth, these buyers and sellers share common impulses and goals. If you don't want something, they do, if they think it might be worth something or useful. Look past the paddle bidding fans and the flat, nasal style of high-end auctions, and you will find junkers scrambling to get the newest castoff, haggling and cajoling and engaging in one of the oldest of human activities—negotiating over who gets what and for how much. Collectors of American Colonial pewter are really not much different from people who collect license plates, in both the broadest and narrowest senses. They are all interested in condition, rarity, and in the significance of something in their collections. Above all, though, these gatherers will spend hours explaining their collections to you, each item with its set of meanings and with a story. "Let me tell you how I found this old jack plane," a tool collector will say, and you are invited along for a tale of the chase, one with pitfalls, perils, and triumphs.

People in this shadow economy also fascinate me because they are off the grid, as energy conservationists say about people who rely on solar or other alternative power sources. These people don't fit into mainstream economic culture: They largely do not need the output of the economy. From their perspective, there is plenty of merchandise already; they need only to find it, a process they find joyful, even essential. Some buyers and sellers of discards have encyclopedic and intricate bodies of knowledge, with discriminations in value based on arcane marks and features. Antique dealers and collectors are as studious and mysterious as alchemists. Other buyers and sellers gather anything, whether they know its value or not. Even antique dealers can't know everything about all their wares, and they will often underprice things and create a bargain for the next person. Others will nearly give something away as long as someone can use it. I have seen great generosity and great chicanery at all levels in the used goods network. If you are looking for predictability, buy new.

People who live off what others discard are experts in reuse, or they'd be unable to survive. They are imaginative, skilled, and optimistic about the bounty of the land. They know that they glean from a largely unreaped field of castoffs. They are all scavengers finally, whether filling a mansion with bronzes from great nineteenth-century French artisans or populating a field with broken farm tractors. Both consumers and sellers find a corner of the market in which they can prosper and expand their holdings. Collectors of American primitives are drawn to the homely, worn paint on a cabinet, while another seller finds the same furniture in need of repair and refinishing. Another collector is so beset with the junk he has gathered that he will rent an abandoned house or store and try to sell some of it, while still other collectors fill old panel trucks with their accumulated riches and become itinerant peddlers at flea markets where they hope people will think they have rare collectibles. Those who buy and sell through eBay, and its predecessor, the want ad, also hope the next log-on or edition will reveal something they have always coveted or help them make a sale, while more castoffs come pouring into the mosaic of secondhand commerce every weekend through yard sales. Finally, even the trash-picker is a treasure hunter. Something left on the curb, earmarked for the oblivion of the landfill, might still be useful. If so, someone will interrupt its trajectory and salvage it, recognizing potential in what others have deemed worthless. In our oft-declared throwaway culture, very little actually gets wasted.

These collectors, merchants, and gatherers make up a great tribe of people who acquire things as part of an American tradition of reuse older than consumerism, one rooted in practicality, frugality, and ingenuity. This facet of American culture pays scant attention to new retail advertising and mocks mainstream, mega-capitalism while thriving on the tail end of its central tenet of buy-then-discard. Although I have attempted to isolate various levels of this commerce, in truth they stymie such pigeon-holing; stuff moves around until it finds its appropriate place, through many hands and across many states. The network of reusers defies neat mapping and discrete categorization. They are capitalist anarchists, happily living on what others have discarded. The antique collector and junk hoarder share one bond: They see value in the abandoned, and they claim it. They are visionary consumers.

Chapter One

❧

At the Top of the Food Chain

In a newspaper interview, Colin Stair, auction and antiques restoration manager, said merchandise enters the antique and used trade through "the Three D's"—debt, death, and divorce. I would add a fourth "D"—discarding—but Colin would see little of that class of castoff as he was at the high end of the jumbled network of buying and selling what others no longer want. In this nebulous system, identifying a top is at best arbitrary, but Colin Stair's auction house had as good a claim as any to that position.

When you think of the pinnacle of the world of the gavel, you naturally think of Sotheby's and Christie's, auction houses that sell the most precious, legendary *objets*—the rare, beautiful, and historic detritus of the world's civilizations. If a truly astonishing work of art, an icon of our culture, a gem made mythic by a fabled curse, or a humble whatnot once owned by the famous must change hands, the deal is done by these venerable auction firms. Their sales make the news, and the prices they fetch are often met with great gasps, and then polite applause. When these houses simply agree to sell something, a high price has been guaranteed. They have strict standards for what they will represent, and their appraisers are antique and art experts. Surely they are the top of the trade. Surely the top was not so hard to find after all.

It isn't that simple; nothing is in the secondhand world. Sotheby's and Christie's are not really in the used business, and they would bristle at the implication. Those houses deal exclusively in art and rare antiquities, one-of-a-kind items that have never been part of the network of used goods. Although a new rare item comes to light now and again, most of what Sotheby's and Christie's sell is already known, part of a set list of things of beauty and renown, and might have been auctioned before. Top auction houses consult old auction catalogues to figure out what price to expect for an item at hand. These important paintings, sculptures, and masterpieces of famed furniture makers or glass workers have been valuable for so long, for hundreds of years in some cases, that they have long ago ceased to be part of the general trade in castoffs. But like other used goods, these prized items will resell endlessly, be restored when necessary, and be coveted for their value. In that way they are not much different from my old chest of drawers. However, most of the auctions handling them are clearinghouses, not true marketplaces.

Auctions that participate in secondhand commerce are less affluent. So, if I wanted to start at the top rung, I had to find where goods go when those rarified auction firms decline them, and that was where I found Colin Stair, a former Sotheby's employee in the used goods and high-end antique markets in Hudson, New York.

Hudson is an old river town that fell on hard times in the 1930s and, with an occasional pulse produced by industry, has continued to fade. Across the Rip Van Winkle Bridge from its picturesque twin, Catskill, Hudson has always been a bare-knuckled town. For decades it was known best for brothels and gambling. Such endeavors had left their mark on the blank faces of the houses, porches long gone, decorations effaced by aluminum siding. Most towns have an ornamental entrance, a way into town on which the failed fortunes of some of its residents do not show. I have approached Hudson from all major compass points, and each leads through a dingy postindustrial tableau. Along its dull streets, small signs either promoted or protested a new factory for making cement. Was it another chance for prosperity or a death knell for the town, simply another layer of grime from industry?

Two other sources of income persist. One, a pervasive trade in drugs, had been the source of a concerted effort by law enforcement to tamp down—with some success. Still, I had been warned the town had a dangerous edge. The other was the secondhand trade. The main commercial streets off the central square once held a full complement of businesses you'd find in any town: furniture stores, groceries, pharmacies, hardwares, and clothiers. Now, block after block has been inhabited by more than ninety antique dealers, each space adapted to varied wares. Secondhand culture has colonized the carcasses of failed retail businesses, and a new breed of merchant has created a new bustle on the streets.

I stopped at one of the antique shops operated by the Stair family. Colin's father and wife each operated one of the Stair Galleries. When I parked across the street, I saw parking meters, a vestige of Hudson's old commercial life. I did a double take when I realized they demanded five cents an hour—another relic of times gone by. I donated a dime to the city coffers, though I suspected I'd not be more than a half hour, and as I crossed the street I tried to recall the last time I had bought anything for a nickel.

Inside I found a woman on the phone. I assumed she was Colin Stair's wife and would be able to put me in touch with him, so I idly examined the shop's goods, waiting to speak with her. The neat shop contained high-priced items; I noted a $20,000 grandfather clock. As the woman ended the call, I picked up a miniature teacup—one of a set of four— priced at $3,000. I gingerly set the cup back on its tiny saucer.

Although the woman was not his wife, she was very helpful, calling Colin's Clavarack, New York, office to see if he was there, then giving me his number and a postcard for an upcoming sale, the first Stair Gallery auction, of the estate of Frederick W. Hughes, Andy Warhol's friend and business manager. The illustration depicted some of the offerings, including an Elvis bust and a crystal top hat.

I called and arranged to talk with Colin Stair in his assemblage of barns on a side street in Clavarack. When I arrived I saw Colin ambling across the lawns in the front. I recognized him from the newspaper photograph. A powerfully built man who walked with an economy of motion, Colin was very calm and jovial, especially for someone preparing to watch millions of dollars of prime used and antique items pass through his hands in a nationally ballyhooed series of sales.

"This was the Clavarack train station," Colin said, pointing to the station building, to a row of barns along the track for grain, livestock, and other goods, and to a blockhouse-style building offset from the rest, the former railroad office, now Building Number One, headquarters of Stair Restoration and Auctions. The 1850s buildings were impeccably restored and painted a classic red with white trim, each barn a sibling of the next. The entire scene, a bit anachronistic in suburban Clavarack, was pastoral and quaint, with the dignified air of a country gentleman. A clear blue Northeast autumn sky capped the scene.

Colin came to Clavarack to head Sotheby's restoration business. His family has a long association with the auction house: His grandfather and great-grandfather had worked for Sotheby's in England, while Colin and his father worked at the New York office. Then Sotheby's scaled back their operations, eventually selling their restoration business. "When Sotheby's said they wanted out," Colin said, "I said I wanted in." He was irritated with the press reporting the auction house had shed this sideline because it was unprofitable. "I came here, and in the first year we broke even. Then we turned a profit each year after that." Colin had a total of sixteen years' experience with Sotheby's, including an apprenticeship—something he said many of the big auction houses no longer do.

Now Colin was poised to enter the top of the used merchandise trade. Though he no longer worked for Sotheby's, he was still in contact with them and with their customers, both buyers and sellers. Sotheby's can sell only a fraction of what is offered to them. Not choosy like Sotheby's, nor as concerned about how what he sells characterizes his business (Sotheby's reputation rests on selling only the absolutely most valuable items), Stair was equipped to handle anything of value. His business was at the cutoff between the world of the *objet* and the object.

The upcoming sale of the Frederick W. Hughes estate was a good case in point. When the executors of the estate offered the worldly possessions of this confidant of great artists and soaring socialites to Sotheby's, they accepted 353 items. Then they recommended Colin Stair to handle the remaining 1,500 lots as the legitimate next rung on the secondhand ladder. Colin was doing a "broom-clean" sale. When he was finished, Hughes's house would be swept clean of unwanted items. Colin was selling everything: dishes, furniture of all types, memorabilia from a life in the glare of the famous, and the flotsam of collecting the curious and the coveted.

"I'm even selling the man's clothes," Colin said, "though he was a small man, maybe five-two." He wondered who was going to buy them. "Maybe a very thin woman."

Colin took me into Building Number One. On the first floor was a library of reference books and auction catalogues, though they'd be hard-pressed to cover the range of goods Colin and his staff were expecting to sell. The world might pass through their hands, everything from hand-kerchiefs to Hottentot masks. Colin said he relied on experts he knew and that he and his staff had cultivated a depth of knowledge in specific fields. I had no idea, though, how arcane such knowledge would have to be or how truly strange the merchandise was.

Colin's office was on the second floor. His mahogany "partners' desk" (a desk with drawers on both sides) sat in one corner faced by two gilded and carved chairs. Colin sat at his desk, and I took one of the ornate seats. Other desks for staff occupied only slightly less prominent positions in the large open room, which had a big wooden door at the end open for ventilation. Clearly Colin had outfitted himself with castoffs—all the furnishings were antique—but, gilded chairs aside, they were restrained, such as a dropleaf table, lustrous with two centuries of age and polish. The table was stacked with some bric-a-brac, including a miniature paint-ing of a South American general, his large head almost cartoonish, as if the artist was lampooning his patron. Colin said the painting was from the mid-nineteenth century, and he had developed a real fondness for it.

Colin spun Hughes's Rolodex of addresses on his desk, and said he had culled it to attract people to the sales, including Jimmy Carter, Jack Nicholson, Bianca Jagger, and the Whitney family. The Rolodex was a ferris wheel of the names and addresses of the rich, famous, and infamous. Colin planned to sell the Hughes estate in three stages. First he was going to hold a "tag" sale for the lowest-quality stuff—genuine celebrity junk. Then, within a month, Colin would hold an auction of the better goods, followed by another of only the best artifacts from the era of Campbell's Soup cans and multiple Marilyn Monroes. Hughes had eclectic tastes and loved the strange and exotic. "He put a lot of value in stuff," Colin said.

"Hello, Mr. Stair," a voice said from the first floor. "Shall I come up the stairs?"

"Now you're going to get a double dose," Colin said, then called out, "Hello, Mr. Stair. Yes, sir, come up the stairs."

And up came John Stair. Colin Stair's father was a man in his early six-ties with a gruff animal magnetism, ashen hair converted from the blond his thirtyish son now wore, a beard and sweeping nineteenth-century moustache. After introductions the elder Stair lodged himself in the second of the gilded chairs and began describing some "English barometers and case clocks" he'd found. John talked earnestly, but in a garrulous rumble of terms and qualities only another appraiser might understand. From what I could catch, these new treasures were in Buffalo, offered by a wealthy man who had turned an old monastery into a fine manor.

"Good man. We need more like him," Colin said. "Is he still in the land of the living?"

"Yes," said John. Obviously another of the Three D's was in operation. The father continued describing the goods to be had. The thrill of the hunt was still with the retired Sotheby's auctioneer, and he fairly percolated with excitement.

Then John got up to leave, joking he was Stair AA and Colin was Stair BA (After Auction/Before Auction), attributing their age difference to the stress of running a big sale. His son took this teasing with a warm grin. The father did appear to be an older, and wiser, version of the younger.

"Tell him what you do when you have an auction and no one shows up," John said.

"What do you do?" I asked, wanting to draw the father into the conversation.

"You wait. It happened once when we were selling Oceanographic." Then he added, as he disappeared down the stairs, "And don't talk to me about French manuscripts." I could tell he was dredging up old war stories to gently worry his protégé prior to his own big sale.

Although Colin was nervous about the sale, he was also enthused over the opportunity to show what he could do, apart from Sotheby's, and with a cache of curious merchandise that had belonged to a star of New York society. The association lent value to some otherwise unremarkable items. For instance, Hughes left behind a box of ancient Roman money which a numismatist had appraised as very common coins of the realm and worth about $10 each. In contrast, a plastic key card to Hughes's posh private club in Manhattan, "VIP" printed on it in large letters, and below his name the appellation "Super Star," would sell for much more. "The coins are thousands of years old, but . . .," Colin said, grinning. He clearly enjoyed the quirky aspects of the business and planned to capitalize on it.

Hughes had dedicated his life to surrounding himself with one-of-a-kind stuff with an attitude. "He liked being like Andy Warhol and tried to live like him," Colin said, having taken the measure of Hughes's life through what he had left behind. Perhaps that is one of our surest legacies. When all the tallies are in, the accomplishments, loves, and adventures, the secondhand merchant has the last say. Our lives are open to gross summation when our drawers and closets are emptied of their resonant secrets.

The Hughes house had been an adventure to clean out and catalogue. Colin had found bootleg jazz recordings, Pop Art memorabilia, folk art, and rare books. "And then you'd turn the corner, and there would be an Egyptian mummy's hand," Colin said, shaking his head. The serendipity of buying used was certainly in force; Colin knew he had uncommon wealth piled in his picturesque barns, some treasures about which he did not know everything and might slip through his expert grasp. When I asked what Colin thought would fetch the highest price, he cited predictable, easily priced items, such as blue and white Staffordshire pottery, but some of the weird stuff might be the sleepers of the day. Perhaps the greatest gain would be publicity. Colin had an eye on launching this part of his business, and National Public Radio had already said it planned to cover the event.

As much as Colin hoped to attract attention and customers to his auction through the glitz and romance of this Pop Art impresario, he did not welcome notoriety. The Hughes estate also contained some Native American artifacts, such as Zuni Kachina headdresses, but Colin said the family wanted to keep most of those. "I'm glad, too. I don't want to deal with stuff like that. The [Native Americans] can come in and say, 'That's from our tribe, and we want it' and take it," referring to the legal right of tribes to repossess artifacts looted from them over the centuries. Throughout our conversation, I gathered that Colin Stair was a gentle, mild-mannered man, content to be working in a dignified form of the business, and he did not invite acrimony or lawsuits. He picked up a ceramic pot and said, "If someone came to me and said 'I bought this pot from you, and you didn't mention it had a crack in the glaze, and I'm going to sue you,' I'd say: 'No you're not, because I'm going to take this pot back and give you back your money, and you can leave, and never come back.'" Then he paused. "'Or come back and try again,'" he added with a smile; he'd never want to alienate a customer.

Not that Colin's auction, like any other, did not operate on the age-old buyer-beware principle. That's what the preview is for; Colin planned

to display Hughes's goods for two days prior to each auction so everyone could examine everything, ferreting out each flaw and researching
provenance or value. And the wise buyer does just that, and more. Colin
showed me a table he had on consignment that the owner purported to
be eighteenth-century French Baroque. Colin thought the wood underneath the top was not sufficiently aged, but he would list it in a catalogue
as Baroque, because that is what the owner said it was.

"What would you do if someone asked your opinion?" I asked.

"I'd say I'd guess it was something someone made to look old in
probably the nineteenth century, and that unless they [the customer]
liked it, not to bother with it as an investment." If you wanted Colin's
expert advice, though, you'd have to ask. Caveat emptor.

"I like to call this the true world's oldest profession," Colin said.
Though Colin had seen all kinds of tricks used by auction houses to make
a sale, he added, "It's not a business that takes advantage of people. I've
never seen anyone get hurt." And he hoped it would stay that way, noting that auctioneering is probably the largest nonregulated business in
the United States, a "multibillion-dollar business." With hundreds of
auctions in New York state alone, and tens of thousands nationwide, it's
important that some unwritten code exist, some sense of fair play, or "the
government would try to get involved, and that would have an impact
on the entire business."

I knew Colin was thinking of the commission-fixing scandal that had
resulted in a federal Justice Department investigation of Sotheby's and
Christie's for violations of the Sherman Antitrust Act. Top Sotheby's
managers were indicted, one received a three-year jail term, and huge fines
were levied against the house. The charges had stunned the art community, as the reputations of these houses had never been questioned. If the
government took a prolonged interest in the way secondhand commerce
was conducted, the ramifications might be felt all the way down the distribution chain, through antique stores and potentially even flea markets.
However, I knew, given secondhand's anarchical structure and serpentine
trade systems, even a stringent bureaucracy would have a difficult time
collaring it.

Rebecca, an auctioneer who worked for Colin, came in and sat down
at a nearby desk, and the three of us talked about how she had learned
the business. I had thought you needed to be trained in how to call, that

fluid mix of vowels and consonants that an auctioneer uses to fill up the silence between bids. Rebecca said such practiced stuttering was for "country auctions." She had learned the business by doing it; she had worked as a runner for a few months, someone who helped the auction-eer by bringing items to the front. After Rebecca had seen how it was done, she decided to give it a try. She and Colin then told me about some of the greats of the auction world, including Ron Bourgeault of Portsmouth, New Hampshire, who had once stood for ten continuous hours at an auction, or Dick Withington, who, Cal Ripken–like, had just led his seventeen hundredth sale.

An auctioneer has to be personable and able to handle finicky buyers and anxious sellers. Appraising an item so a seller knows what to expect to get for it is the hardest part of the job; Colin and Rebecca agreed they have to give sellers bad news 99 percent of the time. The general aware-ness about antiques, and the popularity of *Antiques Roadshow*, has made people better informed. They know enough to call an appraiser when they want to get rid of something old. However, people now expect higher prices. When they protest that they "know it's old" because it had belonged to their grandmother, Colin will respond by saying, "Well, your grandmother bought it new. . . . " Even so, I couldn't imagine Colin bringing the hopes of the owner of an ersatz valuable heirloom down to earth with anything approaching bluntness.

I was eager to see some of the rare items and valuable junk being in-troduced to the used goods market through the Hughes estate, so Colin took me out to his well-appointed barns. At Sotheby's, Colin had seen some bizarre things come across their block. Among them, he cited a sale of Russian aerospace equipment, the leftovers from the once proud flag-ship of Soviet communism. With its dissolution, these prized remnants—the nose cones from rockets that had safely borne cosmonauts into the ether and back—were liquidated for needed cash through this purest of capitalist venues in one of the most exquisite of historic ironies. All deaths, even those of empires, lead to twists of fate.

Another item Colin had seen was both strange and highly touted: a pile of bones. However, these were really *big* bones, a complete Tyran-nosaurus Rex found in South Dakota, and the subject of lawsuits between for-profit fossil hunters and the landowner. Sue, as the dinosaur was nicknamed, was auctioned as part of the settlement. The Chicago Field

Museum paid $8.4 million. In this case, the auction block had been a way of exercising justice—and for finding a suitable home for a fantastic specimen.

We passed through the first two barns; these contained the restoration workshop, an orderly assembly of tools and benches. Then we went into an upstairs storeroom in the third barn where the Hughes collection, and other goods also fated to fall under the hammer, were arranged by owner and type of goods—shelves of clocks and boxes and racks of dishware. Colin stopped in front of some exquisite porcelain, stacks of platters, pitchers, and vases, that a collector had shed. He said the collector had bought a new house in Westchester. The collector's old house contained the most lavish antiques, but now he wanted to decorate "in a country style," with Early American furniture and folk art, and so his interior designer had asked Colin to sell his client's collection. So he did get discards too, I thought.

"Here's some of Freddie's stuff," Colin said, leading me through the heaped shelves to a table in the corner. These must have been Hughes's most esoteric goods. I was drawn first to some statuary, heads of Roman gods stuck into posts and mounted on clear acrylic cubes; and figures from household shrines of the type frequently turned up by plows in fields along the Adriatic Sea. One was whole, a small Egyptian statue. One of Colin's experts suspected it might be a Roman copy of a genuine Pharaonic figure, an example of ancient forgery.

Colin picked up some little frames, gilded but battered. They were reliquaries, bits of saints sold by the church in the Middle Ages, the genuineness of their hair and fingernails certified by a papal bull or certificate attached to the back and graced by a daub of red wax bearing the impression of the pope's ring. Then I saw it: a loam-dark hand in a cardboard box with a clear lid, the kind you'd find housing a Hallmark Christmas ornament. I picked up the box. The mummy's hand was nearly weightless, devoid of the stuff of life and removed from the weight of the body. I was struck by how unassuming it was. I could have been examining any other curio, some scrap of parchment or hunk of driftwood, not what was left of a person who lived maybe four thousand years ago. This was a remnant of his or her humanness, a hand that had combed a child's hair, wielded a weapon, signed documents, or held another's in love. Not only was Hughes's life palpable in what he had left behind, so were the lives of others, even frail vestiges of their bodies.

These old curiosities seemed a degree shy of mysterious in the bright overhead lights in Colin's storeroom. That some of Hughes's esoterica might be museum-quality was without a doubt. However, when not ennobled by a display case and spotlighting, without a narrative provided by research, the statuary was simply crudely made, and even the saints' relics and mummy's hand were merely macabre and a bit sad. "Somebody asked me how I could tell it was Egyptian and old, and I said, 'You just look at it and tell me,'" Colin had remarked when I had picked up the hand, and I had looked at it and had found only more questions. How would he sell it? How would he generate interest in this bizarre item?

Then I noticed it wore a pinky ring with a green stone. "Is that a jade ring?" I asked.

"Yes," Colin said solemnly, but with a hint of glee. He would at least have that as a selling point, as an attribute for the auction catalogue. He knew the right combination of details would attract buyers. Everything has a buyer; nothing is worthless.

Still, Colin had his work cut out for him, because there was no end to the oddities. I noticed the tooth of a prehistoric mammoth, mounted on a plastic base, and then a three-foot wooden statue that Colin said was a piece of Mexican folk art. I recognized it as Saint Sebastian, blood dripping from his wounds—the arrows that once had protruded from his body were missing, and he was leaning against a carved saguaro cactus, another impaling.

When I told Colin how the saint had been martyred under a hail of arrows, he said, "I've just learned something more," delighted over having this bit of added information, anything that might help him sell it. I had just marvelled over how much anyone in the auction business must know, something about fine china, Colonial furniture, fossils, and ancient artifacts, and Colin had responded with an apt aphorism: "The one thing I've learned is how much I don't know."

I had been seized by a bit of melancholy in looking at a fraction of the Hughes estate, looking past the objects to the quality of mind driven to collect them. Taken together they represented a consciousness, an approach to life. I could imagine Frederick Hughes showing his latest find to visitors, offhandedly displaying the mammoth's tooth on a hallway table, or dismissing a friend's astonishment at his owning a mummy's hand with a shrug suggesting he thought *everyone* owned one. Hughes must have decorated his house on Long Island as you might stock a museum, or even design a stage set in which the solitary actor, F. W. Hughes, played out his role as *bon vivant* and eccentric. Now the drama was over, and the set, a bit worse for wear, had been disassembled, the props stored in Colin's barn until purchased and put into service in a new context, a new life. However, each carried some vaporosity of its old owner, some intimate suggestion of a life lived to its conclusion.

Colin didn't find the business sad, though, saying Hughes's possessions were "only objects. Stuff endures and people don't." He had even known Hughes, having done some restoration work for him. "I'm the guy he used to scream at, so it's kind of ironic that I'm the guy selling his stuff."

Colin had made some judgments based on his cleaning out the Hughes estate, though. "He surrounded himself with stuff, really put a lot of worth in it. Probably too much." We were now downstairs, and when I remarked that I had never seen a hearse with luggage rack, Colin laughed merrily. He stopped at a desk in the shop and picked up a photograph. Frederick Hughes was a man of the shape and size once referred to as "dapper," with a witty glint in his eyes. The photo showed Hughes at a party, probably one of his star-studded soirées. In this candid shot he was wearing a pair of magnifying goggles, clowning around with his arm around a female guest and peering down her blouse.

Colin laughed, then picked up the goggles, also on the desk. "These have to go together," he added. The gag goggles would be nearly worthless without this bit of provenance, but together they made a package and achieved a moment of fame.

Chapter Two

❦

Don't Scratch Your Nose

COLIN HAD CALLED AUCTIONEERING "the true oldest profession," and historians can find evidence of auctions being held six thousand years ago in the city-state of Ur. The first comprehensive records of auction sales come to us from the Romans; the emperor Caligula even sold his household goods on the block to satisfy his creditors. More commonly, soldiers used auctions to disperse the spoils of war. A sale would be announced by a spear stuck into the ground around which buyers would gather, hence the origin of the term auction, from *auctio sub hasta* or "increasing [price] under the spear." The spear remains a symbol of the auction house, similar to the three balls of the pawn shop or the striped pole of the barber.

Many other traditions have survived. Though bids are no longer met with trumpet fanfare, buyers still use Roman gestures, nods, or even eye movements, to bid. Others traditions haven't endured. In early British auctions the winning bid was the highest made before an inch-long candle burned out, a practice called "dumb bidding." A "Dutch auction" worked in reverse: A seller shouted out a price and kept lowering it until a buyer agreed to pay it. The pressure on the buyer arose from worrying how low to let the price drop before it tempted another buyer. Auctions were always both dignified and the subject of scandals. They were even banned in Cromwell's England. Auctions were also a handy way to disburse contraband, and clandestine sales probably did a healthy trade in pirated goods.

Auctions thrived, spreading into all corners of the British empire and especially in America, which added a bit of the huckster and snake oil hawker to the staid traditions of the mother country. The banter of the American auctioneer is a close cousin of the sideshow barker's spiel. Although New World auctions had their more sinister chapters, such as an essential role in the slave trade, the primary advantage of the auction, the ability to sell large quantities quickly, made it perfectly adaptive to the land of plenty where they sell even whole farms and their contents. Not surprisingly, floor bids remain at the heart of the way the country does business at the New York Stock Exchange, and although new merchandising long ago left the auction behind as too unpredictable, the used market has kept the hammer falling in every community in America.

On the first day of Colin's auction, to be held at the Elks Lodge in Hudson, I arrived with my friend Michael Sham. On a side street near some abandoned trolley tracks, the mid-nineteenth-century brick building might have once been part of a mill complex, but it had been transformed into a meeting place for the fraternal order, complete with a sheet-metal elk's head on the facade, each horn tipped with a lightbulb. Colin was hoping to erect his own auction building once the business took hold. Inside the main hall, big enough for meetings, dances, and dinners, were displayed the earthly goods of F. W. Hughes, Lilian Reineck, Bert Barkas, and another seller only identified as "a distinguished Greenwich, Connecticut, collector." I guessed the last seller was still of this world, and wanted to preserve his or her privacy; however, that the dead have no right to privacy was made abundantly clear in this business.

Colin's team had transformed the humble hall, testifying to the hard work staging such a highly visible auction requires. A life-size marble composite cast of "Venus Emerging from Her Bath" sat to the right of the doorway where it was sure to catch our eyes. Colin set up a wall of glass to safeguard the finer china and glass, identified in the catalogue as "significant Blue and White Transferware as well as a group of English, Continental, and Chinese porcelain." Colin's father, John, was working there, removing the items prospective buyers wanted to inspect and explaining their signifying marks and features. At the opposite side sat tables of what are known in the antique trade as "smalls": clocks and frames and decorative boxes—anything smaller than a dining room chair, of which there were also plenty in the rear of the room. There, nearest the back doors and the loading dock, sat a traffic jam of furniture, some of it gigantic, such as a towering English wardrobe, a Swiss baker's table, a highly polished barrel on a pedestal where dough would be stored, and a sideboard that could double as an aircraft carrier.

Having things grouped by type increased the impression of plentitude, as the eye discerned one table packed with mortars and pestles, another with a cluster of clocks, and a herd of chairs in the corner. All of this careful disorder had taken many hours of preparation and back-breaking labor. The auctioneer's job appears to be simply standing at a podium and talking up prices, but the job is as arduous as it is intricate. I overheard a guy remarking dryly to a customer, "I *guess* you could say I'm familiar with this stuff. I spent hours photographing every piece for the Web site." He was the photographer Colin had hired to shoot the entire collection for his on-line catalogue. In addition, Colin and his staff had produced and mailed hundreds of color postcards, made innumerable phone calls to potential buyers, and posted announcements in newspapers and trade publications. Each step was orchestrated and timed to provide what public relations experts call buzz, a series of expectations and questions that the next advertisement or mailing fulfills and answers. The payoff would tell whether Colin had delivered the goods.

The Elks hall glittered with the promise of gilt, silver, and brass, and it was warmed by the luminosity of polished, fine wood. The buyers were here in force, collectively bobbing their spectacled heads as though in sporadic prayer, but obviously appraising each item in turn, not giving away their interest. Their faces remained unmoved besides a raised eyebrow or studied squint. In a subtle way, the competition had already begun. Though these goods had been available for inspection for two days, everyone was continuing to poke, pry, and peer. Serious buyers examined every inch of a serving dish or pastoral painting—the latter were displayed on folding panels set up in the corner as a mini-gallery. Even an hour before the sale began, while trying to learn even more about what would be on the block, the buyers were also on display themselves. People were trying to determine who would be their main competition for a particular item. Who might run the bidding up, and how serious did that buyer look? More importantly, what did someone see that you hadn't? What maker's mark, signature, or flaw had been revealed to a competitor so that she or he knows more about a piece and is more or less willing to bid? A serious buyer might telegraph that a clock was not worthy of his attention, while mentally cataloguing its attributes and qualities. Of all the reactions I noticed, a display of admiration for a particular piece was distinctly absent; it would signal to others that a piece might be worth more attention, and money, and predicate a bidding war. Even if something was a prized antique, or filled some gap in a carefully assembled collection, it was best not to reveal it. Better to remain detached, displaying only a poised disdain. Only one thing was certain: Everything, all 479 lots, would be gone by the end of the afternoon. This was the essential urgency of the auction, the driving force behind the urge to buy. If you really wanted something, you must be prepared to bid. Buy now, because you might never see it again.

The runners who would be bringing items from the display areas to the front and then holding them up during the bidding, were strategizing how to move the merchandise through the crowd quickly and unobtrusively. Neatly dressed in green polo shirts, a "Stair Galleries" insignia stitched over the upper left pectoral, some of the runners were gym-built specimens, and they'd be getting their workouts, lifting furniture built large enough to take up space in an eighteenth-century manor. During the auction, when two were straining to raise a bulky English Arts and Crafts–style dining room table to shoulder height, one runner, clearly the more experienced, blithely commented, "This will work on your upper body strength." The other nodded with gritted teeth.

Colin's publicity regimen had done its job, perhaps too well, as the crowd had outstripped the capacity of the rented hall. He'd need his new facility soon. He had plenty of chairs, but not enough space to put them, and a couple dozen remained folded, leaning against the wall. The hundred or more chairs were staked out with little paper signs taped to the backs or a bidding number on the seat. I walked to the back where I stood a chance at finding a seat and saw a couple of unclaimed chairs; I ripped pages out of my notebook, scribbling "reserved" on them.

I had just put down the last one when an agitated man with a thick French accent looked at the signs, said, "Reserved, eh?" and grumbled something about needing a seat. He quickly found another nearby. His was one of the many heavily accented voices I heard in the crowd; the international buyers Colin had expected had come to the sale. After all the seats were filled or reserved, people began sitting on furniture to be sold. I winced as people cavalierly straddled spindly and creaking eighteenth-century Windsor dining room chairs worth a thousand dollars each or plopped down on a cracked leather couch, the cushions wheezing dust.

One customer was sitting in a chair behind the folding panels, out of eyesight of the auction desk. "Do you plan to make bids on your cell phone?" asked another buyer.

"You'd be surprised," he answered, alluding to the inscrutable nature of phone bidders. Colin had warned me that he'd never bid against a phone, implying that a customer never knew if a real buyer was on the other end or if the house was simply running up the price.

As the time for the sale approached, the competitive tenor of the crowd became tense, sharpened by the visceral aura of big money. Some of the wealthy were noticeable because they had brought their little dogs in a cartoonish stereotype of the rich with their pampered pets. When I asked my friend Michael Sham why the wealthy felt they were entitled to take their dogs anywhere, even into crowds of people who might be annoyed by their yapping or even allergic to them, he responded waggishly, "Because they're rich," to which I added, "And by association, so are their dogs." So many lap-bound pooches had arrived you might have thought we were at a dog show.

Dogs aside, you wouldn't have known some of the attendees were rich by their dress, but if you watched closely the movements of their bodies betrayed their social status. They wandered the preview, unawed by the abundance or obvious rarities. They were uncowed by the fragility of the Chinese vase they casually flipped in search of a mark. They brushed by a 250-year-old card table, casually appraising the burled walnut veneer with a caress as if checking it for dust. Some of them were dressed as fine as on a promenade, and others were as rumpled as any junk seller, but all were at home in this temporary warehouse of profound and pricey castoffs. They were in their element as surely as Olympic athletes on the track. This was only another workout of their well-developed discriminations.

As comfortable as the crowd appeared in this venue, I felt obviously out of my element, even in the homely tweed jacket I had hoped would lend me an air of casual belonging. However, everyone was taking stock of everything, so my wandering about with notebook in hand probably did not look strange, despite my diffidence. I was simply another participant in this discreet mating dance of the wanted and those who want. In order to get an auction catalogue, so I might understand a little of what I was seeing, I registered as a buyer, though I was certain I'd not be raising my number 148 card in pursuit of these high-priced goods. The woman at the desk asked me for my dealer number, and I answered I had none, identifying myself as a collector, the bane of the dealers who were the majority here. Dealers bemoan that auctions have become less lucrative as they have become more popular, and people who would normally be *their* customers showed up and bid against them. Collectors have a distinct advantage when bidding against dealers. The collectors know as much as the dealer does, and many can pay higher prices to get what they want because they don't have to worry about a resale profit margin. The only consolation for dealers is that collectors have to pay sales tax, and if the collectors mentally add that percentage to their last bids it might make a higher one harder to offer, and allow the dealer to prevail.

At noon Colin took the podium to open the auction. He explained the conditions of sale as outlined in the catalogue, a thirty-five-page annotated list. Everything would be sold "as is where is," meaning the buyer should be informed about the condition and be able to cart away a purchase by the next day at 2:00 P.M. They also charged a buyer's premium of 15 percent, a fee paid by the buyer, not the seller, and the house expected full payment immediately. Lastly, the closing of the bid was final; the auctioneer must have the last word on who had bought what and for how much. If not, the sale could descend to a chaos of quibbling, backpeddling, or people offering advances on bids that already had closed. The success of the sale rested on the buyers strictly following the rules and despite the heat of the moment accepting the outcome as indelible. Any contested bid would slow down the sale and erode the authority of the auctioneer.

Colin was visibly nervous, but after a few faltering words found his innate poise; his father was nodding in approval and support. And the auction began. The first lot was a pair of Chamberlain Worcester soup plates, on which Colin said there had been "a fair amount of interest." He also announced he had a "left bid" on the plates—a bid that a buyer who could not attend the sale had written down and left behind. The house would announce that bid and give the room a chance to bid higher. The two plates had been valued at $400 to $600, but Colin mustered up a closing bid of $1,100. It was an auspicious beginning; if he often exceeded his own estimate by that much, the sale would be a smashing success.

As Rebecca had said, their auctioneering style did not feature rolling vowels or rattling chants, but it did have its own vocabulary and articulation. For instance, the rhetoric of the auctioneer relies on the use of "the," the definite article, as in "now we have *the* English creamware small tureen and cover" to emphasize the singularity of the items, the not-to-be-missed rarity. That slight touch aside, Colin usually didn't hawk items by singing their virtues; he read the catalogue description, then started the sale. Once, in reaction to slow bidding, Colin commented that something was "a lovely thing," but for the most part he kept to a calm acknowledgement of a bid with a simple "thank you." Once, when Colin was struggling to get an opener on eight Worcester porcelain tea bowls and saucers, he dropped his suggested price to $100. "All over the place," Colin said to indicate he had seen more than one bid, but had to choose only one as a starter. The set sold for $300, well under the estimated $500 to $700, and the exact price Colin had suggested as an opener. Only when the pulse of the room rose during a fierce duel over a pair of "Worcester porcelain oval butter tubs with covers and stands" did Colin's face break its porcelain politeness with a glimmer of excitement, his head swiveling to collect the bids until the two plates went for $1,100.

After ten lots and ten minutes of selling, Colin turned the sale over to Rebecca, saying she would "move things along more quickly." And she did, as she acknowledged the bidding instantly, building the urgency needed to prod the bidder who might be hesitating on the edge of the diving board. After ten minutes she was on lot 30. Rebecca was able to double the pace by not concerning herself so much with waiting for a bid. If she was having trouble getting a bid she did not belabor it, letting the item go for an opening bid or after one or two advances. She even passed on a couple of items, taking them off the block, such as a set of wine glasses. I learned that a sale with numerous lots would more likely yield a bargain because the auctioneer could not waste time milking the bid for a few more dollars. The crowd could get restless, as some would be waiting for an item to come up later in the catalogue, and if it looked like they'd have to wait too long they could lose interest. It was a delicate balance.

Although Rebecca didn't use the rambling style of a country auctioneer, she too had a style. For instance, she would call out, "I have a hundred, and a hundred and a quarter where," meaning that a $100 had been bid, and she was looking for the bidder who would advance it another $25. Likewise, before closing a sale she'd announce, "Fair room is fair warning," a pause to give the room a chance to continue. Unlike Colin, Rebecca hawked items, but with poise and a studied humor. So when selling paintings of horses, she coaxed with, "Did the horseback riders stay home?" She asked, "No other picnickers?" before closing on a Chinese picnic basket, and, when a bunch of mortars and pestles garnered only $80, she quipped, "No more pharmacists in the audience?"

Rebecca's hands were another thing entirely. While insisting on an advance, her hands looked ready to receive it, as though it would come floating toward her through the charged air. When a bid came in, she acknowledged it with a flick of the wrist, with the economy Queen Elizabeth uses when waving to the crowd. During a bidding war Rebecca's left hand was dedicated to one bidder while her right, holding a pencil, followed the other, settling into a swift rhythm. During a four-way bidding war, she appeared to be conducting an orchestra, the bidders following the directions of her hand. Because of her timing and elegance, the bids rushed in.

Some of those bids were as subtle as Rebecca's hands. If a buyer sat close, he or she could bid with a deft flip of the card, leaving the crowd to wonder where the bid had come from, and other buyers to wonder whom they were bidding against. On the other end were those bidders who held their cards high over their heads, indicating they were staying in. During a rapid-fire duel, all the auctioneer had to do was look at these volunteering bidders with cards raised, who would then nod. No one bought accidentally, as legend would have it, by the ill-timed fidget, but after bidding once, the most subtle movements sufficed—that and eye contact with the auctioneer. I wondered how Rebecca or Colin could pick up such solemn, birdlike nods from across the room, but like predators they must sharpen their abilities to pick up motion out of the corners of their eyes. Throughout the bidding I saw the runners catch only two bids among hundreds. Some buyers had positioned themselves on the center aisle so their slight motions could be seen most easily, while buyers in the back knew to make more dramatic gestures. A veteran auction buyer probably made any number of calculations, including trying to move closer so as to make bids on a desired lot without performing histrionics from the rear, and therefore signaling eagerness. On the other hand, a visibly determined buyer might suggest that counter-bidding was futile and discourage competition. Such subliminal messages paid off in real money.

A third auctioneer took over to give Rebecca a break after she had sold ninety lots. Rupert's style seemed a tad stiff; he even rolled his r's, as in announcing a "rrrrectangular mirror." At one point, in selling a painting, Rupert had to drop his suggested opener several times, and he grumbled, half to himself, "Suddenly we're doing a Dutch auction here." He was not as quick as Rebecca, but he was quite capable of handling the sale while she restored her breath and repaired the tattered edges of her voice.

The auction catalogue had a rhetoric as finely tuned as the auctioneers' pitches, creating value through association in the same way metaphors make meaning by juxtaposition. Paintings and sculptures by less-known artists were described as "in the manner of" some great master, while furniture was always "in the style of" some celebrated artisan or movement, such as the Empire period or Arts and Crafts. Furniture was also associated with English or French kings and queens in power at the time they were made; it was assumed everyone knew when a named monarch had reigned. From the kind of run-of-the-mill antiques I usually found, I knew that the term "Victorian" generally applied to most furniture of the mid-to-late nineteenth century, it having seen the long reign of Queen Victoria—a highly decorated style borrowing on classical, baroque, and oriental patterns—and that slightly newer, turn-of-the-twentieth-century pieces were "Edwardian." Here, though, we were being offered a Louis XVI (1774–1793) cabinet, a William and Mary sideboard (1687–1702), a Queen Anne walnut card table (1702–1714), and a rare George I mahogany tray-top table (1714–1727) that sold for $5,500. Two hundred such items, as well as fine clocks and carpets, would be sold before the first piece of the Hughes collection appeared, a handmade, thirty-eight-piece wooden model of Noah's Ark, fetching $850.

They were working bids four ways: room bids, left bids, phone bids, and desk bids. The desk bids were coming from Colin himself. Rebecca had indicated a bid was either a left bid or from Colin by swiftly gesturing to her throat with each advance. If bidding against the phone was risky, I'd consider bidding against the house itself foolhardy. They had to know more about a piece than you do, especially if they were bothering to bid. On one item, a corner chair, the desk quickly bid the price up to $1,800, a hundred dollars at a time, driving away the only competitor by giving the impression of being prepared to go much higher by answering bids with an instant advance, Rebecca's hand remaining at her throat. The catalogue description of this chair showed that Colin and his staff had examined it in great detail:

Carlo Bugatti Corner Chair
Ebonized wood parchment and hammered copper. The curved back rail inlaid in pewter with typical geometric pattern above two parchment covered roundels painted with female figures, pendent from cord, inset with pierced hammered copper roundels, the upholstered parchment seat above a conformingly inlaid apron raised on copper wrapped turned legs (distressed).

I have no idea what any of that means, but those attributes had led Colin to estimate its value at $4,000 to $6,000, so he got a bargain at just under $2,000. I thought the chair was garish, even unsightly, but that was mostly out of ignorance; I was not privy to the charms of a "parchment seat above a conformingly inlaid apron." However, like much of what resided in the Hughes household, the chair was probably rare, even one of a kind, though an acquired taste.

I decided to return for the bigger sale, the one in which most of Hughes's possessions would finally be offered up, including the mummy's hand. On my way out the door, I tried some of the food from the little kitchen in the corner—a fresh turkey wrap and homemade soup, for a dollar each. Colin and company were not trying to make money on food; he was simply trying to keep his classy crowd happy with some fine lunchtime fare. The real money was up front, crossing the block.

Chapter Three

❧

Selling the Mummy's Hand

A WEEK BEFORE THE NEXT SALE, I received an e-mail announcing it, with a link to Colin Stair's Web site. I searched the on-line catalogue and found the mummy's hand. The written description was not nearly as fulsome as some: "1 Mummified Left Hand, with faience ring on little finger, in a glass top box, 6 inches long." Because the hand had no documentation, Colin had little to use as a selling point. He couldn't claim it was from an Egyptian mummy, though he was able to identify the ring as "faience," or set with a kind of pottery—not jade— linking it to another lot listed in the same column, "1 Egyptian 3-inch faience Ushabti figure." Perhaps Colin was hoping buyers would assume the hand was ancient by association.

Colin also specified it was a "left hand," one of only a few definite attributes he could use. Perhaps, though, left hands were more valuable than right hands (such discriminations among collectors would not surprise me), or maybe it made the hand more "sinister," a word derived from the Latin word meaning "left hand" or "unlucky side," because that side usually did not bear a weapon and had to fend off blows. Surely this hand had met an unlucky fate, to be separated from its original owner, but the hand was lucky, grotesquely, to be valued beyond the grave. Lord Byron's poem "Lines Inscribed upon a Cup Formed from a Skull" declares: "Fill up—thou canst not injure me;/The worm hath fouler lips than thine." Perhaps the showcase was better than the sepulchre, the spotlight better than the lasting darkness of the tomb. The hand was only one in a run of lots no less hoary, including the mammoth tooth;

however, I saw no saints' relics. Maybe the family had decided to keep them or to donate them to a church. Either way, no indulgences would be sold at this sale, no sins exchanged for papal bulls.

My friend Michael Sham and I arrived at the next sale, and he immediately stopped in front of a display case containing a cache of pocket watches, so I left him there and made a quick pass around the room as I always do at previews, trying to make a mental note of the items there, hoping to be lured by something. I wasn't planning to bid; in fact I hoped to resist the urge because most things for sale here would appreciably drain my bank account.

Still, I was mightily attracted to much of what was on display. I am a fairly practical person, and I normally won't spend $900 on a fine antique bookcase because a cheaper bookcase would serve the same purpose. But the usefulness of an object is only part of its appeal. Show me a strange bauble, with utterly no use—yet sufficiently arcane, or that touches some fantastic daydream about ancient civilizations, for instance—and I can be compelled to spend out of all proportion to its value, overriding my natural frugality, my will to be rational. This sale was full of such whispers, nudges, and Siren calls. So I planned to bid on the mammoth tooth, which I joked with Michael I could use to crush herbs—feeling compelled to invent a use for it.

I had completed my pass around the room and had not come upon the hand. Michael was still looking at watches in the glass case; I too stopped to look at some of the jewelry on display, mostly heavy silver. A piece caught my eye, a brooch made out of an animal's paw. I looked in the catalogue and couldn't find it, so I asked the woman staffing the case what kind of paw it was. I suspected it was a trophy from a fox hunt.

"We think it's dachshund," she said, showing me how the end of the paw had been tipped with a silver collar, and the pin had been worked into the bottom.

"Someone really liked his dachshund," I said.

"I'm fond of my dachshund, but I want all four feet on him," she said.

More goods than the mummy's hand were of a funerary nature. The potential buyers of dachshund parts were there; lots of tiny dogs had shown up, rich owners in tow. When I saw Colin, dressed in an immaculate dark blue suit, I started to speak and was drowned out by a dog barking spastically. "Well, the kennel club is here," I joked, and he replied with a silent smile, not giving away how he felt about the precious pooches at his sale.

Michael asked Colin where the mummy's hand was displayed, and he pointed to the wall of display cases. "Just ask my father," he said and added, "People have been calling up and asking, 'Can we smell it?'" Colin maintained the same smile—coy, amused, and Cheshire. When I saw the hand on the bottom shelf of a display case, I was surprised to find it smaller than I had remembered, although it was six inches long, and my own, not a large hand nor dwarfed by mummification, is a mere seven and a half. Someone with a twisted sense of utility could use the hand as a ruler, in the same way the king's foot was once the measure of an official foot, and the space between the second and third knuckles of his royal index finger the official inch. The heights of horses are still given in hands—a remnant of those pre-premetric days. Of course the king got to keep his hand where it belonged.

The hand was relieved of being more sinister by being in a relaxed pose. A hand frozen in a grip or scrambling crablike is a horror-movie image. This hand was relaxed, fingers pressed together as it would be if placed with its arm crossed on the chest or meeting the other in prayer. I looked at where the hand would have joined the wrist, and I could see the ball socket of bone on which it once swiveled and the shredded flesh from when it had been wrenched free. The hand had clearly not fallen off, I deduced with a shudder.

The box did have a glass top, as advertised, not the cellophane I had thought. The top had been made by a previous owner, perhaps Hughes himself, by cutting the center out of a faux leather cardboard box top and filling it with a rectangle of glass held in place with masking tape. The homemade glass top was an attempt to ennoble it, as was the white silk lining the bottom, bunched like the upholstery in a coffin. Michael was holding the box, and then he removed the top and said, "Touch it. I know you want to," but I didn't. I didn't want to find the hand as unremarkable as a leather wallet—or worse, that it didn't feel like leather at all but like something I had never felt before. I had touched it already, in a sense.

"I think I have to bid on it," I said.

"You should," Michael said.

"Not that I actually want it. In fact, if I did accidentally win the bid I'd have to take it home and bury it or something." I only wanted to participate in the transaction, to raise the price, and the value, of the item. Bidding somehow seemed like a sign of respect.

Colin began the sale as before, this time announcing there had been many left bids. However, he immediately turned the auction over to Rebecca, who commenced with her graceful bid-catching, hands finding the rhythm of the crowd as she sold thirteen lots of Middle Eastern rugs and then ceramics, pausing to make her trademark pitch, "No one else needs to say prayers tonight?" when selling a porcelain angel.

Rebecca moved quickly through a parade of furniture, the highest price, $6,500, paid for a Louis XVI mahogany table, made by a phone bidder. As Colin had with the Bugatti chair, he picked up a bargain, bidding $950 for a print "from Catlin's North American Indian collection" of a buffalo chasing a mounted hunter entitled *Buffalo Hunt, Chasing Back*. Its predicted auction price was $2,000 to $3,000. Because there were so many left bids, I finally figured out how the house handled them. They were a range of prices a buyer is willing to pay. So, for instance, if a buyer at the preview likes an item, but cannot attend the sale, he or she will fill out a left bid form, promising to pay perhaps between $100 and $400 for it. The auctioneer then is free to start the bidding at $100 as an automatic opener and advance at increments against bids on the floor until the $400 left bid has been topped, at which time the auctioneer announces the bidding is now "in the room." That makes the playing field level. An auctioneer is working for the seller, not the buyer, but is duty bound to be fair with the latter. At this sale each item came with at least one left bid.

The crowd was clearly restless, and even a bit noisy, and I guessed many people were here for the stranger items and were a bit impatient as Rebecca sold a string of fine but common antiques. Rebecca relinquished the sale to Rupert at lot 80, which was the beginning of a run of antiquities. The first contained two French prints depicting the faces, front and profile, of Egyptian mummies. The frames bore skull-and-crossbones designs, exactly like those on a twelve-foot tapestry hanging on the wall that the catalogue identified as a decoration from the Skull and Bones Society, a quasi-secret club at Yale whose membership is rumored to have George Bush the elder as a member.

Rupert himself was bidding on the print, but when he closed the deal at $1,500 I couldn't tell who had won. Rupert would eventually bid on most of the antiquities, and I wondered if that was why he had replaced Rebecca. Some of these items were marked as having once belonged to Andy Warhol. A set of three Mayan pots that had sold in a 1988 Sotheby's auction when the pop artist's estate had been sold after his death and Hughes had been among the buyers had a double provenance. I could tell from the murmuring attention of the crowd that they were here for precisely this kind of merchandise.

The mammoth tooth was coming up, and I made a quick calculation about how high I might bid for it. It was valued in the catalogue at between $50 and $75, and I decided to go as high as $150, figuring twice the price would be a competitive bid. It was a ridiculous figure to pay for the giant tooth of an extinct mammal; it was not rare and was certainly no T-rex relic like Sue. Still, its gleaming enamel was deep and creamy, and when I recognized it was a molar, crisscrossed with ridges for gnawing plants, and I imagined the beast contentedly grinding a mouthful of tough glacial-age grasses, I was hooked. Once you become involved with an item, you become a committed buyer. However, when the molar crossed the block and opened with a left bid of $300, and the bidding ran up to $550, I realized I was purely an observer at a sale like this.

Still, the mummy's hand remained. It was up next, and I spied it in the hands of an older runner. He glanced at the box, then took a longer look which telegraphed a casual curiosity and slight bewilderment. He too was probably wondering how such a thing had found its way here. As the runner walked to the front with it, I surprised myself by being a little nervous, as though I might really buy the hand. I had arranged the card in my hand so if I raised it the number 86 would not be mistaken for 98. If I did make a bid, I hoped not to be so unlucky as to make the winning one.

"And now the item I'm sure you've all been waiting for," Rupert said to a shred of nervous laughter in the room, to which he replied, "To each his own. On the mummified left hand we have a left bid, and we'll begin at $1,200."

A bid came from the floor for $1,300, to which Rupert added the absentee bidder's advance of $1,400. The floor went silent, and the hand was sold.

I was astonished. It was over in seconds, and I never had a chance to bid, though I would never have so much as flicked my card with such a high opener; I didn't dare scratch my nose. I noticed Rupert did not bid on it as he had on every other antiquity. His distaste for the thing was nearly liquid.

In contrast, this absent bidder must have had a serious need for the hand, had made some connection with it that perhaps rivaled Hughes's own when he had acquired the relic. The new owner of the mummy's hand had come in during the preview and had left an opening bid of four times the highest estimated price, obviously to ensure his success. Even so he *did* have some competition in the room, though he had prepared for that with additional advances. Had the bidder left a bid because he needed to be elsewhere that day, maybe running an antique shop in Hudson, Saturday afternoon being a busy day? Or did he find the hand so compelling he couldn't stand to be present at the sale, to reveal his ghoulish enthusiasm by attending and bidding in person? I wondered about the highest figure in his left bid.

Rupert moved on quickly, offering an unidentified "fossilized bone" by saying, "Now, for those of you who missed your chance at the left hand, be the first on your block . . . " However, a crescendo had been reached in the sale. Colin would make a 15 percent premium from the buyer and another 10 to 15 percent commission from Hughes's estate, earning nearly $500 on the hand. The moment was over, the deal was done, and the momentum of the sale was unstoppable. The expensive cavalcade would continue, one lot at a time, until the final hammer fell and all the spoils had been divided among the citizens of this peculiar empire.

Chapter Four

❦

High Victorians on the Block

OUNTRY AUCTIONS CONJURE UP IMAGES of failed farms and closed businesses, of despairing sellers standing nearby as weed-sucking buyers loot the trappings of their lives for pennies on the dollar. However, ordinary country auctions, those not devoted to the finery Colin Stair sells, are not usually so grave, and they are perhaps more rewarding as a result. People don't show up expecting the finest castoffs; they come for a deal, and maybe a steal, if they're lucky. These auctioneers do the same research as their higher-end colleagues, but because their sales are so varied, both in the goods they sell and in the buyers they attract, they are more apt to make a mistake now and again—and that's what the customer is betting, and bidding, on. Country auctions are public rituals, full of humor, drama, and even warmth—as much an excuse for a community to gather as a village parade. The bidding is still competitive and the outcome the same: A wealth of castoffs changes hands in a couple of hours.

These infusions of goods into the secondhand network are held weekly or monthly, as regular as local sporting events, and the attendees grow to know each other. Regulars eye a stranger cautiously, though they take care not to make a stranger feel unwelcome, as your money is as good as any. Still you are a potential rival, perhaps drawn from wherever you hail by some choice bauble about which you have special knowledge. Your presence signifies there might be some rare fruit to pluck this night, and you plan to harvest it and leave the rubes to bid on the rest. It is akin to attending an unfamiliar church. The congregation accepts your presence, but it subtly signals it has noticed you. Now sit down, pay attention, and sing the proper hymns, and not too loudly, if you please.

This is a brief alienation, though. Auctions are advertised events, so regulars expect to see a handful of new faces each time. Show up twice and you're no longer a threat, show up three times and you are treated as a regular, but don't try to stake out a chair front-and-center, where the big buyers sit, unless you can weather the cold stares. They are like the counter seats at a neighborhood diner, or the deacon's pew.

Jack Metzger, an antique dealer in Cambridge, New York, told me Mike Smith's Cherry Tree Auctions should not be missed. "There you will really see something," he said. "He gets dealers from all over New York, Vermont, Massachusetts, and Connecticut." Cherry Tree Auctions are held monthly at the Washington County Fairgrounds in the rural hillsides near the Vermont border outside Saratoga Springs, and the setting would have been appropriate for a sale of farm implements. I was early for the preview so I had the place to myself. The white-painted cement floor of the building probably held Four-H exhibits during the August fair, and it echoed with my footsteps. Auction posters from the past two hundred years displayed at the front door featured wagons and tractors and "Four Fine Bulls."

This sale was full of fine silver and bronzes, some of the former tagged as from the Trask estate, lavishly wealthy, nineteenth-century Saratoga Springs residents. The bronzes had been a college professor's, I learned. There was no catalogue, only a legal-sized sheet of paper crammed with a continuous, single-spaced typed merchandise description. The statues were on classical themes, and I looked for one I might recognize, such as Daphne escaping Apollo by changing into a laurel, but only one intrigued me, a four-foot Greek general, the tag said, playing a lyre. The tag also noted the item would sell at 6:00; the sale started at 5:00. Nothing else had a set time of sale, so I wondered why this piece was special. Everything else would be brought to the block randomly.

"If you buy 'em all you'll get the right one," said a gray-bearded man in a white straw Stetson, his lack of front teeth failing to inhibit a wide smile. A tape measure hooked onto the front pocket lip of his denims, he walked among the growing crowd, joking with everyone; I assumed he was a runner, his job before the sale being to raise the energy level and to build goodwill. A friendly crowd is essential in a country auction.

Longtime attendees are loyalists, ready to give the auctioneer a reasonable opener, but he has to keep them on his side.

Like the Hughes/Warhol provenance, the Trask connection was the high point of this sale. Financier Spencer Trask and his novelist wife Katrina built a stone Victorian mansion on a compound outside of Saratoga Springs. Soon the family suffered great calamity. Their four children died, and Katrina lost Spencer to a railroad accident in 1909, leaving her in a deep drama of grief rivaling Queen Victoria's mourning of Prince Albert. After Katrina died in 1922, the mansion, Yaddo, with formal gardens and statues dedicated to their lost children, became an internationally famous artist colony. This romantic story of great riches and sorrow was now being applied to the value of the family silver, as it would to antique toys at next month's sale. Mike said these were the Trask "Sunday toys," trains and dolls with which the children were only allowed to play once a week and were therefore pristine, including "The Fountain Boat," a steamship that had plied the lily-padded pools of their grounds.

Besides silver, Trask pieces included painted copies of famous works of art, Russian Orthodox icons, and a letter signed by British Prime Minister Gladstone framed with his picture. I saw a woman examine the "Moscow stamp" Mike Smith said could be found on the icon, and a man train a penlight on the silver. Stopping in front of a painting, actually five oval paintings in one gilded scroll-and-leaf carved frame, I recognized the center one as Raphael's *Madonna of the Chair* and mentioned the title to Mike. He responded, as Colin had, with "Now I know more than I knew before."

I added that John the Baptist was the second infant in the picture, and Mike countered by pointing to another oval, saying it was Raphael's self-portrait. Mike didn't want to appear not have done his homework. The nearly triumphant broadsheet showed he thought this sale was auspicious: "Certainly one of our finer sales with exceptional items in many categories. . . . We are pleased to have been chosen by a descendant of Spencer Trask to sell a hoard of Fine Silver and several pieces of 19thC [*sic*] Italian Art used by Spencer and Katrina Trask. . . . " To be selling such revered local merchandise was a bit of an honor.

Was this an important provenance, though? The household had broken up eighty years ago, probably at an even more exceptional auction, but did their having owned the demitasse cups and toilet sets still add value? A buyer said, "The Trask provenance will last forever, forever" when I asked him about its significance. "How would you like to own a Washington table?" he added.

"But Washington's provenance is a bit different," I said. "He's a national figure. The Trasks are only locally famous."

He agreed. If this merchandise was selling outside of the area, in Pennsylvania for instance, the provenance would probably elicit a pregnant "Who?" from the crowd. I had seen license plates from four states in the parking lot, as Jack had said I would, and the distant buyers wouldn't be impressed by a Trask connection. Pricey used goods, like fine silver, have a secure value everywhere, but the impact of provenance can be tied to a geographic region, thinning considerably when farther flung.

"I appreciate how you've put this sale together," one buyer said to Mike. "No oak."

"Well, it's not an oakey sale," Mike answered. Oak furniture is a hallmark of a "country antiques" sale, as it was not used often for furniture before 1900, and even then it was stained to look like cherry or mahogany. Mike had added items from elsewhere to complement the Trask goods. One of the few exceptions was a primitive corner cabinet in a fleshy maple—the only thing that truly appealed to me. An elderly woman at my elbow declared the cabinet "homely." She was there, like most of the others, for Victorian frills.

Bidders had reserved all eighty-four of the seats during the previous day's preview, Mike said over the microphone. The place was packed now, and many attendees would be standing. The competition for seats did not spill over into a tense expectancy, though, as many buyers seemed to know each other, and they called out to friends by name. Cherry Tree Auctions was like a club, where the rules were clear and simple: Mike found the stuff, and these folks showed up to buy it. As Mike explained, "If you have never been to our sale, listen closely. If you have, half-listen. We do not take credit cards. We do not charge a buyer's premium. You pay what you bid and in cash or good check." Mike joked if you were used to paying a buyer's premium, feel free to pay the extra 10 percent. Then he said, "Everything every single person wants will be sold in the first hour." Laughter followed, but I missed the joke until he added, "It's inevitable in a sale like this we'll be selling very nice things at 9:00." He wanted the overfull crowd to stay for the duration. If people drifted away, the end of the sale would see less bidding and lower prices. Mike took no left bids or phone bids. His auction was among the most aboveboard and traditional I have attended.

Another aspect of Cherry Tree Auctions was equally traditional: I overheard one buyer joking with another over her "healthy dinner." A vendor outside was selling carnival food from a cart—no fancy wraps here. I chanced a hot dog and a hot chocolate.

Besides the primitive cabinet, the only piece of furniture that attracted my attention was a tall, six-drawer chest called a highboy. One of my friends had been looking for one, so I entertained the idea of buying it if the chest went cheaply, which at first seemed unlikely. This one was in the style of early-eighteenth-century chests, with scalloped carvings on the top rail, the kind fussed over by the Keno brothers on *Antiques Road-show*, which sold for many thousands. It needed work; one drawer was tight, and the finish was mottled and crusty. If this was a true antique, it would be a crime to refinish it. Perhaps it had stood in a basement for years, dampness puckering the finish and swelling the drawer. It was barely serviceable.

I decided to spend some time with the highboy, testing my ability to discern its age. I folded the flyer, in case its age was listed, and looked for clues to whether the piece was from the eighteenth century, a nineteenth-century copy, or even newer. Opening the drawers I saw dovetailed joinery, but wide and regular, not the thin, irregular type of an "early" piece. The brass pulls were original, tarnished black, with no wear signs on the drawer fronts showing another kind of hardware had ever been used, but the screws on the inside holding them on looked machined, not handmade.

Those details alone were enough to convince me the chest wasn't from the eighteenth century. I next decided the wood inside was too bright, and saw writing, in a black wax pencil, near one of the drawer runners. It was upside down, but when I turned my head I saw "⅜ x ⅝." Dimensional lumber. Until roughly 1900, all lumber was sold at full size. So, if you bought a 2x4, it was a full two inches by four inches. When the vast, old-growth forests had fallen, lumber barons realized wood was not inexhaustible, so they began selling what was called "finished" or dimensional lumber, making a 2x4 a half inch thinner and a quarter inch narrower. A drawer runner measuring ⅜ x ⅜ would have been made by splitting a 1x1 (¾ x ¾). The chest was probably not even a nineteenth-century copy. This was confirmed by "C-17" stamped on a drawer back, a furniture company model number. The piece was probably from the 1920s.

While determining the age of the chest, I had also found some flaws: two turned spindles that had adorned the top had snapped off—I found them in the drawers—and a drawer back was splintered. Add these flaws to the highboy's dubious age, and the piece had serious problems. How would Mike sell it? Surrounded by genuine nineteenth-century pieces, it could have passed for much older to a less scrutinous buyer. If Mike had gotten it on consignment, and the owner had said it was "early," would Mike sell it as such, even if he could tell it wasn't? I'd soon find out, as Mike stepped to the podium to begin the sale.

Mike announced the seats should now be occupied by those who had reserved them; a few minutes later he declared any unclaimed seats were now up for grabs, grumbling about people reserving seats at the preview but not showing up at the sale. A couple near me had anticipated this and had stood in one of the narrow aisles; they rushed in to grab two. I sat in the back on the edge of a shaky card table holding embroidered linens, keeping one foot on the floor to carry part of my weight.

The sale began with silver. Mike would suggest an opener he thought was a fair price, $900 for a tea set, for instance, but when no one bid, his opener plummeted to $250 in order to get the bidding started. Usually Mike got the price back up to his original opener, and above, but the crowd made him earn it the old-fashioned way, a short advance at a time. The buyers knew Mike had no left bids in his pocket, nor phone bids up his sleeve. He was a skilled auctioneer, though, and had the goodwill of the crowd, so no one was stealing anything.

Mike also had his own idiosyncratic cataloguing system and banter. For instance, lots tagged PFM meant "Print-Painting-Frame-Mirror" or, as Mike said, "Pretty much anything that hangs on a wall." His rhetoric was a bit euphemistic, so faded and threadbare Persian rugs showed "good age," a sign of authenticity. Vowels and syllables rolled like marbles in his mouth, but with a series of phrases embedded in them. An opening bid of $140 would elicit a "Thank you," followed by:

"150. Do you want it?"

"160. Do you care to?"

"170. Do you be?"

"180. Do you need it?"

"190. Would you go?"

"200. How about it?"

These insistent questions seemed to revolve as long as the bidding lasted.

I was getting better at detecting the bidders' buying techniques. I saw one guy who seemed to have come for Middle Eastern carpets, bidding on almost all of them. Because he was standing in the back, Mike would acknowledge him by saying, "In the far left." After the man got four carpets, he slipped to the other side of the room. This, I realized, kept Mike from immediately looking to him for an advance and to keep the others from knowing where he was and bidding harder against him because he had prevailed against them on the other rugs.

When I stepped outside for a coffee, I met a disgruntled buyer. "It's crazy," he said, "like a feeding frenzy." He thought the Trask items had drawn buyers with deep pockets, though he admitted their silver had not brought more than others. Any sale with lots of paintings and silver was high-priced and drove up prices on other stuff, he said.

"I thought when lots of buyers only want one or two kinds of things, like silver, other stuff is underbid," I said. After all, that was why Mike had grouped like goods together.

"Last month, furniture from the 1700s was selling for $50," he said, but I didn't believe him. Then, grinding out his cigarette, he added, "Most of those paintings I wouldn't have hanging in my house."

I returned inside to see the Greek lyre player come up. Mike said he had received so many inquiries about the piece he decided to sell it at a specific time so all would get a chance. A quick duel reached $2,000, the most earned by any of the old professor's bronzes. You really didn't need to buy them all to get the right one. The Raphael copy sold for $1,100, and as the buyer carried it out a chunk of the frame fell off. I'd say he was stung, though I'm no judge of paintings. Still, for old paintings not made by a great artist, the original frame is a big part of the value. I don't think the provenance would help it much.

Next Mike sold a metal rack I had seen while registering. A hoop of iron from which hung hooks and decorative shapes, like an upside-down crown, it had stumped the house, the woman at the counter said. It was clearly handmade, and I thought Jack Metzger might like it. If I could buy it cheaply enough, I might sell it to him at a profit—trying my hand at being a picker. I told her I suspected it was a rack for hanging pots over a hearth, and the decorations were fleur-de-lis, a traditional French design. It was as good a guess as any, I suppose, and likely accurate.

And that's exactly how Mike described it when it crossed the block: "A pot hook, possibly French." She had reported my guess to him. Had I been really serious about buying it, I should have kept my mouth shut.

At 9:00, a third of the buyers were gone, what Mike had been trying to avoid, and most of the silver, rugs, and paintings had left with them. Now the highboy I had examined was up. The runners didn't bother to bring it to the front; one simply draped an arm across the top. Mike described it as an American chest from the 1920s. It sold for $450, and as I left I heard Mike complain, "That's a good price for such a fine piece." Still, he had not tried to pass it off as older.

The Cherry Tree Auction is itself a kind of antique, being held at a fairground and forgoing left bids and buyers' premiums. Fairgrounds themselves are cultural curios, remnants of our agrarian, marketplace past. For the last few decades, malls have taken over as community meeting places. In many places, though, malls have become beside the point in the face of big-box stores. New York's Capital District has been declared "overbuilt" with malls; half of these concrete substitutes for traditional downtowns have been demolished in recent years. Before meeting the wrecking ball the malls underwent one more resuscitation—as centers for secondhand commerce.

One of those struggling malls, the former Clifton Country Mall, renamed The Clifton Center, in an attempt to eschew its mall-ness, had been closing by inches. Now it hosted antique stores, and the monthly "Acorn Auctions." "We're inside the mall next to JCPenney," read the flyer I picked up in an antique store. The big store remained an "anchor." Acorn's spot had probably been a large clothing store and had undergone little remodeling. The walls still bore the backdrops of the various departments within the store: mirrored walls stopped at faux Victorian wallpaper leading to a painted mauve section.

This was a less busy auction, in terms of customers and merchandise, as it mostly contained stuff from one house, described in the flyer as "the contents of Virginia Monroe's Albany home. Ginny is a descendant of

Mary Stuart and, true to her brave and adventurous Scottish heritage, is heading south with just her suitcase and her cat!" Discards. She must have been an antique collector, as most of her goods were from the nineteenth century or earlier.

I had gotten pretty good at picking out the dealers from the amateur buyers at previews. Amateurs glide through with equal interest in everything, hands behind their backs. A dealer confidently handles each piece, having handled plenty like it, accustomed to the weight and balance, flips the dish to check for marks, and strokes the lip to feel for chips. I saw one stoop-shouldered dealer with a mastiff face rifling through a suitcase full of dolls, like someone looking for the proper piece of cordwood to start a fire.

Another aspect was also familiar: the food. "Worst cup of coffee I've ever had in my life," said a buyer. When I registered, a woman at the desk said to her coworker, "It's not even 6:30, and I'm already on my second soda. Looks like I'm going to be a five-soda girl tonight." You are as apt to gain weight as spend money at an auction.

Jim Carter, the auctioneer, chatted to the crowd, reporting one of his runners had been in an Amateur World Strong Man Competition and had lost some skin on his hands "from lifting an S-10 pickup and rolling it forward like a wheelbarrow." When I looked at the nearly seven-foot, thick-limbed runner, I couldn't decide if Jim was kidding or not. Jim wouldn't be lifting anything; he had hurt his back and was letting a younger man, Ed Finney, Jr., handle the sale. Ed was a sizable fellow, too, and had probably also started as a runner.

The auctioneer is the focus, but the runner plays a pivotal role. Not only must runners find and lift items so everyone can see them, they must keep an item moving, motion being visually magnetic. Two runners will hold up a chest of drawers; then, with one hand, one will open and close drawers, or together they will turn the piece to show the back or tilt it to show a burled veneer on the top. A single runner will hold a cut-crystal vase high, moving it hand-to-hand, swiveling it to catch the light—all while keeping his or her hands out of the way, so it can be seen fully. These gyrations match the pace of the bidding; when the bidding slows, the item begins to spin.

Runners *present* an item, and their postures and facial expressions are attitudes of offering. This is up *now*, so now is the time to bid. It will soon be gone, the arched eyebrow suggests, and you know you want it, so come on and bid! It is part taunt, part invitation, and as the runner looks out expectantly, he or she is also required to call out bids the auctioneer misses, to be an extra set of eyes. These things must be done simultaneously. A night of running must be exhausting.

Ed started the auction, and at first he tried overly high openers, then cut them by half, then half again, until he got a bid. The bidders signaled they might bid half the price by making a horizontal, slicing motion with their cards. Were they giving Ed a hard time because he was a substitute-auctioneer, the way students bedevil a substitute teacher? Were they trying to take advantage of him because he was young and inexperienced? Ed made his first sale after much coaxing: $175 for a folk art whirligig. Ed was a capable, but not stylish, auctioneer; his chant was slurred, his pitches stock: The pictures were all "cute" or "scenic" and the furniture "nice" or "clean and ready for your house."

Most of the bids started at $50, and they appeared to be coming from buyer number 31. He seldom won, and it made me a bit suspicious. Once, when number 31 bid on a pair of porcelain dogs, Ed took his opener, then closed the bid. Was the buyer obliging him with gift openers, and Ed rewarding him with a good price on something he knew number 31 wanted? Such an agreement would not be unheard of and was certainly not provable. Even if true, no one was being exploited; pieces were going cheaply, such as a nineteenth-century blanket chest for $200.

Ed could even be getting his $50 openers out of thin air. Colin Stair had called them "chandelier bids," and Talk of the Town auctioneer John Christman had labeled them "kicked-in" bids. This trick involves an auctioneer pretending to see an opener in the crowd. No one can contradict him or her, because all eyes are on the moving merchandise and on the auctioneer, not on the other buyers. Who knew what subtle bid had been caught. The risk is that if no one advances the chandelier bid, the house, or the auctioneer, has to buy the piece.

I saw this backfire for an auctioneer once. The house, which I'll call Crooked Tree Auctions, was handling a run of fairly good antiques. The auctioneer, M. Mumbles, figured each of them was worth a minimum of $100, and he steadily picked that figure out of the air for an opener. The crowd bid up each piece, until I could feel the mood flatten. They had figured it out. The auctioneer had kicked in $100 one too many times, and without calling out a location or pointing to a buyer.

Mumbles kicked in a $100 bid on a table, got an advance at $125, then nothing. He kicked in another $100 on an oak desk and got no advance at all; the room stared at him. Mumbles had to eat the next six items, until he let the opener arise naturally—this time $50—and the bidding resumed with a great exhalation, from both the crowd and auctioneer. If the buyers suspect they are being taken for a ride, they will collectively punish the auctioneer. The auction is in real trouble if the room begins thinking in unison.

"People have some psychological thing about making the first bid," John said, and getting the opener is the hardest part of the auctioneer's job. John claimed you can judge an auctioneer by timing how fast things sell. If the auctioneer is only moving 50 to 65 items an hour, the auctioneer is struggling. John said if he is selling 100 items an hour, he is doing well, and that he has moved 350 lots in three hours at the Talk of the Town.

Buyer number 31 could also have been a plant. John told me some auctioneers will station a buyer in the audience. Some complain these plants make high openers—the same as a chandelier bid—but John said an ethical auctioneer will use an agent only when he wants to buy something, like Colin's desk bids. The significant difference is the room doesn't know it is bidding against the desk or if the auctioneer's buyer is simply running it up.

Left bids, phone bids, desk bids, plant bids, chandelier bids, gift bids—clearly anything could be going on. The smart buyer learns an auction house by observing before ever buying anything, learning how the sale works, and what forces are in play—still, tricks might elude you. I'm not saying anything truly fishy was going on at Acorn Auctions. However, even the most aboveboard auction could be tweaking the results.

One of the reasons furniture was going cheaply was the presence of dolls and ceramic Hummel figurines—one of the first manufactured collectibles. Collectors and dealers of dolls and Hummels were here in force, and the rest of Ginny's estate was being shortchanged. One buyer knew this and was aggressively bidding on other items. Elderly and frail, with a cane between his knees, the buyer's thin body was incongruently covered in bib overalls and what looked to be a black silk shirt. When one of two case clocks came up, what are commonly known as "grandfather" clocks, the buyer grew attentive, the deprivations of age lifting.

He snapped up the first clock for $1,000, a high price for anything at this sale, but not for a case clock, which can be worth twenty times that amount. He bid briskly on the next one, identified as French, and the bidding halted at $1,300. Before Ed could shout "Sold," his runner said, "It has 1835 written on the back!" and the bidding restarted and rose to $1,800 in no time. The old man eventually won that bid as well, but he was grimacing. He'd seen that date and had hoped no one else had. It was one of the few times I ever heard a runner hawk a piece. Was it timed to jump-start the bidding?

The old man entered one more bid, on a hall mirror, but did not come out on top, slumping back into his body. The mirror, attributed to having graced the Grand Union Hotel in Saratoga Springs, a giant Victorian hotel that burned in the 1950s—another local provenance, like the Trasks—sold for $2,400. The crowd applauded. It was the highest price paid at the auction, but what did the applause mean? Were they lauding the skill of the auctioneer, the value of the piece, or the buyer's discernment in acquiring a fine piece?

Later, when the auction was over, I saw people crowded around van rear doors and pickup tailgates, looking through box lots, boxes of stuff bought for one price. The wheeling and dealing continued in the mall parking lot.

Chapter Five

✌

All-Purpose Auctions

VEN A COUNTRY AUCTION can have a legacy like the generations of Stairs. The Doins of Waterford, New York, Sonny and Dean, have run auctions for at least forty years. They hold three auctions a week, and so they don't liquidate estates exclusively; they gather stuff from flea markets, yards sales, and on consignment. Likewise, they don't group stuff to attract one kind of buyer, and they rarely advertise. Everyone knows the Doins and when they hold sales. Country auctions come and go, but Sonny's Auction Barn is an institution.

I first went to Sonny's ten years ago, and the family barn was little changed from when it had stored machinery a generation before. Sonny, a brisk little man, bald as a lightbulb, conducted from a high podium while several runners hustled, including his red-haired son, Dean , whose high-pitched yelp when he spotted a bid was startling. Dean was learning the business, and he called the auction for part of the evening. His father was the real attraction, though. Sonny cajoled and good-naturedly insulted his crowd when they wouldn't bid, complaining they were "stealing this stuff." Mostly, though, Sonny would perform for the crowd's amusement, which would egg him on. When selling a radio, for instance, someone would invariably shout, "Does it work?" Sonny would say, "Sure it works," then, holding it beside his head, start singing a burlesque of a country-western song into the microphone—until the bids started. Sonny was all show.

I once attended an auction of a closing hardware store and was delighted to find Sonny in charge. He was having a tough time of it that day, though. The sale was outside, and it was a drizzly, spring day, so the crowd was sullen. What's more, Sonny was selling the small stuff first, hand tools and hinges, and buyers near me grumbled about waiting for air compressors and lawn tractors. Sonny had decided, I suppose, to hold off on bigger items to keep the moist crowd there. Nothing was selling well, however; even brass-trimmed mahogany carpenter's levels, elegant precision tools, went for $10 apiece, and sets of socket wrenches sold for $5. I bought one of each.

Then Sonny noticed it was noon, and the crowd, which had been standing for two hours in the rain, wanted lunch, so he started selling the candy bars the hardware store had sold by the cash register. Sonny's instincts were dead-on; the crowd began hungrily bidding. Candy bars were flying out of the boxes, and Sonny started selling them a handful at a time. At one point he held two fans of Hershey's bars high over his head, and as the price rose he began a little clog dance to his rolling banter, that white-noise scat of the country auctioneer, his face ablaze with the moment. Sonny was in some rare auctioneer's zone, a moment when he had what everyone wanted, when time had stopped and the bidding was endless.

Sonny's Auction Barn was now Dean's Auction Barn ten years later when I returned with junk aficionado Bob Miner. I expected the son's more laid-back style would dominate. The barn was paneled now, not the whitewashed utility of Sonny's day. I had hurried there after work and knew I'd have to eat auction fare for dinner, so I went straight to the makeshift grill in the corner. There a woman with auburn hair and her young daughter were cooking hot dogs and hamburgers. The mother smiled at me in a beautiful, overworked sort of way. I left, wondering about her life.

Sonny didn't make an appearance, though when I had called for the time of the sale his voice still graced the answering machine. And the tall podium remained, and the single ceiling spotlight the runners used to twinkle glassware.

Dean also ran an antique store in one of the emptying malls. He had branched out from his father's calling. Once I saw Dean at an estate sale, showing another buyer a box of fishing lures. "Yeah, I know what I have," he said. He knew old lures had become one of the hottest collectibles, some fetching many hundreds of dollars. Dean was savvy, while his father had been tireless and ebullient.

One tradition persisted at the Doin auction: junk night. On Mondays and Saturdays the Doins sold their best goods, including antiques, but on Wednesdays they peddled the most desperate castoffs. On this night part of the parking lot was taken up with junk, rows of half-full boxes, pipe-framed furniture, a jackstraw pile of pickaxes, a wooden-handled scythe, tattered modern wicker furniture, wire racks, and an exercise bike. People squatted over the boxes, raking through them to find an enticing curio.

Bob and I joined the hunt, and he locked onto a log splitter lying nearby. Dean had not bothered to put lot numbers on anything, so it was hard to distinguish between what was for sale from other junk. When I asked Dean if the log splitter would be auctioned, he said, "A friend of mine dropped that off. It doesn't run, and the pump needs new seals, so I'm not dealing it. He wants $80, if you want it." Bob had said he'd pay as much as $100 for one, so he was mightily tempted and spent time stooped over it, like a detective looking for clues.

The absence of lot numbers made me hesitate about bidding at the sale. I once got burned at Sonny's because I didn't know the number on a bookcase. Sonny had three bookcases for sale, all made of oak. One had curved glass doors, and a second was plain and square with flat doors. The third was rickety, with warped shelves. His runners brought all three to the front at once, and I bid $300 *on the wrong bookcase* and got it! It was my fault: Had I known the lot number, I wouldn't have been confused. To add insult to injury, the curved book-case sold for the same amount, and it was clearly worth more than the one I had bought. Someone got a real deal. I kicked myself for the rest of the sale.

I glumly took my plain bookcase and my stupidity home with me, and over the years have grown fond of the former, deciding its simple, unadorned lines suited me more than the fancier one. Never mind that it wasn't even a bookcase. It was a china cabinet. It holds books as ably as it would dishes.

None of this Wednesday night junk would sell for $300. A steady customer told me how this part of the auction worked: "Dean will stand over these boxes, five or so at a time, and ask for a bid for your choice of box. Be ready to bid, because he'll let them go quickly."

"He really sells them fast?"

"Oh yeah," he said, "he'll move this stuff out."

Dean started, as the customer had said, with the junk outside. With one runner to help, he'd point to a row of five boxes and ask for one- or two-dollar openers—and sometimes settle for that. The highest priced box went for seven bucks, a box of tools chosen from six. The remainder sold for less. Dean sold three pickaxes for two dollars and failed to even get a bid on a store mannequin and the exercise bicycle. He barely tried with the bike; he put his hand on it and asked with a sheepish grin, "Will anyone give me anything for this?" When no one bid, he told the runner to "take this to the Dumpster," adding "I don't want to catch any of you poking around my trash." He knew this scavenger crowd would rather trash-pick something than pay a single dime for it.

Dean had negotiated a freewheeling set of ground rules with his junk-night regulars: He was free to say anything he wanted about an item, and they were free to believe anything they chose. Dean did what he could to sell his parking lot castoffs. If a rocking chair rocked, he rocked it. If a pair of shears worked, he snapped them in the air. Dean pitched a garage door opener, work-booted foot on top of the machine, declaring: "Used three times or for three years, I don't remember which." He tried to get an opener of $50 for the wicker, claiming it was "antique." When no one budged, he grinned and said, "Well, it looks *old*, doesn't it? Come on, just a coat of paint, and it's ready to use, and now's the time of year to buy it." Dean would have said that at any time of year. He crowed, "Baseball cards!" when he hovered over a box of sports cards in albums, knowing they were collectible, but I had looked at them and had seen they were off-brands, not the venerable Topps, and only of *umpires*, not actual players. Moving quickly, Dean pulled a knife out of a box. "Look at this stuff," he cried. "A knife, possibly military, I don't know." The rows of junk sold in less than thirty minutes.

The scavengers trailed Dean inside where the sale resumed on less forlorn merchandise. He claimed some things were "good buys if you were just getting into the business," a line he had used outside as well, probably noticing one young woman was buying liberally, especially glassware, perhaps building inventory for her own junk shop or antique store. She was an easy mark, and Dean worked her hard for bids. Before long she was surrounded by plates and tea sets. John Christman's wife, Heidi, said people building an inventory for a fledgling antique business were usually foolish—at first. She had once watched a new dealer at an auction buying Roseville pottery, checking a price book he had in his lap. She took him aside and told him he had bought a pile of reproductions, hundreds of dollars' worth, and he was devastated. She gave him some valuable advice: If you are going to buy a particular type of antique, look at it and get used to seeing it so you can spot a replica.

I saw a veteran antique dealer I knew who would not be likely to make such a mistake. "I haven't seen anything I want here," he said. "I'm just here for the abuse. It's free." He was referring, I thought, to Sonny's banter, but soon I realized Dean had his own to dish out. Dean was selling a console television, trying to get a $25 opener. It was like the Ransom of Red Chief—no one wants old televisions, especially one from the 1970s with dubious color quality and a chunky wooden stand.

Then Dean said, "Give me ten dollars. If it doesn't work, bring it back in three days and I'll give you a refund." His father would never have offered a refund; he would have claimed it worked and, crouching beside it, made up a news report.

Still no one bid. "Okay, will anyone give me five bucks? But if it doesn't work, you can't bring it back."

A woman raised her hand.

"Sold," he said, then asked, "Do you own a boat?"

"No," she replied.

"Well, you just bought an anchor."

More antics followed. Dean sold a traveling trunk, spray-painted brown, for $20, and then a runner brought up a primitive little box with straps like a trunk. Dean kicked in: "This was a salesman's sample, a salesman selling trunks. He sold thousands of the kind that just sold, but only had a few of these. Do I have $500 to start the bidding?"

No answer.

"Well, it was worth a try. It's a good story, don't you think?" A couple of people laughed. Though Dean clearly had the goodwill of the buyers, purchased with humor and an infectious smile, this junker crowd wasn't biting.

In the parking lot, my friend Bob approached a woman who had bought three boxes for five dollars during the parking lot sale. One had contained a toolbox Bob wanted, so he pointed to it and said, "You don't want that." She agreed, and he gave her a dollar for it. Better to pay four than five, the woman probably thought. Better to buy only what you want for one, than to pay five for stuff you didn't, Bob reasoned. Both were right.

Talk of the Town Auctions, where John Christman calls, is in one of those shopping centers that can't keep tenants. Everyone has seen these retail locations permanently dipped in failure. Someone builds a string of stores, and it looks like a good bet; after all, it's on a busy street near big retailers. However, inexplicably, no store prospers, and a stream of ill-conceived eateries and novelty stores come and go. Eventually some spaces are used for office space—a death knell—and the strongest contenders for permanency are a karate school and a video rental. The stores that remain obstinately empty attract used goods peddlers.

Carousel Village in Ballston Spa, New York, is one such luckless location. Once across the street from a major grocery store, the owner must have watched in dismay as the big chain declared bankruptcy and no longer anchored the three shopping centers that laced it. As Carousel Village began slipping into vacancy, Talk of the Town Auctions moved from its former host, the county fairgrounds, to the basement under three stores.

This was a general merchandise auction, not exclusively antiques but not all junk, as on Wednesday night at the Doins. The owners, John and Beverly Stanislowsky, liked to offer a variety of goods, something for everyone, so nothing garnered fire-sale prices—contrary to the specialized auctions I'd so far attended. One buyer told me if he ran an auction he'd "sell a Stanley tool with a Hummel figure in the same lot, and get the tool collector to bid against the Hummel collector." He was only joking, but it's indicative of how an auction house strives to manipulate their customers' desires.

Beverly Stanislowsky said they tried to run an aboveboard auction, stressing they did not have a buyer planted in the crowd or charge a buyer's premium, practices she thought hurt the business. A customer had recently paid $5,200 for a fishing lure, a transaction John Christman had mentioned proudly, it being probably the highest price they had ever seen at their auction, or ever would again. Beverly said the buyer was thrilled when he realized he didn't have to pay another $520. Premiums keep prices low for the seller, she said. Buyers will pay more if a buyer's fee is not tacked on.

John established a bidding schedule: When an item was selling for under $100, the bids had to be in increments of $10; over $100 in $50 advances, and over $1,000 in $100s. He had told me a bidding schedule sped up an auction. He would rather run the sale on "$10 bumps." You can get more players in, and the bidding goes faster. "Sonny taught me that," he said. Likewise, larger bids slow the sale and make for fewer players. Despite John's schedule, I saw him take even $2.50 advances—especially if a piece was being "stolen."

On this night, glass items, especially figurines, were going high, but the furniture finished cheaply. John ran a quick sale, though, and the energy was high. One buyer was standing on the side, and John and his runners missed his bid. The buyer complained, and John firmly told him if he wanted to bid he should sit with the others. John maintained control over the process, as he did when shushing the crowd when it got noisy. When two Texaco gas station attendant uniforms came up for sale, nostalgia for the days of uniformed pump jockeys cleaning your windshield triggered a bidding duel. This quieted the room. The uniforms sold for $150 each.

I had noticed a large brass kettle sitting on a corner cabinet and planned to bid on it. Though not handmade, the vessel was old and originally used for making jelly. I had seen one in Jack's antique store for $200, but this one sported a big patch on the bottom, fastened with clumsy iron rivets, what dealers call an "old repair," and not as serious a flaw as a modern, brazed patch would be. Still, condition in buying used is as important as location is in real estate, and the tinker's crude work would seriously discount the kettle.

I figured the kettle would make a grand birthday present for Bob Miner. Bob would love it because he has a pure junker fondness for repaired and salvaged stuff. Such things, for him, bore the stamp of human use. What's more, he wouldn't be using it to reduce juice into jelly. He'd use it to hold kindling for his woodstove; the patch would be only so much ornament.

When the kettle came up, John Stanislowski was running it. He pointed out the patch, and Christman, predictably, cited it as an old repair. In a split second I had my card up and found myself bidding against someone in front, in fast $5 bumps. After the other buyer bid $30 over my $25, I hesitated, shaking off John's glance to me. Then I succumbed, going the extra $5 and winning. "Sold. Number 299," Christman said with a broad smile.

John knew I'd been bitten, that I had paid the last $5 simply to compete against the back bid (the next-to-last bid), simply to *win*, and I was exhilarated when mine was the closer. Winning the bid is like being chosen, singled out for a moment on top, and the runner carries your purchase to you with a congratulatory smile. Then it is over, the highlighting fades, and perhaps there's a little disappointment ringing. The object now in your lap is not quite as precious as you had thought. What had gripped you? Why had you been so impulsive? Did everyone know you had paid more than you wanted? Perhaps they are thinking you have been swindled, prey to the orchestration of light, rhythm, and sound. Still you can redeem yourself; you too can get a great deal, be the clever one in the crowd. Bid again, but this time know when to stop, when to let the other guy overpay. Show some restraint next time, for God's sake.

The emotional reactions to being a player in an auction are complex. One is constant, though: Everyone gets a better deal than you do. Pam, a friend who came with me to Talk of the Town, was planning to bid on some ephemera (old paper goods), a box that included a program from Futurama, the General Motors display at the 1939 World's Fair predicting what life would be like in the 1960s—now amusing for its overpredictions about automation. I saw a runner looking through a tray of papers, so I got up to see if the World's Fair document was in it; neither of us had jotted down the lot number. It was, and Pam got the lot for $15, finding it also contained 1920s New York City tourist brochures, with photographs in which the Empire State Building is absent and the cars all gangster rigs. One of the brochures was easily worth the full price. Another buyer picked up a wooden case I had admired, with little drawers and trays full of crystals, fossils, and minerals, also for $15. I saw him outside after the auction. "Nice buy on the box of rocks," I said.

"Did you see the petrified root?" he gushed, pulling out a glorious, polished piece of petrified wood, probably an old souvenir from the Petrified Forest national park in Arizona, where collecting such specimens is now illegal. The stone was easily worth the entire amount he had paid, as was the box, with its multiple drawers and partitions.

Talk of the Town also held auctions for firearms and related outdoor sporting goods, and John Christman told me I should attend one. He said gun buyers were a separate breed. "You should see these guys. You'd think they don't have five bucks, then they spend a thousand." There were no regulations, no waiting periods, or background checks. Gun auctions are legally private sales—a gun owner using the auctioneer as a broker to find a buyer. If secondhand buyers and sellers are fiercely independent of mainstream culture, at a gun auction I was liable to see this magnified.

Bob Miner came with me again. While passionate about lower-phylum junk, he especially loves old guns. Bob's devotion is unorthodox: He loves old military rifles, scarred and rusted hulks, particularly those from the Near East and Eastern Europe used during World War II and in the revolutions afterward. Like any good reuser, Bob is thrilled by the narrative of the gun. Bob has a personal connection with them; he grew up in Turkey and Greece during those days, when these weapons were smuggled in to support various factions in the power vacuums that arose after the war. At the sale I watched Bob caress a Mauser .30-caliber rifle with a Turkish stamp on the receiver. I imagined Bob seeing it in the hands of a ragged rebel in Macedonia, smuggled on muleback by Bulgarian rug merchants, and peddled by Portuguese arms dealers.

We browsed the tables strewn with dented, oiled weapons, while Bob recorded facts about them, planning to check their values in gun digests in the public library. Some he probably wouldn't find, such as a muzzle-loading blunderbuss broken in half and patched with a sheet of brass many decades ago. It was described on the flyer as a "wall hanger," meaning it wasn't safe to fire. Bob and I fawned over the ancient rifle; it was so ruined I imagined no one would want it, and Bob urged me to bid on it, but I told him I wasn't there to build an arsenal. I was only there to infiltrate the tribe, not be initiated. Still, though I hadn't been to the gun auction before, I was a known entity at Talk of the Town, so Bob and I got to tag chairs with our names.

I wasn't under any illusions about truly fitting into this crowd. It was mostly male, and either pot-bellied, gray-haired veterans or lean, chain-smoking loners—I only saw three women at the sale. These guys were largely concerned with firepower, with the rare romantic like Bob mixed in. Bumper stickers on their dented and rusty pickups and SUVs, apropos of vehicles actually driven in the woods, signified they belonged to the National Rifle Association. Other stickers made clear their stance on social issues: VEGETARIAN: INDIAN WORD FOR POOR HUNTER and GUN CONTROL IS BEING ABLE TO HIT YOUR TARGET. I didn't recognize anyone from the house's antique sales; this was a specialty crowd. Even the food was affected; they were serving venison chili and venison stew.

I grew up around guns, and I know more about them than I will ever need to know, so I can fake it at a sale like this, helping a guy close the bolt action on a Japanese military rifle, for instance. Bob's enthusiasm helped, too. Other buyers could see the gleam in his eye and felt he was one of them; it was like having a local guide when you are abroad. However, when I talked to a couple of them, I found out they either knew very little about guns or were pretending ignorance. When I asked one customer about the age and value of a Winchester carbine, he said, "I don't know what these guns are worth because none of mine are for sale." That was either an honest admission, or he was playing his cards close to the vest.

"I don't know anything about guns; I'm just here for the animals," another man said. He looked to the walls where dozens of taxidermied heads hung. There was quite the menagerie: deer heads galore, a standing black bear which looking more foolish than fierce, a pine marten, a pheasant, and plaque-mounted fish. Later I saw there was a vigorous market for these goods, too.

With almost two hundred in attendance, the basement room was warm for a May evening. People were carrying chairs to the front, lengthening the rows; a fulsome guy set a chair beside me, and one of his thighs overlapped my chair. I had to sit cross-legged and tilted left to avoid being partially in his lap. Many of the men had yet to shave their winter beards, or perhaps they lived in the Adirondacks and hadn't yet noticed it was almost summer. There was something grim about them, a coldness of purpose shot through their eyes, a leaden camaraderie. There was weaponry to be had, and they were here to get it, to squirrel it away in their personal bastions. The auction rules reflected their mood: All guns and ammunition stayed behind the auctioneer until paid for and taken away. The crowd would not gradually be armed by runners handing out their purchases, and the thought of this possibility made my skin crawl. Likewise, the sale was videotaped, a camera mounted on a center post. Beverly sat beside it, her lap full of left bids. She bid for those who couldn't attend.

This was a sporting goods sale, though, and the house was selling as much fishing as hunting gear—especially rods and reels. Pretty soon the crowd settled into a bargain with the house; they would pay between $50 and $100 for a reel and $100 to $200 for a rod. John Christman's calling became predictable. The guns were more variable. John didn't spend much time pitching them; he read a description his runner handed him. When John mispronounced the calibers and model names, I realized he didn't know any more about guns than what was on the cards. The guns were sold in the order listed on a flyer mailed to the buyers, beginning with the most valuable. When the patched-up gun was brought up—the last one—I raised my hand to offer $10, but John just smiled and took a bid for $25 elsewhere. It closed at $45.

Anything associated with hunting or guns found a buyer, even advertising items for ammunition or old calendars from sporting goods stores with pictures of white-tailed deer and other game animals. The stuffed animals were the biggest surprise. When a stuffed mountain lion came up, a buyer immediately accepted John's $500 suggested opener, then ran it up to $600. I always thought the point of having a taxidermied trophy was it was evidence of your hunting prowess, not auction savvy. Bob thought the buyers were supplying rustic restaurants with faunal kitsch, as good an explanation as any.

Some of the items were military, not hunting-related, such as a National Guard uniform from the 1870s, which John proclaimed was "fresh to the market, hasn't been shopped around," saying someone had thrown it away. "Fresh to the market" is a common claim on auction handbills. Auctions are like a lubricant to the used trade, moving goods around the market, and between dealers, until they find the right buyer. Goods that haven't been "shopped around" are a blank slate. None of the dealers have tried to sell them in their shops, so they don't have the stench of white elephant. Later John said, "That story was absolutely true." He had discovered the uniform in a trunk being thrown out and set on the curb. Only the hat was missing, and he had found one to go with it elsewhere. John hoped the uniform ended up with a militaria collector because the soldier's name was written on it, and a collector would research the name and learn the story behind it. Rescued from the garbage, the old blue uniform would pass hand to hand until it reached a buyer who would unite it with its story, reclaim its lost meanings.

John later said he had spotted six key players, who then spent most of the money. When something was hot, such as the rods and reels, he often had a hard time telling "who was bidding what." If John asked for a bid and a dozen cards went up, he just pointed to one after another, raising the bid until the hands returned to their laps. The gun auction had been so lively I saw a runner spot a bid, a rare event; John had thanked him by saying, "Nice catch."

The many rods and reels had all come from one collector, someone who bought Orvis equipment whenever the tony sporting-goods retailer came out with a new product. "Even if his family didn't have food on the table, he just had to have the newest one," John said. The man had died, and his widow got $10,000 out of the sale. "That's going to help her out," John said, satisfied he had been able to contribute to alleviating her distress.

Half of the buyers were there for the fishing gear, half for guns. The buyers were "all business," John said, a somber bunch. "And I was telling some pretty good jokes," he laughed, admitting it was the wrong crowd to entertain with comments on how "cute" the taxidermied animals were. The trophies would travel through the used network to upstate hotels and bed-and-breakfasts. The newest trend in tourist traps was the "Adirondack Room," decked out in rustic accoutrements, unlike the usual B&B decor that John described as "Victorian and done up frilly." The blank stares of white-tailed deer or plastic snarl of a mountain lion would complete the picture of a room in a lodge.

One of the marginal items had been an eight-foot-long Nazi flag. It had hung on the back wall during most of the sale, lending the proceedings a clandestine feel. I had scanned the crowd trying to guess who would want it. When two runners finally brought it up, the crowd sat on its hands, telegraphing, "We're into guns, but we're not into that." Many in attendance wore hats bedecked with the insignias of their units from World War II; they certainly didn't covet this castoff.

A couple of bids arose, and a young man in cargo pants bought it. I would have never guessed he'd be the buyer. He and his friend, a young Asian man with a mullet haircut whom I'd seen buying a painting at Mike Smith's auction, got up to leave. They were stone-faced, not giving away their feelings about it, though I speculated they were eBay sellers.

Heidi Christman said she didn't like "dealing in that stuff," though they used to handle more Nazi curios. Once, when selling a Nazi police cap, they were beset with collectors wanting to know what kind of tag was inside and which direction the arrows were pointing on the medallion on the brim. Collectors of military uniforms are exacting. They know precisely how a seam should be stitched, and they examine cloth items like flags under black light to spot repairs; newer thread will glow. It was risky to buy a flag you intended to resell to collectors without such laboratory techniques; if the guys who bought the old Nazi banner sold it on eBay, they'd have to be dealing with amateurs, not seasoned collectors.

Eventually Heidi asked John to get out of selling Nazi items; it made her nervous, like being involved in something illicit. I told them the creepiest thing I had seen sell, so far, had been the mummy's hand. When I had mentioned it to John, his face furled, and he said, "I thought selling something like that was illegal." Heidi also chimed in, saying they had once dealt the contents of a barn. In cleaning it out, they discovered a human skull and had been told selling body parts was against the law. Perhaps because the hand had a celebrity provenance, such restrictions did not apply. After all, the mummy's hand was a cherished old relic in a display box, and it possibly came from an ancient Egyptian, while the skull in the barn was just a run-of-the-mill head. Anyone's head. Nothing special.

Heidi Christman said you seldom lose money selling at an auction because there are two kinds of buyers: those who know what something is worth and those who have a hunch. There's nearly always one of each, and they are guaranteed to run up the price. Once she and John had seen an early American flag at a sale, and though they weren't certain about it, they thought it might be really valuable, so they bid on it. "I just knew we could get our money out," she said; they were the hunch bidders. The guy who outbid them said later if the Christmans hadn't been there, he'd have made the "buy of the century." He knew all about the flag. "People think they're going to come out here to a so-called 'country yokel auction' and steal stuff, but it doesn't happen," Heidi said. John admitted, though, that sellers still make mistakes. Once he sold a lot of sewing supplies and thought he had done well for $45, that is until he found out the supplies were in a Shaker-made box, a religious sect known for its skilled woodworking and elegant designs. It alone was worth $2,000. Every auctioneer has one or more of these stories to wake up to in the middle of the night.

Losing control can also give an auctioneer night sweats. Gary Guarno, who runs a Salem, New York, junk shop and antique store, once ran an auction house in Westchester. "There's lots of ways to lose control," Gary said. He saw it happen to his own auctioneer. The crowd might "stall" him or "make him beg" for bids. John Christman said, "You start, and you can just tell. The money's there. The buyers are there. On other nights, you know it's going to be slow."

I saw this happen at the Niskayuna Auction Gallery. The owner of the former "Duane Toyland" rented the upstairs to junkers and collectibles dealers, and the downstairs was an auction house. The entire building was painted red to resemble a barn. They had even nailed sheets of plywood to the 1960s Modernist building sides and painted them with white Xs to imitate the cross bracing on barn doors—a symbol of the rural origins of the auction. I was also reminded, pathetically, of Colin Stair's headquarters. A sign out front called the red building The White House, perhaps left over from a previous life.

It was a slow night, and the auctioneer, a middle-aged man with a ponytail that remained reddish while the rest of his hair had gone iron gray, was hustling for every bid from a crowd in dented metal chairs and, in the back, a pew with a dirty yellow vinyl pad. The top item was an Edison phonograph; a couple of collectors showed up to bid on it. I should have guessed the auction was in trouble when the auctioneer drafted someone from the crowd to work as a runner. His girlfriend said, "My honey: Auction Extra," and giggled. The tall buyer got up to help, turning to give her a bucktoothed grin. The auctioneer gave the volunteer a few pointers, then began the sale.

The auctioneer tried to keep control. When he couldn't get an opener on a couple of items, he set them aside, so as to signal he'd not be intimidated into giving stuff away. "I'm only going to sell you what you want," he said. The runner was slow, and the auctioneer was forced to simply grab anything nearby and try to sell it. "You'll like this better than your money," he quipped. Once the novice runner tried to hawk some cups and saucers himself, and when it didn't sell, the auctioneer whispered something to him—probably telling him to leave the selling to him—and sent him into the back room for more goods. When the runner came up with a box of toys, the auctioneer had to remind him to "Show what's in it," and took the box from him to pull out some of its contents.

The auctioneer tried humor, but the crowd heckled him in response. When a signed and framed letter from President Clinton came up, he asked, "What's Bill Clinton worth these days?"

"Two cents," said someone in the crowd.

"We want Monica's dress thrown in," said another. The letter sold for $17.50. When another customer bought some crystalware and it slipped out of her lap, the auctioneer asked "Did it break?" She said no, and he answered, "Too bad, that way'd you have more for your money." She groaned. With customer number 11, he made the joke about his number being upside down each time he bought something. He tried being wry, but also to no avail. When a customer asked whether a silver teapot was marked, he answered, "It's marked whatever you want it to be." He tried to suggest uses for items, declaring a Chinese checkerboard, without game pieces or box, was "better to hang on the wall in a kid's room than a picture."

No matter how much energy the auctioneer brought to the sale, the crowd refused to get on his side. The auctioneer struggled, the room getting smaller as the silence of the crowd surrounded him, backed him into a corner, savaging his self-confidence. I could see an anxious flit in his eyes, and the crowd could sense, with a mercenary satisfaction, that he was hurting up there. Increasingly the auctioneer sent the drafted runner away with unsold lots with a disgusted wave. He was losing them, and he knew it, so when he missed a bid and the customer was visibly peeved, he asked, "You going to throw a stone at me?" The next time the same customer bid, the auctioneer halted the bidding. "Sold," he said. "We're even." However, he had no real chance at getting even with the control so lopsided.

"WE CAN TURN your items into CASH-CASH-CASH with an auction by CORINTH AUCTION SERVICE . . . 35 Years in and around the auction business. Our experience pays off for you. Call Today."

Sitting at the counter in Jack's, a diner in Corinth, New York, paper millworkers at each elbow, I spied this advertisement in the *Pennysaver*, a want ad circular, open in front of one of them. The display ad announced an auction of the contents of "Two partial homes from Dix Avenue and Bay Road. 10 percent buyer's premium. Charles Witherbee, Auctioneer." At the end was teaser about a future sale, a "Toy Car and

Truck Auction, combined with 1000s of Comic Books . . . Combined with *Playboy* collection . . . Combined with ???"

Somewhere, I knew, was the obverse of the fine antiques auction, a place through which any castoff would travel, where every night was junk night and provenance pointed to a garbage can. This looked like the place. It was Sunday morning, and I guessed Charlie Witherbee would be in his establishment, waiting for buyers to pick up items from the Saturday night sale. Toys and *Playboy* magazines at the same sale? This had to be a singular auction house.

Charlie's was in an old furniture store with gaping holes in the eaves, a flat roof sagging from too many heavy snows, and a rotting pressboard sign, rain-soaked and shredding. The front windows were stuffed with oak furniture and boxes stacked on top of each other, not so much as on display as because the interior was simply full to bursting. A sign propped akimbo against the wall said AUCTION 6 P.M. and another on the front door said the entrance was on the left side, but I saw no apparent opening there, as everywhere broken furniture lay heaped against the wall, overgrown with weeds. A rickety ladder was propped against the wall, perhaps left the last time someone had thought to repair the roof. Now a sun-faded rag doll was jammed between the rungs. For a moment I thought the place had been abandoned, that I had gotten the address wrong. I saw several doors, all nailed shut but one, a steel door with a length of clothesline looped through the lockset hole. I pulled the rope, and the door opened.

For a scavenger, walking through the door was like entering the Tabernacle of Junk. Rows of pews, with racks for communion cups and hymnals still attached, and cushioned with scavenged pads, faced the "altar," the auctioneer's stand. The place had an exhausted air, as though it had been the scene of a tumultuous sale that had gone into the wee hours. It was lit like a theater, spots trained on select corners piled with treasures, and I was drawn to browse. To the right the building revealed a fathomless interior where lurked mounds of junk, separated by narrow pathways through the spacious old store, acres of refuse, like an immense, roofed junkpile. The auction hall was only an annex, a chapel in the cathedral.

I rounded a pile and saw a man sitting in a little office behind the registration counter. He was staring at a computer screen with his back to me. I called out hello, and he jumped.

Charlie was tall and broad, with a mop of gray hair, sad dark eyes, and a wracking cough. He was too busy to talk to me, he said, and when I asked when would be a good time to come back, he said he would be busy then, too. After a little prodding, I learned he had been at this auction house for fourteen years, though "I've been in the business for forty years," he said. "At least it feels like forty."

At first I chalked up Charlie's weariness to having conducted a sale last night, but then he added, "There's too much stuff. You never get rid of it all, never get it sold. I have to just sell something and move on to the next thing." Of course there was. Charlie had plunged into the general trade of castoffs, and his heaps and stacks of junk were monuments to the immensity of the enterprise. I sympathized with him immediately; he was overwhelmed because he felt that everything had some value or utility, and he hated to see anything wasted.

Charlie said he didn't have much time to think about what he had to sell, so he didn't have much to say about it. I mentioned eBay, thinking that might provide an additional market for the surplus, and he said, "I was just listing stuff on eBay. You can sell anything on eBay, and for more than you'd get at an auction, because it's worldwide."

"But it would take you two hundred years to list and sell all the stuff you have here on eBay."

He grinned, but that was erased by a fit of coughing. "Lots of stuff has to get thrown out; there's too much," he said. "Too much stuff," he repeated wearily.

Wanting to keep the conversation going, I asked if Charlie auctioned all of the stuff himself, and he said yes, but lately had hired a woman to help.

"Did you go to auctioneer's school?"

"No."

"I hear there's one in Kentucky. Self-taught, huh?"

At first Charlie didn't answer; he clearly wanted to get rid of me. "There's one in Missouri," he said finally. Then he leaned on a counter with both hands and coughed explosively. I hoped it was only a cold, something picked up in the drafty auction hall.

Later I asked a local dealer about Charlie Witherbee, and he asked, "Have you been inside?" I said yes, and he replied, "Then you know what to expect." He wouldn't buy there. "You don't know if the chest you are buying is infested. It takes only one bug, and then you're done. You don't want that. He'll sell anything. He'll pick up a sweater out of a box and just try to sell it." He shook his head.

Another dealer had told me he had seen Charlie lose his temper and break glassware on the floor when he couldn't get more than a lowball bid, and when I asked about that, a picker in the store said: "All you need to write is that Charlie is a crook." I told him I refused to believe that until I saw him in action.

Charlie's place was a bit cleaned up by the next Saturday sale; most of the broken junk outside was gone. I heard Charlie tell someone he had taken two loads to the landfill that week, but one look around the inside revealed he had barely dented his accumulation. The old store was still full, with floor-to-ceiling moraines of junk, most of it under sheets, not to be previewed or mistaken for being part of the night's auction. The old store proper was off-limits; only the goods on display in the tacked-on auction house were open for perusal.

These few exposed rows contained common household goods, from several mounds of bath towels, sorted by color, to boxes of used dishes. I could discern no theme linking the merchandise, besides it being yet more mongrel junk, but some of the offerings were curious, if not fetching. I found a box of playbills, probably saved from a lifetime of theater-going, and a box of sheet music, most of it martial, like the Marine Hymn. One box on the back wall contained plays, handwritten manuscripts by students in "English II" in 1912 and graded by their teacher. Some stuff at least looked useful, such as a shiny Coleman camp stove and a smattering of jewelry, watches, necklaces, and pins, forty pieces that Charlie would later try, and fail, to sell as a single lot for $100.

The scrapbook of Marjorie Baker, from Boston, Massachusetts, whispered a story, so I flipped its pages, reading the events in her life. At first it contained birthday cards and letters and postcards from traveling friends and family members. A community college graduation program made a clear demarcation in the scrapbook. It was followed by plane tickets and boarding passes, then cocktail napkins from hotels in Pennsylvania and Virginia, with plastic swizzle swords glued to them. The remaining pages were empty. Why had the scrapbook been abandoned? Why was it for sale, together with a box of old high school yearbooks and other memorabilia? What detour did the bar napkins suggest? If still alive, Marjorie would be in her forties. These castoffs were even more ominous than Hughes's leavings.

On a lighter note, Charlie had lined the room with a collection I had not noticed before. A shelf ringing the room near the ceiling was occupied by ceramic cookie jars of all shapes and sizes: a basketball-sized apple, Cookie Monster, hefty matrons with wide aprons, a squirrel sitting on a stump. They looked down on the assembled like surreal angels. Charlie also had a collection of tavern beer lights and, on one wall, like at Cherry Tree Auctions, historic auction posters, including one announcing the sale of the surplus goods of a farmer heading to the Oregon Territory in 1849. He was going to sell "All of my ox teams except for Johnnie and Bessie, Jack and Jill." Presumably they would be conveying him westward. He was also selling "six Negro slaves." Someone had stuck a note on the framed poster that read, "We've made some progress."

The crowd certainly didn't look like either dealers or sharp-eyed collectors. They were mostly older, the women with purses the size of hay bales, the men with suspendered ample girths and webbed plastic caps. One man in front of me had a farmer's tan—red forearms and V-neck. A couple beside me had brought a young girl. She appeared bored and was putting in the time reading *Fried Green Tomatoes*, a Tigger bookmark protruding from the pages. At one point she look up and eyed me uneasily.

Charlie ascended to a high desk in the back of the hall, gasping like a beached bass when he got there. A waifish young woman sat beside him drinking from a half-gallon cup of soda and chomping fistfuls of corn chips. She would record the numbers of the bidders. A man in a black T-shirt strolled in, flirting with some of the older women. He stopped at a table, picked up a maraca, and shook it.

"Going to do a dance for us, Carl?" someone yelled.

"Just a minute," he shot back and reached for his belt buckle like he was going to remove his pants. He was one of two runners.

When Charlie started the sale he must have also sensed a slow night. He registered his frustration with the low-bidding crowd by asking if there was any interest on some items before chancing the opening of a bid. He even let the openers go down to a single dollar, but he'd set an item aside rather than accept a pocket-change bid, as he did when unable to get a buck on four crystal candle holders. He even refused some low-ball bids. "Do I have any interest in this Foosball table?" he said, and when someone shouted $10, he ignored it, saying with asperity, "Our next item is . . . " to show he wouldn't entertain that amount. The buyer grumbled to his companions in the back. When someone gave him a charitable opener, $2, on a typewriter, Charlie closed the bidding, trying to joke his way out of it by saying the near-worthless item someday would be collectible and that it had a correcting ribbon, implying the buyer should use it to erase his mistake. The customer took this ribbing good-naturedly, luckily. Dean Doin could get away with such high jinks, but Charlie always seemed to be walking a line between angering his crowd and losing his own temper.

Charlie seemed tired, bored, and at times even confused. In trying to sell a newer brass chandelier, he didn't know if the glass globes lying nearby fit, but he offered them with the lamp, saying, "You don't need shades anyway with the flicker bulbs they have." He sold a blender with the half-hearted pitch, "This thing whips and beats and grinds and whatever-the-hell you need it to do." When a runner brought up some wooden spindles, Charlie reminded him that they went to a wine rack, but they couldn't find the other parts. "Maybe it will turn up," Charlie said, as though losing interest in it, and they put them aside. When he couldn't sell a couple of cheap art prints, he sighed, "Looks like we'll be taking a load to the dump again this week," though I'd bet he'd find a place for anything unwanted in his hoard. Charlie added a mirror and a print of a Monet landscape to the other prints and tried to sell them all together, joking, "We're the only auction in the state of New York that's got a Monet for sale tonight." He got a laugh, but no bid. Charlie had to keep adding junk to the lot: a mystery box with paper and cloth items, the wine rack spindles, a stack of plates and bowls, and metal picture frames. Finally he got a bid for $2, and sold the pile.

One runner seemed to be specializing in books. Maybe he wasn't up to any heavy lifting that night. Charlie tried to get the crowd involved by taking one out of the runner's hand—a craft book on reusing old panty-hose—and making a couple of jokes about it, but still he couldn't get a bid. When he sold a washboard for $2, one of the buyers shouted, "Is it cordless?" His audience had better lines than he did.

The cookie jars looked down with pity as Carl ran two dozen plastic party top hats through the crowd, holding one out like he was begging. Someone put in an empty popcorn container, but no one bid. When Carl added four Disney figurines to the lot, Charlie growled, "There's nothing in this whole building to go with those hats but Disney figures?" He knew Disney items were collectible and could sell on their own. Still the lot did not get an opener. Charlie and Carl then started arguing about what to add next to the deal.

Charlie did a little better when selling a wood sander, which Carl plugged in to show that it worked. Charlie said a woman had brought it in to raise money for her son's medical bills. He had been in a car accident in Stony Creek two days ago. "I hate when they come in and tell me that," he said. The story was undoubtedly true, because everyone in a small town knows the intimate details of local misfortune. The sander fetched $35.

Next Carl held up cartons of "brand new, never been used" eggs from a local farmer. He walked through the crowd, joking that the farmer had "squeezed the chickens extra hard this morning." Clearly this auction sold anything. When one buyer bought a dozen for a dollar, Charlie chimed in, saying she should buy more because "I'm inviting everyone over to your house tomorrow morning for eggs." He sold twelve dozen, all the farmer had brought in.

In my assessment Charlie was a successful auctioneer because he could truly sell anything he put his mind to. He sold nearly useless junk, such as an exquisitely ugly set of brass pole lamps that looked like bug antennae, for $5, and a stack of framed certificates, including a law degree diploma from Boston University, for $4.50, for which I could hardly imagine a legitimate use. Perhaps the most useless lot Charlie sold included nine bound books of wallpaper samples, which he gamely claimed could be used by a dollhouse builder, even though the patterns would be oversized. The leather-necked farmer in front of me bought them for a dollar. When Carl brought them over, he trotted away and came back with two more books, saying "This is your lucky day." The buyer carried them out to his car, and though I am an inveterate scavenger and reuser, I was baffled by how he planned to use four vertical feet of individual wallpaper samples, no two pages alike. I reminded myself that a junk collector will buy anything if the price is low enough.

Charlie sold toys at this sale, too, but no copies of *Playboy*. The couple beside me got a stuffed Tigger for their daughter, who looked up from her book and watched the bidding eagerly. Her mother cried out,

"We got it!" when their last bid of $4 won; the child hopped up and down when it was carried over. Next Charlie sold a stuffed dog. Carl joked about its phallic tail, wagging it suggestively. "Not everyone has a tail like this," he said.

"Yeah," Charlie said, "but I'm not even going there." Another little girl in the crowd got it, and she ran up to grab it, hugging it all the way back down the aisle. People sighed.

"You ought to give it to her, Charlie," someone shouted.

"No problem," Charlie said, "just charge it to you." The shouter agreed.

With the crowd starting to thin, I stepped outside to talk with some of those leaving and got into a conversation with a picker standing near the door smoking. He spied my notebook and figured I must be checking prices, as there were no lot numbers to record. "Are you a dealer or a collector?" he asked.

"A collector, I guess."

"What do you collect?"

"Tools," I said, for lack of another answer.

"I bring stuff in for sale, sometimes, when I find something." He didn't look too prosperous, sporting a Sno-Cat cap with a torn brim, an old oxford dress shirt, and cotton work pants. He took a drag on his generic-brand cigarette.

"Where do you get stuff?" I asked, hoping for a trade secret or two. I did not often find a picker who would talk; they are usually close-mouthed and gnomish.

"Yard sales—all around. One time I got a whole box of wood planes for a couple of bucks and sold them for $100. The guy broke his arm getting his wallet out." He was obviously proud of that deal—his best tool sale. He lit another smoke.

A man in coveralls stepped through the door, and the picker asked, "Are you done?"

"Yeah," the other man said, "I'm going to load up." He walked to the back of the building.

"Who's he?" I asked.

"He buys stuff everywhere. He has a whole warehouse full of stuff. He's going there to load up a truck to sell to the shops tomorrow." A picker with a cache of goods big enough to require a storage building. Perhaps his acquisitions rival Charlie's.

"Why is Charlie's place loaded with stuff, but he isn't selling it tonight?"

"'Cause he's afraid someone will get over on him." Charlie would rather hang onto something than risk getting a low price, though his customers were all nickel-and-dime scavengers.

"Are all the people here pickers?"

"Yeah, most of them," he said, and a guy walked out with an old wooden console radio. The picker called out, "So you got that?" The guy calls back that he paid $35.

"That's a pretty good price," I said to the picker. "He'll probably make some money on it."

"I only paid five for it. Got it in a yard sale today. I'm surprised it made that. It's the only thing I brought in tonight." He said the guy with the radio was an eBay seller, but most of the others sold on the picker circuit.

"Well, I gotta go help him load," he said, meaning the fellow with the warehouse. "He's the kinda guy you want to get to know," he said with a wink. "And check out the auction in Schuylerville, on the east side of the river. Wednesday nights. No buyer's fee."

I thanked him for the information and stood alone listening through the dented metal door to Charlie heaping up another pile of castoffs, building another deal for his gaggle of scavengers. Though I was headed home, something almost drew me back in. Maybe Charlie would take a chance and reach back into his reserve, try to sell something really precious, some long-hidden treasure. The picker had given me a couple of tips because he saw I could as easily succumb to the trade, turn picker, and hit the road. For a moment, I had entered the network. I had been confirmed and was a member of the congregation.

Chapter Six

✌

You Should Have Seen
What My Grandmother Had

BEFORE I EVER WATCHED *GONE WITH THE WIND*, I visited Tara. The antique trade is nearly as old as the auctions that feed it, but these highest-priced used goods were narrowly defined—people have always coveted what are considered "antiquities." In our own time, any handmade object of quality predating the Industrial Revolution was called by the French term "antique," and strictly speaking this definition still holds among the most discriminating. However, in the 1960s, nostalgia for an agrarian, pre-auto, pre-television America spawned a vigorous trade in the ordinary artifacts of the lives of our grandparents, whether handmade or bought at the general store. These crates, crocks, and rocking chairs were coveted because they had been pushed aside by Tupperware, Frigidaires, and La-Z-Boys.

Whether recalling the antebellum South or childhood summers, the soft focus of nostalgia is a powerful force, and this bittersweet cyclone soon gathered nearly everything old within its path, spinning out categories of collectibles that encircled stuff no longer gracing department store shelves. Even product tins and advertising items became valuable precisely because they were meant to be disposable and were subsequently rare. Antique toys, for instance, are often absurdly valued because they were usually cheaply made, played with roughly, discarded when outgrown, and are now as scarce as comets. Add syrupy memories to rarity, and these discards assume values beyond reason or utility. A toy truck or doll can viscerally recall lost experiences and intimate details of the past, and when we buy these remnants we might be hoping for a long-gone innocence in the bargain. Those who sell such reminders traffic in more than substance.

The antique stores of my youth introduced me to this heady realm. Tara was the name of a store in Vienna, Ohio, the town where I spent much of my childhood. My friend Jay and I watched as a bungalow on the main drag sprouted a twin—a new building—connected by a covered walkway. This was before antique dealers learned to exploit historic buildings and barns as settings for their wares. Soon the woman running the store had it aptly decorated, a porch crammed with barrels and crates, and a front path rubbled with farm implements around which sprouted a fan club of wildflowers. At nine years old we didn't even know the word antique, but we knew this place was uncommonly enticing.

A fascination with antiques was inevitable for two young boys who entertained themselves by hoarding anything odd that came in variations: stamps, marbles, insects, and fossils—the latter growing to a passion as we were transformed into nascent romantics by the signs of a prehistoric inland sea in the flat farmlands of Ohio. We had lately taken to prowling these farms, many now fallow. The houses and barns of some were vacant as well, and we found them irresistible. Walking into an abandoned house was like being Carter in the Valley of the Kings. They were a musty mess, and we assumed the occupants had left in a hurry, or transients had caused the spilled boxes and avalanched closets. It never dawned on us that the houses had been looted by scavengers as had the Pharaohs' tombs. We seldom took anything; we were merely curious, looking at the detritus of unknown lives and piecing together their fates. I once tore an old stamp off a postcard; I recall the picture as being of Niagara Falls. As trespassers, we were terribly respectful.

That all changed after we visited Tara. Jay must have already gone there, because he knew you had to go to the house to get the owner. Tara, as we called her, never learning her real name, opened her store catch-as-catch-can; she worked as a nurse. She seemed ancient, though probably only in her fifties, and she certainly was kind, with the patience to show her precious stock to a couple of curious, penniless boys and to answer their questions.

The store was not unlike the derelict houses we had been exploring. Tara Antiques was like a well-dusted attic, crowded with mostly smaller merchandise: dishes, lamps, and tchotchkes. I loved the back wall where she had hung a miscellany of tiny items, such as ornate brass hinges, a cut-glass drawer knob, a lead soldier, and a wire-rimmed monocle. I remember picking through a box of photographs, recalling my grandmother's trunk of snapshots and daguerreotypes. Years later, my grandmother's mind waltzing with Alzheimer's, one of her last sentient acts was to sit for hours and scribble on the backs the names of those captured on film, working against time and sense to conserve their identities. How had the cherished pictures in Tara's box slipped through their heirs' fingers into anonymity? Perhaps more so than other castoffs, photographs require context to have much meaning.

Tara once gave me my pick of these photographs. They were not very valuable, and she kept them only for the ambience they lent. And I still have it. It shows a storefront, planked sidewalk leading to it where two men lean against porch posts, hands pocketed. In front rests a buggy drawn by two horses, not a matched team because one is all black or brown and the other has a white blaze and white left socks. This is not a fancy equipage but a farmer's going-to-town rig. The horses were chosen not for looks or speed, but because they were used to the harness from pulling the plow and stoneboat.

I chose the picture, though, because of the two people in the buggy, clearly the center of the picture. The father seems anxious to leave, with a smile scratched on for the camera, his angular hat completing the geometry of his face. While the father is slouching, the son is preening, bolt upright, his shirt buttoned to the throat, probably unaccustomed to being photographed and considering the occasion of high importance. His impatience stems from elsewhere: He looks anxious to escape, to leave his life of planting and reaping. With the forward thrust of his jaw and the distant cast in his eye, he might be imitating the etchings he'd seen in books in the public library of the visionary postures of nineteenth-century poets. While the father appears intent upon the literal road ahead and the chores he has left that day, the boy is looking years down the road to loftier goals. "Let's get this over and get going," the father thinks. The son, though, begs the viewer to consider him, to deduce he is going somewhere noteworthy if only given the chance.

Both father and son are gone now, their names lost, but they had inhabited the space in this image, in which everything has also vanished: The stores have been replaced by shopping centers, and the buggies have gone the way of buggy whips. Looking at the photograph in Tara's, I first realized the past was once palpable. Soon everything I saw in her store had a backstory. I credit Tara with introducing me to the epic string of meanings tied to used merchandise, though she probably had no idea she had given me this along with the picture.

My grandmother had acquainted me with antiques as a concept. She and my grandfather had bought a forty-acre farm after he retired, and while my grandfather, Jake Leslie, was a scavenger, tearing down the farmhouse and saving lumber and barn stone, even straightening nails, my grandmother had another angle. The trappings of her Appalachian childhood were growing valuable, so she gathered them, particularly rocking chairs. Soon she had a half dozen of them. Jake was a practical reuser, but, my grandmother, Margaret Leslie, was a collector, and I listened, enthralled, as she showed me crocks and oil lamps. I was launched early in my predilections.

The pieces all came together after Jay and I visited Tara. I saw things like those my grandmother had been gathering—with prices on them—and Jay saw the junk we'd been stumbling over in deserted farmsteads. So we became scavengers.

Don't try this at home, because it's obviously not legal. However, it was a common practice when little nineteenth-century family farms were being abandoned in the booming 1950s and 1960s. Jay and I searched these places for things to sell to Tara. (We knew no other dealers, so she had a monopoly on our finds.) These had been humble Ohio farmers, however, with few fine dishware or fancy decorations to leave behind. If the trade had begun then for advertising items from the 1920s and 1930s or for old farm implements, we would have had loads to sell, but such stuff wasn't yet sought after, or at least Tara didn't handle them. Nevertheless, the thrill of the hunt was upon us. Although I can't speak for Jay, I was also motivated by happening upon another glimpse of the past.

I don't recall our having much luck. Jay once found two wooden candle stands that Tara bought, but she declined most of what we offered. With little success in the barns and houses, we turned to dumps on fencerows. Old bottles, especially those hand-blown or embossed with dates, were becoming desirable. So we whacked away weeds on tumbled, split-rail fence lines, or in the woods where a row of larger trees would reveal an old field edge, and dug with our bare hands. Our parents must have been chagrined and puzzled by the cuts we'd come home with from broken glass. We'd find milk bottles and blue canning jars with ceramic-lined lids. They are very collectible now, but then only the finest and oldest bottles were valued. Most of the bottles were shattered from generations of roving children who would, as we had before enlightened, use them as targets for pitched rocks.

Then one day we hit pay dirt. Half buried in the woods, three miles from our houses, we found a ten-gallon crock. We had seen lots of old crocks and jugs at Tara's, and though hers had blue glazed inscriptions identifying their maker, and this one only had a plain "10" on the side, we knew it was old, and likely worth more than either of us had ever earned. It took us an entire afternoon to unearth it. By then we both had to go home, so we covered the crock with branches, planning to return the next morning and deliver it to the antique store.

Stoneware is heavy. On the next day we learned we were unable to carry the crock together for more than a few feet at a time. Finally we settled on rolling it, careful not to mar the glazed finish by avoiding the gravel sides of the roads. We got to Tara's door after hours of pushing the crock over bumpy fields and portaging it over creeks. Jay rang her doorbell; I hung back, always shy about approaching her with something, not believing what we could find would measure up to her treasures. I was right. Tara turned down the crock because of a fine crack in the bottom. Today such a defect would only discount the piece, but at the threshold of the country antiques business only perfection would do. Although Jay and I were a bit discouraged, we were too committed to scavenging to give up.

During that period I'm sure thousands of items in the antique market were "rescued" from tilting barns, derelict farmhouses, and obsolete Victorian mansions, and that source is reflected in how the trade is conducted today. Antique stores are the retail end of used selling, and most things at least forty or fifty years old that do not sell to a collector at auction or in a lower venue like a flea market or yard sale will drift toward one. Depending upon the dealer's aspirations, a store can look like a hushed art gallery, a cluttered barn, or a cobwebbed old mansion. Because antiques must evoke or contain a narrative, the setting in which they are sold is a powerful ally.

Colin Stair's wife was a gallery dealer, for instance. The Stairs operated at the high end of the business; they had clients who offered choice goods, and the Stairs displayed them in a spacious environment befitting their singularity. Such presentation incorporates the rhetoric of awe and respect; it takes me nearly as long to survey a gallery store as a crowded shop because each Limoges watch, Tiffany vase, and Georgian fruitwood stand demands attention. You are led to take in every detail because this might be the only time you see something like it. They are places where catalogue illustrations pop and vibrate into real life. Besides a price you might find a written description of its significance—or not. These dealers expect buyers to *know* why something is priced so high.

Gallery stores are museums where you can touch the exhibits, sometimes. Glass cases prevail in antique galleries, though you can *ask* to touch anything, if the dealer is convinced you are a serious buyer. I believe cases produce one other effect, deliberate or not: They arouse our inner cat burglar. The whalebone scrimshaw is in plain view, and you can see every scratched detail, every sail on the flotilla of ships, each waterspout and breaking wave. What is on the back? How much does it weigh? Can you still discern the touch of the bored sailor on the surface, silkened by his callused palms? You could ask to inspect the bone, but that would be a minor fraud; you can't spare $3,000 to back up the ruse. What's more, you'd be too nervous to handle it under the dealer's scrutiny. Still, only a thin barrier denies you the *presence* of the object.

Such a fragile impediment would inspire the thief to return in the night with a glass cutter, but the honest merely entertain the thought of giving in to the spell and buying what otherwise can only be had illicitly. Money can complete the heist. Then you'll be able to extend the dialogue, though with your thin checkbook nagging for attention.

Some galleries are so gussied up, so full of trumpets and pedestals, I often can't settle down long enough to lose myself in what I'm seeing. Mark Lawson Antiques, in Saratoga Springs, sponsor of the local broadcast of *Antiques Roadshow*, struck me in that way. Nothing was free-standing in this narrow store. Nearly all was encased, and it was staffed by a small, hovering clerk who asked me one too many times if I was looking for anything in particular. I felt I had to *invent* a reason to be there and pointed to Persian carpets hanging near the ceiling—out of reach. These carpets had drawn me like jeweled visions from the sidewalk. When inside, I saw Lawson had *spotlit* the carpets, like stained-glass windows.

I don't go into gallery stores often. Not only can't I afford anything in them, I have a disconcerting feeling I simply don't belong there. If you are not there to buy, a gallery suggests, you have no business ogling around. Their stuff is so expensive, so rare, gallery dealers don't try to attract impulse buyers. Instead they expect committed collectors to walk through the door and buy instantly when something fills a hole in a passionately linked collection of mechanical banks or fine porcelain. Of all the used venues I frequent, galleries give me a feeling similar to the one I get when I make a rare trip to a retail store. Here is an entire building filled with goods I either don't want or can't afford, aimed at an immense population with which I have little in common, people who live in ways unfathomable to me. Everything they want is reliably priced and available 24/7. You don't have to know much beyond what advertisements have told you to make an informed purchase. When I go there for something I can't get secondhand—flashlight batteries, for instance—I feel exposed under the light as an alien to the aisles and racks. I hustle along as though late for an appointment in the electronics department. When I leave, the automatic doors are never fast enough, and I am certain I have escaped something psychologically lethal.

Whether using a gallery-style display or a more jumbled arrangement, antique dealers are usually found in old retail stores, but antique dealers also capitalize on the sad fortunes of once-grand houses. American settlement patterns have changed often in the past two hundred years, orienting to rivers, canals, railroads, and lastly highways. Each change has created new residential districts and ruined others with industrial or suburban sprawl, isolating former staid country manors or proud Victorian mansions in a new landscape of warehouses, gas stations, and fast-food restaurants or in a neighborhood frayed by poverty. These quaint survivors, like William Faulkner's Miss Emily's ancestral seat, are sometimes recast as retail locations, offices, or even cubbyholed into apartments, erasing their original grandeur. Some become so buried in lighted, hollow-core plastic signs and display windows, you have to step back and use your imagination to see the old Queen Anne gables or remnants of a Colonial Revival porch.

Antique stores, in contrast, are a gentler revision. In fact, dealers count on customers' curiosity about the remaining fancy architectural details, fireplace mantels and lofty foyers. The Manor Antiques in Glens Falls, New York, was a dignified example. This three-story, thirty-four-room country mansion from the early 1800s had been rescued from its latest role as an apartment building and was filled with dozens of dealers. The owner/main dealer sat at a desk in the spacious foyer and held claim to the parlor to the left.

The stately house was now a maze of rented rooms, and the dealers' specialties gave them precise flavors. The former kitchen displayed mixing bowls, spice racks, plates, teapots, and Hoosiers, the latter free-standing oak or maple cabinets from the 1920s with a cutting board, flour sifter, meat grinder, felt-lined silverware drawer, and pot and pan organizers. I can imagine the traveling peddler pulling out a miniature model and hawking it as "a kitchen-in-a-cabinet." The den sported enough rolltop desks to outfit a squadron of Bartlebys; the bathrooms were galleries of wooden medicine cabinets, straight razors, and leather strops; and the bedrooms were chock-full of blanket chests and bedroom suites. Even the closets were open and filled with shelves on which dealers displayed "smalls." The third floor was accessible through a winding back stair, and the slanted ceilings, dormer windows, and pine floors hinted this had been servants' quarters. The social stratum was preserved in the quality of goods there, such as bamboo lawn furniture not thirty years old. The owners were using the house with a consciousness about its past and about the scavenger-impulse that would have led their customers to rummage in an abandoned mansion, although this building was not deserted, only marooned among malls and discount tire stores.

Historic houses provide dealers with a great contextual collateral, but they are pricey to maintain. The architecture that gives them their appeal must be preserved with caulk, paint, and sweat. Old houses have to support themselves in some way, and many owners put them to work as bed-and-breakfasts. Antique selling offers another line of work, allowing the owners to live in part of the house while the rest is public space.

Sometimes, however, it's hard to tell the difference between living and selling. A Federal-style house from the 1830s in Hudson had been harnessed by its dealer/inhabitants. I pulled over in front of it with my friend Pam a few days after the World Trade Center tragedy. Pam had been attracted by the display of patriotism and grief it bore: a larger battalion-sized flag hanging on the front with black bunting obscuring it, draped from the high Doric porch columns. "Not many people know the proper way to display a mourning cloth," Pam said to the owner. A bunting is supposed to block the flag from view, but not touch it. The owner was pleased she had noticed.

The house was furnished with Victorian wares only a couple decades newer than the house itself. Walking through the store was eerily intrusive, though, because the living quarters of the man and his partner were open for viewing, too, though cordoned off with gold braided rope, probably scavenged from a closed movie theater.

"This is a work-in-progress," the owner said when I commented on the display. Sometimes, if they forgot to put up the rope, people would appear in their private rooms. The owners would be sitting in their kitchen, and a sidetracked customer would wander in, gaze at the cupboards, and ask distractedly, "Why isn't anything priced back here?"

Their house was in the context of an entire town of used merchandisers, and many towns have been reinvented as antique versions of themselves. In Lebanon, Ohio, for instance, main street businesses that had not switched to antiques still reflected the theme by setting other nostalgic tripwires. Lebanon had one of the last working ice cream parlor and soda fountains, complete with twisted steel–framed chairs and tables and a marble counter. The town also had the collateral of The Golden Calf, an inn dating to 1809 and further distinguished by having hosted Charles Dickens during his 1832 tour of the United States. However, when I checked Dickens's *American Notes*, I learned he had been displeased; it was then a temperance hotel and unwilling to serve him brandy. Yet up the twisting staircase through three floors of rooms, I found one dedicated to Dickens and other rooms dedicated to period luminaries who might (or might not) have stayed there. The tiny rooms were clotted with antique dry sinks and highboys, including those four-poster beds that require a step stool to reach—perhaps to elevate the sleeper from cold drafts. A day-tripper could stay in one of these archaic rooms, breakfast in the storied inn, then browse for antiques, stopping for refreshment at the ice cream parlor. A day in Lebanon was a total immersion in the past.

Taking over a town affords a group of dealers both advantages and disadvantages. An old town is a coherent retail space, with established traffic patterns, parking spaces, and storefronts. Dealers have only to plug in their wares, and the setting again begins to function. The stores were designed to display, so little adaptation is needed, though most retailers will fine-tune them to some historic context. Old signs, like the GREEN-WICH HARDWARE in stained glass above the door in a shop in Greenwich, New York, are left to maintain the look of a classic small town. Like dealers in old mansions, dealers in downtowns must preserve their locations.

Ostentatiously named, The Antique Store was located in what had been the village hardware. Ballston Spa, New York, had rapidly become an antiques town, with a dozen dealers in the former jewelry store, diner, shoe store, and grocery. Across the street from The Antique Store was another building that had housed a half dozen dealers in a decade. If you stepped back, you could see the outline of a mid-nineteenth-century duplex for workers in the paper mill on the Kayaderroseras Creek. At some point, it was made into two stores, with apartments above and attached to the back. Then the stores were united into one and pressed into the used merchandise service.

For some reason, though, no dealer could make a go of it there. Everyone who tried had tempted customers with curb-appeal merchandise: stick furniture, traveling trunks, brass pole lamps. and other eye-catchers outside on the sidewalk. To the uninitiated, this display might suggest the dealer was being evicted, but for a veteran it evokes a yard sale, a scavenger's favorite source of bargains besides the trash. Back home in Vienna, Ohio, Tara had used weathered barrels and farm tools as a decoration, but that was before yard sales were a weekend mania. Dealers now know their customers search nearly every source for castoffs, and an assortment outside—particularly wooden items—will slow traffic like neon. It is the reverse of the display case; rather than impart preciousness, dealers hope to intimate give-away prices.

I suspect the ill-fated store simply couldn't compete with The Antique Store across the street, and that's one of the drawbacks of an antiques town: competition. Most customers have a threshold of diminished attention span. If you stopped at The Antique Store and went through the owner's multitudinous offerings before visiting the other dealers, you'd expend your ability to study a cluttered shelf or curio cabinet. There simply would be more than you'd have the mental energy to consider. That's why I like to go antique shopping with someone else, to benefit from an extra set of eyes. Brent, the owner, had so much stuff because he ran what was oxymoronically called an "antique mall." His store contained sections rented by other dealers, places even fuller than most because they will jam a rented space to capacity. They also provide yet more sets of eyes, each dealer having another perspective on the trade, a different knowledge.

Brent's shop was well organized, with high, twelve-pane windows to admit lots of light. Another feature was less obvious: the floor. A well-trod wooden floor is a musical instrument, booming and crackling in a pleasing, reciprocal way, recalling the empty houses Jay and I used to invade. Modern stores, built on cement slabs and filled with the white noise of ventilation systems, have erased even this modest, human-scale interaction of person with place. Sometimes Brent had a 1930s cabinet radio on, tuned to a big-band station playing Bix Beiderbecke songs, but usually he let the building itself speak to his customers.

Brent knew his building was an ideal setting, and he had done what he could to enhance it. The upstairs, probably the home of the original owner, had an ornate balcony that Brent had meticulously restored, as he had the inner staircase. Likewise, Brent either had a real knack for window displays, or he hired someone who did. On patriotic holidays, Brent brought out his stash of historic red-white-and-blue bunting, window aprons, and banners. He pointed them out to me when he first bought them, proclaiming his the only store in town suitably attired for Veterans Day. A brass cash register and period light fixtures completed the picture.

Ballston Spa was also the home base for auctioneer John Christman, whose little blue-painted shop was two blocks down in half a building; the other half was a barber shop that hung leeward over the Gordon Creek. The Christmans lived across the street in an 1860s cottage with a wraparound porch. Heidi said the cottage was haunted. Once John had been cruising yard sales and brought home "an ugly lamp with an ugly shade." The next day they found it near the front door. They had seen a sideboard door swing on its own, and their daughter said the ghost pulled her ponytail. Heidi even claimed the specter set the table for coffee when a friend was coming to visit, but I caught John rolling his eyes at that one.

The Christmans' antique shop was haunted by another ghost, the long-gone country general store. Gordon Creek Antiques also sold soda and penny candy, the latter kept in glass canisters. One late Friday afternoon I watched a gaggle of children file through the door. Each grabbed a soda from the cooler, and presented pocket change to John, saying how many of which candies they wanted. Children often stopped on their way home from school, John said.

As John gave out candy, I was reminded of the general stores of my youth, particularly Henry's Store on Scotch Hill in the Allegheny Mountains, down the road from my grandparents' new house. When we visited, my grandfather, with Scots frugality, would send my sister and me out to the country lane in front to scrounge in the ditches for discarded soda bottles to take to Henry's for the deposit. After we each had an armload, he'd give us a paper bag to hold them and a nickel from his change purse, and then he'd send us to the tar shingle-sided store with a single gas pump in front.

Henry's was so packed with stuff an adult would have to twist around tight corners and duck beneath pairs of Wellingtons hanging from the ceiling. My father used to say you never expected to find what you needed, but the brothers who ran it, Blaine and Jim Henry, knew where everything was, and they seemed to have it all, from pickaxes to paper plates. We went there for less practical provisions, though: soda and bubble gum or hard candies kept behind the counter.

Blaine Henry carefully counted out our candies, putting them in little paper bags, but with his brother Jim we went through a mysterious ritual. Jim would simply grab a handful of each candy we had selected, filling a bag to a rotundity that would have angered his parsimonious brother. We had to pretend not to notice, and never acknowledged his generosity; we would wait and squirm, casting sidelong glances to judge how many extra pieces landed in the bag. We'd thank him, trying to register our delight with our best manners, and outside dump the bags to count our take, thrilled by getting something for nothing.

Once Jim had given us so much extra candy, our consciences dictated we return and mention it. "If you kids can't count any better than that," he said, stone-faced, "you'd better go home and tell your parents I said you should be in summer school working on your arithmetic." I secretly suspected Jim was the one who couldn't count, but when he died years later my father said his obituary listed his college degree. Whenever Jim reached for our candy, his hands shook terribly, I recalled then; perhaps he had been too ill to pursue a profession beyond running a country store and had few joys beyond exciting children with extra candy for their nickels.

Ever since, I have had an affinity for country stores pressed into service by the antique trade, like the dueling antique stores of Fort Anne, New York. Tollpath Antiques had lots of curb-appeal with churns, spinning wheels, and plows, while inside the dealer specialized in another class of castoffs: signs, postcards, and other ephemera. However, they were hard-pressed to answer the riot on the porch of the antique store across the street. Most prominent were two life-sized dummies sitting on a bench, an elderly man and woman posed like *American Gothic.* Inside I found Charlie Chaplin. Then I recalled a wax museum in Lake George, a tourist trap from the 1950s, had closed recently, its exhibits funneling into the used market, the deathless images put to work as another kind of attraction. The place was parsed into cubicles with a different class of goods, such as an area with a sign calling it GRANNY'S KITCHEN, for dishware, pots, skillets, and strainers. On my way out the wax couple startled me, even though I knew they were there.

Any building that evokes the past can serve as a context for antiques, and many one-room schoolhouses and water-powered mills have been preserved because they can embody some part of the past only knowable through old photographs such as the one Tara gave me. Country stores aside, my favorite setting is an old barn. Of all the buildings that remind us of the past, barns are iconographic. Most are slightly dilapidated, suggestive of the deserted farms Jay and I had ransacked and bespeaking the kind of amnesia a barn has always fostered. A giant old barn, perhaps larger than the house nearby, rapidly became the repository of everything no longer needed, but somehow too valuable, or potentially useful, to discard. If you are lucky enough to own an old barn and have not yet become a hoarder, you are probably a soulless wastrel. Why throw something out when you can "just put it in the barn," a limbo betwixt rubbish and active service, where things can live on in its dusty corners? Barns are a netherworld of the not-needed, and "just put it in the barn" becomes a refrain. Every scavenger knows this and eagerly expects barns to yield alluring finds. The nation's barns are still erupting with forgotten goods.

Naturally, antique dealers would take advantage of these expectations and use barns to make their offerings seem like lost hoards or to appeal to people who go "antiquing" in the countryside. John Christman said, "Summer is when you gather. Fall is the best time to sell around here. People walk into a shop on a crisp fall day . . . "—pausing to emphasize the powerful sales potion made by a conjunction of time and place. "We sell a lot to the apple people and the leaf peepers," he added, meaning those who day-trip to orchards in the fall and tourists attracted by the autumnal foliage.

Anyone with a barn can rely on fitting into the agenda of those on rural forays. Jim Clark, a dealer in Galway, New York, converted the stalls in his barn to cubbyholes for antiques after he quit raising horses. The barn had a dirt floor, so Jim carefully covered it with crushed white limestone. Overhead a center beam of oak, two feet wide, kept the entire roof up, rafters nested into mortises. Uncommonly fine carpentry is a frequent feature of barns. A farmer could always depend on his neighbors to help with a barn raising; odds were one of them was a good carpenter. The house might be a slapdash affair, but the barn would contain minor masterpieces of timber-frame joinery.

"I know of people who have bought old farms and paid for them with what they found in the barns," Jim claimed. Though the story has to be apocryphal, I once had a similar experience when I bought a fourteen-room Victorian house. What really sold me was the two-story carriage house in the back, part of a complex of barns left from the original owners' family business: a livery stable. The house had been cut up into apartments since 1935, and generations of tenants had left discards in the barn. When I bought the place I had to accept the barn sight unseen because it was hard to walk around inside.

"The owner will have all of this cleaned out," the real estate agent said, trying to mollify what he assumed was my disappointment in the clutter.

"Tell him I'll take care of it," I said, aiming to appear magnanimous and forgiving, but secretly rejoicing. It took three years, but eventually I culled, sorted, and saved everything of value in the barn. There was no end to the treasures. When I finally got through a trapdoor in the ceiling and into the second floor, big enough for a basketball game, I found wooden moldings and trim that had been removed from the house during an "update," the mahogany stair banister, doors, storm windows, enough original 150-year-old locksets to repair the locksets in the house, and even furniture I still use today.

With a barn, dealers don't have to build a shop, as Tara had, or share their living quarters with the business. A barn trumps all other settings. Dealer Gary Guarno had an entire hotel for his wares. He lived on the third floor, but he was most eager to show me the barn in back. Half of the downstairs was crammed floor to ceiling with stuff he was going to throw away, though surely some picker would give him a token payment for it.

"Isn't it a great building?" Gary asked me, and I obligingly admired the post-and-beam joinery. His barn was untouched, simply a place for his surplus, but most dealers will enhance the barn-ness of their settings, such as a store outside Scranton, Pennsylvania, where the owner had created loft rooms out of rough-cut lumber on either side of the barn. Barns are adaptable because, aside from animal stalls, they are largely open spaces, waiting to be reconfigured.

Another shop, Longmeadow Farm Antiques outside of Schylerville, New York, had settled into a comfortable partnership with its barn. The owner had sided it with rough, vertical boards, covered the seams with thin strips of wood, and filled in the bay door, narrowed to a typical doorway. Against the front wall, the dealer had propped two hayracks, partially sheltered by the eaves, and a set of primitive "country cupboards," one stripped to battered bare wood and the other left with the worn paint some collectors love.

The barn had been carved into little warrens dedicated to types of stuff. Dealers create groupings akin to still lifes or Joseph Cornell's boxed assemblages, though not aiming so much at the sublime. New retail stores make displays with mannequins or furniture, but a dealer must be more associative. A space might be anchored by a drop-leaf dining room table, but no chairs, no dishes, nothing else associated with dining. Instead you have a jewelry box, three wooden yarn spools, a set of rearing elephant bookends, some embroidered doilies, an umbrella stand, and a mother-of-pearl-handled mirror. Few of these things would normally inhabit the same room in a house, but the tabletop cannot be wasted, so the doilies are draped off the end with the stitchery hanging in full view, held down by the spools and mirror, the bookends are placed on either end of the jewelry box, serving to announce its presence, and so forth, until the items are in conversation, presenting a united front in which the shapes of the things, not their functions, relate to each other. Wood will always provide a pleasing counterpoint to glass; a leather pouch should contain postcards and other papers; a barrel will always nicely corral hand-forged tools; canes, drapery rods, and yardsticks can sprout from an umbrella stand. The jumble of an antique store is a medley of the subconscious. When I have bought something at a store, I have often seen a dealer's eyes dart to where it had been, then around the room, trying to find the right item to replace it.

The Longmeadow barn had been expanded in recent years, and to make the addition sufficiently barny, the owner had nailed the barked sides of logs sheared off at a sawmill to the ceiling to imitate beams. Everything seemed to belong where it lay or hung. On the day I stopped, a customer was buying a blacksmith-made mowing scythe, a wicked-looking instrument you'd expect to find in the hands of the Grim Reaper.

"My wife is going to kill me," he said as he wrote a check.

"Has she done that before?" the dealer bantered.

"Sure, all the time," the pleased new owner of the scythe said, though he was obviously very much alive.

I looked at the wall where the blade had been hanging, and the empty space yawned, the pieces around it forlorn. I don't know how long the tool had been hanging there, but I suspected the dealer would have to rearrange the entire wall to adjust to its absence.

Chapter Seven

❧

THERE'S A FINE LINE
BETWEEN A HOBBY AND INSANITY
—from a sign in an antique store

MOST DEALERS ARE COLLECTORS, TOO, funneling their madness into a sideline. At first they might have only surplus from their collections in their stores, but soon other opportunities open up, and their offerings grow more faceted, anything that can help support their habits. Antique dealers sell as often to each other as to other customers.

Junkmeister Bob Miner, his novitiate scavenger daughter Allison, and I had wound through Mechanicville, New York, looking for the Hudson River Trading Company, on the main street in a town built around a waterfall, two canal locks, and a major river. The town was down on its stockings rather than only its heels. After we had crisscrossed the town twice, we found the store in a commercial building that looked wholly derelict; had Bob not spotted the sign, we would never have guessed it held a working business.

And the place was not actually open for business that day, though we had marched in the unlocked door before we knew it. David and Cathy Petronis were collectors of militaria, and as Bob plowed into a conversation with David about the endearing qualities of deadly weapons, Allison and I fanned out among the other offerings.

Their card said they dealt in "china, glass, furniture, fishing, trapping, old ammunition, knives, military collectibles, specializing in collector firearms, swords, old toys, Hall china, and Depression glass. We also handle estate sales, tag sales, moving sales, and auctions." Their collecting quest had lead them into every level of the used hierarchy. David said he had started as a collector and then became a dealer as he improved his collection through "trading up." He also did some scavenging. Among the piles of stuff near the cellar stairs was a corroded Winchester. A tag said it had been dug up on the Chisholm Trail. Although the barrel was rusted through and the stock had rotted off, the tag declared, "Will clean up into good condition."

The Petronises had been in business in this building since 1986, "and people still don't know where we are," Cathy said, when we recounted our difficulties in finding them. The old store was as much a place to house their collection as a place of business—in the window display nothing was for sale. They had done little to improve the place. A fire had scorched the ceiling, and the blackened beams were still exposed, while the storefront had been stripped of its decorative facade by a tornado a few years before and left that way.

When I tried to show my interest by asking about a Sako, a Finnish rifle, David said, "Sure I have one," and turned to the wall rack behind a long counter. Then he spun around and said, "It's not for sale anymore," his heavy face sombering.

I feared I either had offended him or that he wanted to be rid of us, but Bob later explained that as a collector David was afraid I might actually make him a too-attractive offer and then he'd lose a prized part of his collection.

Many dealers don't actually sell or display the kinds of items they collect for that reason. Gary Guarno housed his store in the Ondawa Hotel, built in 1840 in Salem, New York, later the Abrams Department Store until the 1960s. Opening a desk drawer by pulling on a screw protruding where a knob should be, Gary fished out a photograph of Abrams standing in his shoe department. Gary had been living in Westchester County when he saw the building advertised in a newspaper—and an opportunity to expand. Now painted summer squash yellow, the store bore no trace of the orderly shoes of Abrams's day. Gary had it jammed with antiques and less-aged junk.

I also saw no trace of what Gary collected, "contemporary paintings and sculpture," though he claimed his collection came from his own store. "I have about 120 paintings and 40 to 50 sculptures in my apartment. Luckily I have lots of room, 2,000 square feet."

Brent, in The Antique Store, was also a collector; he liked goods connected to the history of Ballston Spa. The antiques town had once

been a world-famous resort, featuring restorative springs and bottling the
waters for sale. Brent collected village and resort memorabilia. I once
sold him a mirror I had found in my barn, a painting of the downtown
from the early 1900s. The image had been painted in reverse on the back
of the glass, so the old hotels, now gone to fire or disrepair, appeared in
the proper orientation when viewed from the front. Brent said he would
hang it in his store, but I have never seen it there. In fact the only Ballston item I've ever seen him display was a sheet of uncut postcards made
from local, historic photographs. It was clearly marked "Not For Sale."

Collectors are one of the few predictable aspects of the trade. The
urge to collect is a noble passion, requiring a belief in value that defies
explanation, a leap of faith. Now that we have a knowable globe, few
mysteries remain for ordinary minds to plumb. Try wrapping your
mind around the last great questions of physics, for instance. The rest
of us have to construct quests out of humbler materials than the space-
time continuum. Most antique dealers will ask what you collect the first
time you stop by, because it is key to making sense out of what they
have, limiting their store to a few items. Dealers understand impulse
buyers and know they must appeal to them as well, but collectors are
their best customers. John Christman had sticky notes near his counter
with names, collecting interests, and phone numbers. Whenever he got
"good stuff," meaning something imminently saleable, he moved it fast
with a phone call. If you are looking for a something and tell enough
antique dealers, one of them is bound to turn it up. They are like a
huge staff of detectives for whom no request is too trivial. Expect to be
hustled, though.

For instance, my mother once used a ten-inch porcelain water sprinkler, shaped like a Mandarin Chinese man, while ironing. With me a toddler at her heels, she used her imagination to entertain me while still
getting her work done, making up stories and songs about the man,
funny adventures that always ended happily. The water sprinkler was
either broken or lost, and I forgot about it until I saw one in an antique
store and then I was again playing at her feet, hearing her voice. Despite
an antique dealer's adage, "The Time to Buy an Antique Is When You
See It," I picked it up, rapidly replayed the memory, then set it down and
left. Days later I mentioned the sprinkler to my mother. She said I should
have bought it for her, but when I returned to the store, it was gone.

One weekend I decided to make a quest out of the little Mandarin. I headed out to Route 30, a north–south two-lane road in New York state with so many antique dealers they have published a brochure with a map. On Saturday I managed to canvass the southernmost stores, describing the sprinkler to each dealer. A blanched man with a barn store said he had one in storage and would bring it in the next day if I returned. I did, and he brought out a sprinkler shaped like a Chinese man. This one was glazed green, not painted in naturalistic colors as my mother's had been, and shorter and squatter.

"I'm looking for one that is taller and painted to look lifelike," I said.

"This is a good one, though," he snapped, "You won't find one like you're looking for." He had assumed I was a collector, either of Chinese figurines or water sprinklers, and would buy what he had as long as it fit those criteria. He also wanted to bully me into compromising, to believe one identical to my mother's was too rare to hope for.

"Yes I will. I've seen one before," I said, thanking the grumbling dealer. Later that day I found one, enshrined in a case, not standing on a cluttered table like the first one. This one was also five times the price. I bought it, though, and sent it to my mother, who gave it pride-of-place in a china cabinet. When I asked her why she didn't use it, she said, "You don't need a water sprinkler with permanent-press clothes."

Collecting is even more irrational than the nostalgia that drew me to buy the figurine for my mother and that imagined her using it. I think it was more important to me that she have it than it was to her. A collector would have bought that green sprinkler, too, and a red one and a blue one. A collector would have wanted one in an original box, with a price tag from the 1940s, and would buy a catalogue advertising it. A collector would have coveted the mold used to make them. Collectors are so besotted with the objects of their desire, they attempt to capture the entirety of them. It is not unlike bird-watchers who yearn to sight an ivory-billed woodpecker. No one has seen or heard the bird in more than half a century, and biologists believe it is extinct, but it lives on for those who pore through their Peterson's guide and imagine adding it to their "life-lists."

The search for the ivory-bill is surpassed by those who love castoffs, though. Once, while waiting for a plane, I wandered an airport looking at the art exhibits planted to alleviate boredom. An observation deck had been turned into a gallery, and that month's exhibit was unorthodox:

collections. Some were predictable, such as salt-and-pepper shakers, but others were unlikely. The gallery had lunch boxes, paper clips, and even a child's collection of bird nests, but also electric, artificial fireplace logs, all of them plugged in and flickering. The collector's statement said his wife didn't allow him to display them at home. Likewise, a collector of cow weights, to which a farmer would tie an animal he wanted to graze in a field without fences, admitted they were a nuisance when he had to move. Who'd have thought there would be much variation in lumps of iron, but the collector had assembled about three dozen disc-, rhomboid-, and loaf-shaped weights.

My favorite collection was described by its owner as "bad autobiographies by minor celebrities," such as Jamie Farr's *Just Farr Fun*, with a picture of the *M*A*S*H* star in shimmering drag on the cover. The curator was hanging that exhibit, putting each book on a pedestal shelf next to a speech balloon containing a memorable quote. I haven't read Farr's book so I won't say whether the collector was accurate in including it, but taken as a whole, the assemblage was emblematic of the incredible versatility of the urge to gather like items.

I met one collector who had yet to decide whether he wanted to be a dealer or not, but he had built what looked like a country store with a low-brimmed front porch and had erected a sign declaring it a TRADING POST. The proprietor, whom I'll call Edwin, collected clothes irons and washing machines and had them stored in the building. Two walls inside were a veritable "history of clothes pressing," with scores of metal flat irons that were heated on a kitchen stove, in all weights from one ounce to several pounds. A dozen or more were lined up on the lip of a wood-stove rescued from an old tailor shop. Edwin had brass Chinese irons, even thumb-sized irons on shelves shielded by Plexiglas. "Because I want them to stay there," Edwin said. His collection evolved to irons heated by charcoal, kerosene, and finally early electric varieties. He had several of each, arranged to highlight differences in form or size, one morphing into the next.

The washing machines were a little more cumbersome to display, and perhaps that's why Edwin, a real estate agent who planned to retire and make his compulsions pay for themselves, wanted to erect a larger "museum and gift shop" dedicated to what you would have found in "a Colonial kitchen." He had even built his own wooden dry sink when he found an eighteenth-century one too costly. For the time being most of the washing machines were stacked on the porch, leaving only a path to the doorway. The handful inside were among the rarest, I presumed, including a wooden one, a tight oak barrel with a three-pronged agitator inside, operated by elaborate gears and flywheels. Another was a pristine 1953 Maytag wringer washer, coincidentally exactly like one my mother had used, and like the Mandarin sprinkler, it brought back memories. I thought of the dry, sweet smell of detergent and steam, the sight of my mother doing laundry, at a time when doing laundry meant more than simply waiting for it to be done. The clothes had to be pulled from the agitator tub and fed through the wringer, two rollers that squeezed out the soapy water. Then, after soaking in a tub of clear water, the clothes were rolled again and taken to the clothesline. Now I can't imagine how my mother withstood the monotonous chore, but then I was riveted by the power of the rollers. I was warned to never get my fingers in them, as they'd surely be crushed, bone and all.

Unlike the ceramic sprinkler, though, the clunky machine did not have the power to move me to buy one for my mother, nor would she have been pleased if I had. She was relieved when she finally got an automatic washer. That didn't stop Edwin from collecting them, though. His fascination with them went well beyond memory. He was simply unable to resist their multiple variations. Collecting outmoded household appliances, or cow weights, or electric fireplace logs, is a deep-seated enterprise.

Edwin saw his trading post as a tourist attraction and a boon to the local economy. The town in which he lived had once been the site of a Revolutionary War fort, but now only historical markers distinguished the place. Edwin planned to rectify this, though. He had built a wooden model of the fort—another museum exhibit—and planned to turn his house into a replica of a Colonial fort. He already had several life-sized cannons made from scrap lumber and old round porch posts. His house would become the ramparts, with gun emplacements on the roof and mannequins in military costumes. I wondered how grateful his neighbors were toward his civic largesse. "You're a man with an understanding wife," I said.

"She's always known I was a little strange," Edwin admitted with a grin.

Edwin actually had few antiques for sale, I realized after browsing The Trading Post; the bulk was simply an exhibit. Mostly he sold miniature cannons, replica flintlock rifles, felt tri-cornered hats and display boxes he had made from scrap lumber and scavenged Plexiglas. These toys, and accessories for other collectors, were all he had to defray his costly habits.

What exactly is, and is not, an antique? John Christman said it's hard to sell only true antiques, those that fit the original definition. He sent his "real good stuff" to another dealer, "where I can put $100 on a little spoon or something and the customers don't care." He was content to deal country antiques and collectibles. Some deal even newer stuff. And newer stuff warrants caution, especially if you are intent upon surrounding yourself with reverberations from the past. These include reproductions, imports, and forgeries.

Because antique stores provide a fine-tuned context for selling anything that looks old, some new furniture makers have turned to copying the most popular items, such as curved-front curio cabinets, claw-footed dining room tables, and T-back chairs, and offering them to antique dealers who have room in their shops. These are usually made of solid oak, in imitation of early-twentieth-century Golden Oak furniture, and are actually fairly well made and serviceable if you don't mind not having the real article. From the dealer's perspective, little is lost by handling such imitations. At a distance they resemble desirable antiques and add the bright light of oak to fill what otherwise would be gaps in a store's displays. For the buyer they are affordable versions of classic furniture.

Beware of the dealer, though, who stocks reproductions and doesn't mark them as such. In a department store-become-antiques mall in Brookfield, Ohio, I saw plenty of replicas, and most were unmarked. To be fair, dealers might assume most customers can tell they are not the genuine article. I can tell a reproduction across the room, but the people with me couldn't. Over and over one of them would exclaim over a piece of faux Golden Oak, until I pointed out it was not what it seemed. Some of the tell-tale features are hard to explain, but the sprayed polyurethane finish is always too smooth and consistent. If you chalk that up to refinishing, look at the oak itself. Oak has an open grain, and few refinishers can get all of the previous finish out. Some paint or stain residue will remain, especially in the cross-grain on turned legs or tabletop edges. If it's too clean, be suspicious.

If the wood isn't a giveaway, the hardware is usually a certain indicator. The companies are not really trying to make fakes; they simply want to satisfy some part of the market for old things with new merchandise. The hardware will look like the real deal, though the patina on brass will again be too even, as it was done chemically, not with the nuance of time. Hidden items of hardware, such as corner leg braces, will not be disguised, and are dead giveaways; and the companies use Phillips-head screws, not older slotted ones, as the furniture is assembled with power screwdrivers, and slotted heads are harder to drive. Reproductions will bear the signs of newer mass-production methods.

John Christman said you have to be particularly careful with primitives. Primitives are rustic, handmade items mostly rural in origin. However, "country cupboards" of rough pine and scabby with worn paint, or hand-carved troughs, bowls, or tools, can be easily faked. John pointed to three tool carrier trays. "The one in the middle is old. That one on the left some carpenter in New Hampshire made out of old wood," he said. That's what makes fake primitives so tricky to detect: They are old in part. Lots of restorers use old wood and hardware to repair furniture. Colin had showed me racks of eighteenth- and nineteenth-century wood taken from hopelessly ruined furniture. They weren't doing it to deceive, though; they simply wanted to bring back something damaged to as close to its original condition as possible.

Still, some crafters use old wood to fabricate antiques. Herb, a hobbyist who scavenged some paneling I was throwing out of my barn, kept a pile of pine board behind his shop, where the sun and rain could age it, so he could make country cupboards once it was sufficiently silvered. He would hide freshly cut edges with a stain that imitated aging. I have yet to meet anyone who can artificially age anything so well I can't tell; distressing furniture by banging on it with sacks of chains or aging brass with beer still speaks to me of its origins. Yet if someone uses genuinely old materials artfully, I too could be fooled.

I made an antique once. Because my barn was jammed with lots of old wood, I had enough wainscoting, crown molding, and hinges and latches to make a wall cabinet. First I stripped the old paint or varnish off the wood so after the cabinet was built I could make all the wood match using cherry stain in which I had soaked coffee grounds overnight—a trick a furniture restorer had taught me for imitating age-darkened varnish. I had to do little else to make it appear old, because the wood was already dinged and dented in the variety of ways only wood that has been used, not abused, can show.

When finished, I showed my cabinet to a handful of friends, all of whom knew of my scavenging, and all asked, "Where'd you *find* that?" It would not have fooled an expert, no fake can, because, among other things, I used round nails rather than square cut ones from the nineteenth century. The signs were there. However, when I sold the house, keeping the cabinet was one contingency the new owners put into the contract, overlooking the genuinely antique cabinets I had hanging about. I told them I had made it, but I don't think they believed me. If they ever remove it from the wall, they will find my name and the date I made it, 1999, penciled on the back.

In general, dealers who have newly made rustic pieces in their shops will label them as such. One dealer had contracted with a carpenter to make them to order; a board hung in the shop with scarred paint samples so you could pick the color. Another dealer had started a fad for painted and scuffed furniture. The style of furniture he offered was called shabby chic. In his Hudson shop everything was painted white and distressed in the same way. No one would mistake the wear as genuine, and that was the point. People who bought shabby chic could afford any style of furniture they wanted; they chose this stuff as a statement on their own affluence. The trend was a great boon for dealers, who could unload any piece, without need of provenance, age, or quality, with a quick coat of white latex and the application of sandpaper afterward. No one was being told these castoffs were prized or rare, just shabby.

Not all dealers are so honest, of course. I met one in Maryland who sold stuff that he suspected of being reproductions to dealers "out West" where he claimed people were less knowledgeable. He sold fake baseball posters advertising match-ups of classic teams, the New York Dodgers and Yankees, for instance. He would jab tacks and pins in the corners so they looked like "they have been hung up all over," crease them, walk on them, and sell them for $90 to dealers in the Midwest, six times what he had paid for them.

Honesty usually prevails, despite opportunities for lucrative scams, and dealers hope for informed customers. Fakes and reproductions are common, and not just in furniture. An antique store in Coxsackie, New

York, had an entire aisle of fake smalls, such as a glass bowl with a nesting-chicken lid and a cast-iron bulldog doorstop. NOT FOR SALE, FOR YOUR EDUCATION, a sign read. If you are dealing in genuine antiques and collectibles, you don't want the market diluted by an influx of cheap replicas. Nor do you want to buy them. John Christman told me a friend of his, a novice, decided he wanted to buy fine art and antiques as an investment. He called John one day to brag about the deal he'd gotten on a 1920s impressionist painting and on some majolica pottery. John said the canvas painting was attached to the frame with staples, and the marks on the bottoms of the majolica were deliberately blurry—not Italian, he speculated, but newer reproductions from China. His friend had been taken.

The trap that had led John's friend to waste his money was magnified by the fact that majolica originated in Italy. When you are buying or selling imported used goods, you are venturing into a beguiling fog of fakes. Like most collectors, I am most secure in judging American stuff, because I spend most of my time around it, know its historical context, and understand what I should see. They are familiar as part of our culture, the set-pieces of our group-memory. In judging an American antique, I put a lot of value in my instincts about whether it has been tampered with or dressed out to look older. I'm no expert, and I wouldn't want to second-guess the Stairs or the Christmans, but my gut feelings are pretty reliable.

A new type of old stuff starting to appear in the trade has me stumped, though, and coyote-wary: imported antiques. Used goods have long been imported, especially English or Continental goods. A dealer told me "ship container after container of stuff" pours into the business, all of it between 50 and 100 years old. Antique buyers overseas are only interested in things made before 1850, sticking with the original definition of "antique." While I don't pretend to be as good at judging the relative value of French sideboards or English wardrobes as I am of their American cousins, they don't spook me because they are usually comparably priced and familiar enough. The Victorian style was a Pan-Atlantic cultural phenomenon.

Items from the western Pacific rim make me leery, though. I have stood in front of one of the Asian "antiques" now gushing into the market and found it both compelling and suspicious. The wardrobe/

cabinet—I couldn't be sure of its original use—had forged iron hinges, teak and mahogany with what looked like well-rubbed wear, a deep oil finish, and joinery unlike any I had every seen, both crude and delicate at once. Like an American primitive, its door openings were out of square, and the doors had been shaved so they would close. What bothered me was the chest was too compellingly cranky and ancient. Like looking at a Hudson River School painting, I knew I wasn't seeing exactly what was there, only a romanticized rendition. The elements segued too well, like the parts of a sculpture, something consciously designed and integrated. Because I don't know the stages in style or development of Chinese furniture, I had to rely on my instincts. And they were sounding sirens.

What's most frustrating about Asian antiques is that some of them must be genuinely old, but no dealer has assuaged my suspicions. Even Rebecca at the Stair Gallery was not fully convincing. While standing in front some Chinese cabinets, I remarked I found pieces like them dubious. "We were sold these guaranteed they were nineteenth century," she said, but she added they were hard to date. I noticed the gallery's tags did not cite dates, as they did on other pieces. Rebecca added the items were often too crude, and that tipped her off because she knew the Chinese were better craftsmen than that.

Another dealer whose shop was fairly given over to Asian pieces said she went to China to pick them out.

"Where in China?" I asked.

"Shanghai," she answered after a slight pause, and I suspected she had struggled for the answer. "They refinish them over there, so that's why they look like they do."

"What finish do they use?"

"Hand-rubbed shellac," she answered, the finest finish you can apply. "Someday they'll discover polyurethane."

As I examined a desk, looking at a drawer pull, she immediately offered, "Of course the hardware is reproduction." I nodded, pretending I had been suspicious. It had fooled me.

Antiques are pouring out of China in particular because of its most-favored-nation trading status. In a remote shop in the Adirondacks, far from where you'd expect to see imported goods, I saw a wooden container marked "Unusual basket," and it was. It looked like a cross between a bucket and a picnic basket, held together with iron straps. When I asked about it, the dealer said, "I think it's Chinese; it came out of a summer-house. It's got some age on it," she added, but neither she nor I could be sure.

Part of the trouble is that antique dealers are suspected by the general public of being a little crooked, a reputation I haven't found widely warranted. However, these overseas goods open the door to lies and invented provenances. At Cherry Tree Auctions in Greenwich, New York, I talked to a buyer about low prices bid on the few Asian pieces there, and he flatly said, "No one wants them." I've even seen Asian furniture with elaborate certificates of authenticity that could as easily be fake.

There's nothing wrong with buying and selling imported goods, of course, as long as everyone knows what's what. Rural New England is an unlikely place to find an importer, but I suspect the owner of Ebenezer II in West Stockbridge, Massachusetts, had been retreating from the antiques business to embrace another trade. Stockbridge proper boasts Norman Rockwell's home and museum and Alice's Restaurant, balladized by Arlo Guthrie, and it draws tourists year-round. However, John Christman was right: In high leaf-peeping season the town was overrun and traffic-jammed, and the antique stores were shoulder-to-shoulder with tourists wanting that New England Autumn Experience. I retreated from the hubbub to West Stockbridge, founded thirty years later (1779) and with less cachet.

Ebenezer II was a little picket-fenced house on the bend of the creek feeding Card Pond near the restored Shaker Mill, an ideal setting for antiques. Inside, though, I didn't find many; Joe McConnell dealt mostly in Turkish rugs and brass or copper pots and platters, not what you'd be looking for when on a ramble in the Massachusetts countryside.

In the back room were a few antiques, and above a fireplace hung two muzzle-loading muskets. One was priced at more than a thousand dollars, the other was not priced. A sign read ASK FOR HELP WITH THE GUNS OR SWORD, but I didn't see a sword.

"What's the price of the other musket?" I asked a woman nearby, and she sent for Joe.

"I bought those in New Orleans," Joe said, adding the unpriced one was probably French, and that he knew little else about them, besides they had cost him too much, after paying to ship them. "I couldn't bring them on a plane," Joe explained. He asked me to make an offer.

I told him about the Stanislowsky gun auction as a place to sell them and suggested he contact some of the militaria dealers in Gettysburg, Pennsylvania. "I need to research them," Joe admitted, though the sign on the wall was faded; he'd had them for a long time.

Joe was making real money on imports, though, bought in bulk from "a dealer in Maryland." Imported goods, old or not, have a more predictable profit margin. They didn't need much research.

Imported antiques and "recentiques" slip into the trade because dealers always hunger for what they call "fresh merchandise," wanting to offer what the others don't, something unusual. That's what would tempt Joe McConnell to ship home two pricey blunderbusses from New Orleans. John Christman doesn't like to buy stuff at local shops for resale in his. "Everyone knows it, and no one's excited by it," John said. It has already passed hand-to-hand and without selling.

Auctions are good sources of fresh merchandise, of course, but they also simply shuffle the deck among the players. I saw a dealer I knew at Dean's Auction Barn in Watervliet, New York, and after a four-drawer oak chest of drawers sold for $50, I asked him what it would fetch in a store. "It's English," he said, "Maybe $75." I have never seen a single chest sell for less than $150 in a store, so I suspected he simply didn't want me to know their profit margins. I trusted his next answer, though, when I asked him how long he let something sit in his store before running it through an auction: "Six months." If something hasn't sold after your regular traffic has cycled past it, you might as well put in on the block and at least get some money out of it.

Because there is no certain market for anything, keeping stuff moving is key. Gary Guarno said when he was in Westchester dealers from the South and West would come to buy truckloads from him. They really liked "Depression furniture," he said, stuff from the 1930s he claimed was considered old in the West. "The Northeast is where all the oldest stuff is. We've been here the longest." Now a twenty-five-foot truck pulled up each Sunday loaded with stuff "fresh to the area," and dealers from all over the Northeast passed through to get it.

Gary served as a clearinghouse for dealers, a warehouse of the unwanted. "We all know each other," he said. He gets his stuff from estate sales, and other dealers sell stuff they can't move to him. "Sometimes dealers put ridiculous prices on things, and they just don't sell." Fresh merchandise is crucial; "That way you don't have somebody come in and say, 'I know where you got that and how much you paid for it.'" For instance, Gary used to export and import antiques to and from England. Once a London dealer was excited to show him a set of chairs. When Gary saw them, he had to admit they were good ones; he had sold them to a dealer in Bath a year before.

A large man with graying reddish hair and a distinct New York accent, Gary was exuberant about the business, though he'd been in it for twenty-eight years, and his trade had spread to include everything old. Bedroom suites from the 1950s and 1960s, Formica furniture, and space-age floor lamps kept company with primitives and late-nineteenth-century stuff. Wherever Gary's truckloads came from, they were obviously not very selective. His card suggested he was not picky either: "Compulsive Buyer and Seller."

Still, Gary said the business was "not as good as it used to be" because some of what entered the market came from "people who furnished their homes in the 1960s or 1950s, and that stuff is just not as collectible." He also thought the market was dropping off because the new generation's parents had collected antiques, and so the new generation wanted only new stuff, though I'd so far seen absolutely no evidence to support the contention.

One of the central tenets remained, Gary said: Collectors enjoy making pilgrimages to seek their chosen talismans. Gary said people will travel any distance to look for used and antique stuff, and shopping is always a surprise because "everybody's inventory is unique." He thought some of the allure is the chance "to see America." That's why failed retail locations can become successful secondhand businesses: Whatever had kept customers away before does not apply when "shopping is a treasure hunt."

Gary was not interested in making Salem an antiques town though, believing that while having a few stores there helps make it a destination, too many ruin it. A newcomer to the area, Gary was viewed with suspicion by the locals. "I think he might be doing something illegal," a local merchant said after watching trucks pull up. Across the street from Gary's hotel was another tiny junk shop, Ray's Useful Things. I wondered how he could compete with Gary's warehouse of castoffs.

Chapter Eight

❧

What's It Worth?
Or, Is It Just Trash?

O NE OF THE SUREST AND LEAST MEANINGFUL ways of answering
these questions is by using the economic equivalent of reverse
engineering: If it's worth something, it isn't trash. Unfortunately for those who want a definition, and fortunately for those of us
who require a steady stream of castoffs, this way of measuring the value
of something excludes practically nothing. Yet one of the delightful
parts of the pricing of antiques and all castoffs is that no value is carved
in stone. While haggling remains only part of large mainstream purchasing, such as cars or real estate, it is part of even the most modest sale in
secondhand culture.

You'll pay what the market demands, and you'll have to allow the
dealer a profit, but you have much more control over the price than you
might think. No one can predict how a bit of dickering will work out,
nor is any method sure, but the process requires intuition, wit, a sharp
eye, knowledge, and tact. None of these skills come into play in buying
new; sales and coupons aside, new retail consumers have a paucity of
opportunities to save money. And the exquisite contest of the dicker
must be learned and refined through trial and error.

Those who sell in the used market are always going to be better at
getting their prices than a civilian, but you don't have to be at a complete
disadvantage. You simply have to learn to dance. The first step begins with
the seller, as you examine something. Always scrutinize something before
checking the price. This telegraphs to the dealer—who *is* watching—that
you can *see* what you are looking at, the failings and virtues, and these are

more important than cost. Once I was looking at a machinist's tool chest with an eye toward buying it. These look like miniature chests of drawers, usually made of oak or maple and studded with nickel-plated hardware. I opened the drawers, removing a couple to look at the backs. Next I ran my hand over the top and sides before inspecting the bottom.

Then I set the chest down and walked away, looking out of the corner of my eye to see if the dealer was watching; he was of course. I stared at a shelf of porcelain, then returned to the tool chest and looked at the price, running a finger over it. I winced and pulled my hand back as though the box was hot, took a step back and looked at it again, as though sizing up a work of art, then stepped forward and again pulled out a drawer.

That's when a dealer will join you, saying, "I just got that," meaning it was too fresh to discount; "That's a real unusual one"; "Those are really getting collectible"; "Those are getting hard to find"; or as in the case of the tool chest, "I don't get many as nice as that one."

The last comment really puts you on the defensive, but the dealer can only use it when it's at least partially true. You are hard put to work down from a comment like that, because if you find a flaw on which to hang a lower price, the dealer will make a show of taking it personally, as if you have said he is a poor judge of quality. Also, if you cite too many flaws, you will appear disingenuous. If it's such a lousy tool chest, why would you want to buy it? When dealers are buying, they can nitpick because they are only planning to resell; you, however, want to keep the item, so there must be something you like about it.

You have to go ahead though, because the dealer expects you to. You have two choices: either agree that it is nice, but then finger a crack in the top or a chip in a drawer front, and allow the dealer to admit to a flaw or two; or play hardball and say, "I don't know, it has a couple of problems," or "I was looking for one with . . . " and name a feature the box lacks.

Only now will numbers start to go back and forth. If you have played it right, the dealer will drop the price first. Most dealers will have a set of numbers and letters on a tag, a code that tells him where he bought it, how long ago, and for how much. How often I've wished I were a cryptologist. The dealer will look at the tag, and lower the price a bit.

Now you must begin to hem and haw. It helps to have a broad vocabulary of movements and phrases; "I don't know . . . " trailing off into a little shake of the head is a good one. A long exhalation of breath is another useful response. The dealer will counter by citing a virtue or two, or mark time by telling you about the provenance, usually some story about a widow he has helped out by buying her husband's tools and other stuff, implying he has paid too much for the chest out of the goodness of his heart. Nod sympathetically and make a really low offer.

This exchange can go on for as long as you want, as long as you can extend the choreography; however, etiquette requires that the longer the dicker, the surer you must be you will close the deal. Haggling past the first or second price and then not buying is bad form. If the process is simply too exquisite for you, you can take one shortcut: Ask what the dealer *needs* for it. Paul Ferrara, veteran haggler, tipped me off that this phrase works best. It acknowledges that the dealer has to make a living, but it signals you aren't interested in paying more than what's fair. If something has been sitting in the store for a while, asking what a dealer *needs* might get you a low, break-even price. Selling it to you at even money or at a slight profit is safer than running it through an auction.

The joys of haggling are an acquired taste, but once you get the hang of it, when you take something up to a register at a new retail store and pay the ticket price, you will chafe. That's one reason why I'm not as fond of antique "malls" as other venues: The dealers who rent the booths are not present, so there is no one with whom to dicker. Some proprietors will call the dealer if you have a counteroffer, but making a deal through an intermediary over the phone is a poor substitute. Some dealers are averse to dickering. I have seen grumpy signs in their shops reading I FOUND IT, APPRAISED IT, HAULED IT, AND CLEANED IT. YOU WANT ME TO TAKE LESS FOR IT? Those dealers need to find another line of work.

You'd think appraising an antique should be fairly easy; after all, a trip to your local bookstore will reveal that someone has written a price guide on every category of antique and collectible. However, there are too many variables to make such guides useful: context, provenance, and condition. Auctioneer John Christman said price guides are "the biggest scam there is." He said something is worth only what someone will pay for it. He pulled out a book on Griswold iron from his reference shelf. This maker of skillets, frying pans, and pots is easily identified by the large GRISWOLD stamped on the bottom. "We reared a whole generation of people who believe the prices in these books," John said. "And they will go to an auction preview, look at the prices in a book later, then figure they can pay $45 for an item listed for $65 in the book. If you can sell it for $65, tell me about it." When John started selling antiques for his father, all they had were classic price guides written by the Kovels, the original authors of antique guidebooks.

Heidi Christman added that the regional variations in price can be wide. Once a dealer called her and said a guy was coming her way in a beige truck, a dealer from the Southwest on a shopping spree. Heidi had "the book" with her, a list of what she and John had paid for everything in the shop, and when the dealer arrived she offered him rock-bottom prices. He said, "You can't help me. I can't get that back in Arizona." John said the difference in price was due to there being "more money in this area," but it was also a matter of style. Southwesterns want Santa Fe furniture, painted primitives age-faded into pastels, which are not common in the Northeast.

Gary Guarno said you have to learn the business and its pricing through hands-on experience. "No one is born an antique dealer. You make mistakes, then learn from them," he said. Gary also agreed you can't learn much from price guides. "From the pictures you can't tell the difference" between what makes a thing valuable or not. "It's a tricky business. I once sold a pair of chairs to a friend for $7,000 who sold them for $10,000 to someone who sold them for $400,000." Gary was leaning back in his desk chair, hands locked behind his head, but now he sat up, arms crossed. "I still beat myself up about that three times a day, although it's been years ago. Thanks for dragging that out of me. It's time for you to go now," he said, but with a smile. Gary had thought the chairs were from the nineteenth century and Italian, but they were actually English and from the eighteenth century. The kick-myself moment came when Gary saw them on a fancy auction catalogue cover, he added, teeth gritting.

Gary had found the chairs at an estate sale and had watched a lot of other dealers pass them by. "See? Sometimes you let other people's opinions affect yours." Even so, Gary had some real wins in his career; he sold two Italian paintings he had bought for $700 for $50,000. Gary knew they were valuable, so first he took them to Sotheby's where he said, "Some twenty-two-year-old kid tried to tell me they weren't worth anything." He then asked to see the department head, who raved over them. Even the big auction houses make major mistakes, Gary claimed, "Dealers park out front of Sotheby's to buy stuff they turn away."

A dealer can't spend too much time agonizing over whether a piece has brought top dollar, because something else needing research always presents itself. Joe McConnell at Ebenezer II said, "I know you're not supposed to look back. Just make a profit and keep moving forward. I know I've given up some home runs." He once had a flintlock pistol that he suspected was a reproduction. "I finally sold it, and I never really knew what it was. I guess I should be glad I doubled my money." Joe had stopped going to auctions because he started finding it harder to get a good deal. "Too many retail buyers, and the auctioneers started pulling too many tricks."

As difficult as it might be to get a bargain at an auction, it's even more futile to second-guess a dealer, to size up a shop and guess if the business is struggling and use it to your advantage in dickering. Dealers are experts at shaping appearances to serve their ends, and even the owner of a humble or chaotic shop is savvy enough to wait for the right price. I love prowling the back roads looking for shops in the vain hope I'll stumble onto an antique dealer who is starved for customers and ready to deal, though I know they are all plugged into the network. Whitehall, New York, is off the beaten path these days because Interstate 87, the main north–south arterial, veered so far from it people could live on the New York–Montreal corridor and never have an excuse to go there. Most of the town is boarded up, despite the efforts of the good people of Whitehall to make the place attractive, mostly to history buffs who might want to visit the "Birthplace of the U.S. Navy," a claim based on Benedict Arnold having built three gunboats there that he took up Lake Champlain to slow the advance of the British. The town was also a crucial port during the War of 1812, and the remains of another naval vessel from that conflict, the USS *Ticonderoga*, sit in a park by the Champlain canal, its exposed ribs and keel sheltered in a screened cupola.

Carmine Cottage Collectibles on the southern outskirts of the town was indeed in a Victorian cottage, but it could hardly be seen from the road because it was covered with antiques and junk. The front porch was full of chairs, baskets, pails, and cupboards, even a giant cutout of a mermaid, painted in vampish attributes, there for no reason I could tell except the owner had found it somewhere and decided it would help pull people off the road and into her shrinking parking lot, winding around the spring tide of castoffs, as I did, to find a spot.

Curb appeal works, but Carmine Cottage had taken the practice to the absurd. The stuff outside was weathered and sun-bleached. I doubted the owner brought it inside at night. It was all posed, though; even the edges of the path to the house were lined with teacups half buried among the marigolds, recalling a dump with enticing objects just below the surface.

When I got inside the shop I knew she left most of what was outside there year-round. The cottage was so wadded with smalls, two people had barely enough room to sidle by each other in the narrow passageways. Still the owner had arranged everything with a precise consciousness, every spoon and gravy boat positioned to highlight it. The effect was an oddly pleasing sensory overload. The owner was sitting in a makeshift office at the foot of the second-storey staircase, surround by vases, teapots, and dried flowers, looking for all the world like an animal peeking out of a den. She was studying a book on glassware.

A customer approached her, "My wife runs a day care center, and there's a white rocker in the yard that looks like it would be good for rocking babies. How much do you want for it?"

"Seventy-five dollars," the owner said, without even leaving her den to look at it. She either knew everything out there or had made up a price off the top of her head.

"Seventy-five dollars?" the man asked, incredulity steepening his rising inflection. Had he used the story of rocking babies as a bid for sympathy? Had he figured the stuff left outside was nearly worthless? Bad call.

"Seventy-five," the owner said again, looking back at her book.

"I'll tell my wife." he said.

I was looking at canes. An old friend in Key West had just undergone knee surgery, and I wanted to get him an unusual cane. He was interested in something that reflected the Adirondacks, something he couldn't get in the Conch Republic. I picked out a few canes and approached the woman, telling her about my friend.

"So I want to buy him a cane," I said, "but it has to be one that he can actually put his weight on."

"That's very thoughtful of you," she said. "There are more around the corner." I went there and saw a couple more that might do and came back.

"He's a little shorter than me, so I don't know about some of these," I continued. "What do you think about this one? Does it look sturdy enough? I like the fact it has a rubber tip on the end. That'll give him confidence, knowing he won't slip."

We chose a cane of hand-carved, native hemlock. It had been a sapling, and the nubs where the many branches had been attached were left on. The head was a stout, perfectly curved root. It felt reliable.

The owner immediately gave me a healthy discount on the cane, and I like to think it was because I had asked her to help me choose. I had gotten her involved in my gift-buying. The rocking chair customer might have fared better had he asked her which one *she* thought was best for rocking babies.

What I liked best about the cane was it was both handmade and well used, obviously made by an old Adirondacker whose knee or hip had worn down, then used so long the handle had a velvety patina only the human hand can give after gripping it thousands of times. My friend pointed out the handle was shaped on the end like a horse's hoof, and he wondered if the North Country whittler who made the cane would have guessed the next person to use it would be a gay man on the southernmost street in the continental United States, more than a thousand miles away.

Had the old cane not seen the kind of use that gave its handle a creamy finish, I might not have been so drawn to it. An aspect of antiques, and of used goods in general, that new goods will never be able to approximate is the value added by the signs of human use. Primitives most of all rely upon this attribute for their attractiveness, but most antiques are considered more valuable if in "original condition." It would be helpful if that were true all the time, but like the highboy I saw at Cherry Tree Auctions, some things must be repaired and refinished if they are going to still be useful.

Auctioneer John Christman advised people who feel tempted to strip and refinish something to "leave it alone." He didn't even clean off the cobwebs and said customers like to see stuff that way, though he admitted to vacuuming out chests of drawers, saying, "You're going a bit too far when you find rat shit in them." Some dealers claim it's easier to sell something with cracked paint than one cleanly refinished, though the point is debated. John showed me a recent copy of the *Antiques News* with the cover story "Should You Strip Painted Surfaces?"

For the last word on condition and refinishing, I'd ask Jack Metzger. The day I visited him was hot and humid, and I drove the twisted country lane with my windows down. On a tight curve a hornet blew in and landed on my steering wheel; I careened off the road, barely avoided a close look at the Battenkill River, then tried to chase the hornet out the window. When it landed on my leg I did a Saint Vitus dance, jumping out of my truck as someone rounded the corner; the car slowed, the driver stared at me, then sped through the curve.

I was risking insect venom and rural ridicule because Jack had heard of my interest in use and reuse, and he had called me, saying I had to see his collection of handmade tools and other curios. His shop was in what had once been a furniture factory in Cambridge, New York, a town colonized by art galleries, with a refurbished hotel that claimed to be THE HOME OF PIE À LA-MODE. JACK'S OUTBACK, the sign read on the long porch that shielded two other businesses: Battenkill Books and Over the Moon, a giftique shop. Jack's end of the porch was replete with rusted iron— axes, hammers, pots, giant wrenches and hinges, shovels and toys— crowding the edges of the steps and the porch rail. The porch was so attractive it was pictured on the sunflower seed packet Jack gave away as a promotional.

I opened the door—the handle was a decorative chunk of some ancient machine—and saw a group of men talking. When I announced who I was, the tallest one with an Amish-length, lead-colored beard said he was Jack Metzger. I recognized Jack's voice immediately, as we'd had an animated, long telephone conversation about the charms of castoffs, during which Jack had rhapsodized about his love of hand-made hayracks and iron strap hinges. He had a pair forged in Pennsylvania during the Colonial era. Jack was possessed, and I soon found out just how thoroughly.

Jack had prepared a list of things he wanted to show me, but first he described how he got into his niche of the used goods business. His great-grandfather, the original John Metzger, had been in the construction business after immigrating to the United States from Germany. He had nine sons, who "made quite a labor force," and the business thrived.

The business passed down to Jack's father, and Jack grew up around people who made things. Jack, however, found himself drawn to another aspect. The family had a warehouse behind the house where they kept salvaged architectural materials, and Jack loved poking through the old doors, windows, and other things found when demolishing or remodeling a building. He spent all his time in the warehouse, and whenever anyone was looking for him, his mother would say, "Jack's out back," and that was where he got the name of his shop, though he had a kangaroo on the sign because he knew the phrase was apt to suggest the Australian countryside to his customers.

"So I feel this sense of continuity through this stuff," Jack said, and I followed his sweeping hand to look at the shop. Jack's Outback was packed. Every inch of the walls bore a tool or sign. Every cabinet was full of other things, and every ledge or surface was inhabited by a whatnot. To my eyes, every place a thing could be, a thing was there.

Then I got a personal tour. Jack specialized in handmade farm implements and tools. Even a pair of skis, hand-carved and bent, were not used for sport, but by a farmer to get across his winter fields. Jack seemed to revel in tools whose uses were at first puzzling; on his porch I saw several thick iron troughs the size of large bread pans. These, Jack explained, were wagon brakes, fastened to the wheels when going downhill to slow the rig and keep it from rolling out of control and over the horses.

According to Jack, his best treasures were modest and easily overlooked. For instance, he lovingly brought out a snow shovel made out of scrap sheet metal, perhaps part of a cabinet or appliance, wired to a chokecherry branch for a handle. Wire, Jack said, was the duct tape of the past. Jack's Outback had portholes to the past aplenty: Eighteenth-century hearth hooks for hanging pots at different heights (today we'd simply adjust the burners on the range), a rack for making toast over a fire, and wooden clothes-washing tools, which looked like churn handles with a three-pronged end. "The technology is the same," Jack said, showing how the agitator would have spun in a washtub. "Only the power source has changed."

Jack liked to read a tool, to decipher the maker's intent and the challenges faced in making it. He showed me several "commanders," wooden mallets for driving wood pegs in post-and-beam carpentry. The head of one had split, and a blacksmith had reinforced it with iron rings; the repair made it Jack's favorite. Likewise, he prized a homemade rake with nails as teeth, or one with teeth replaced by wooden ones. "I do presentations in schools," he said, "and the kids ask why they didn't just get a new rake, and I say, 'There wasn't a True Value Hardware on every corner. You had to make what you wanted and fix what you had.'"

Jack was holding the rake in front of him like a ceremonial standard. "I think the repairs make it a work of art. Imagine, sitting down and actually carving new teeth for a rake." Jack's face took on an appreciative warmth as he stared at the tool and once again heard the conversation between its parts, the juxtapositioning of metal and whittled replacements. I too could see how the rake's owner had schemed to extend its useful life with whatever was at hand. The rigidity of the head had been cross-braced with thin wooden lath.

I asked Jack if he had a personal collection, and he said he had a few things at home and a bunch of stuff in a storage bin, but that was all surplus.

"It's all for sale," he said.

Jack was ready to show me more when a customer came in, only one of a steady string. Since Jack was busy, I started talking to one of them, a lean, gray-haired fellow who appeared to be one of Jack's friends, though everyone who walked in the door appeared to know Jack well.

The man said that he came to Jack's because he was friendly; he thought a lot of the shop owners were stuffy. He also didn't trust a lot of them, believing they peddled fakes, especially primitives. "I never saw the attraction in 'distressed furniture' until I saw the originals, you know, the old stuff." The man swung his arm around Jack's store. "Now I can see what they're trying to imitate." He was a collector, but he liked the interaction as much as he did acquiring stuff. Talking to dealers about antiques reminded him of his days hitchhiking around the country in the 1970s. He would make up stories about himself to entertain the people who gave him rides. That's what provenance is for many antique dealers, he said. They told stories about where they got something, and maybe even embellished. He didn't mind though, as long as the story was good. He liked to buy antiques when the stories meant something to him.

Jack was free of customers again and wanted to show me a candle chandelier he had made, all out of found materials. It hung on a wooden gambrel, a curved stick used to separate the legs of a pig when it was being butchered. "I have sixty or more of them," Jack said, and he wouldn't sell the chandelier until he had enough parts, iron hooks and candle platforms, to make another one. The gambrel was actually quite beautiful, made of bird's-eye maple and smooth from wear.

Jack loved the patina left behind by use, and he had me feel the inside of a yoke. It was small, and I wondered what kind of animal it was designed for. "It was for people," he said, and he pointed out several others hanging from the ceiling.

I immediately envisioned slaves coffled together, but Jack said the yokes were used by farmers "for carrying water pails, one on each side. I have one I use when I'm watering my garden. It's better than walking bent over."

If someone made an item, especially from unlikely materials, Jack either had it or wanted it. He showed me a homemade fly-swatter, a branch wired to a square of window screen, and a handle from a scythe joined to a tin can lid to make a hide scraper. "I have a high price on it because I don't want to sell it," Jack said. Then he pulled two sticks out of his desk: clothespins. "I like to think about the R&D involved in making these. The inventor finally had to figure out he needed a stick with a knot in it, so he could split it, but it wouldn't split the whole way. Imagine saying, 'Tonight I'm going to sit on the porch and whittle clothespins.' They say the Shakers invented clothespins, but I figure lots of people made them. I keep these in here, because I don't want people to ask about buying them. I just think they're great folk art."

So some things actually were not for sale. Another thing I'll bet Jack would have trouble giving up were the seats from the outhouse from the one-room schoolhouse renowned folk artist and painter Grandma Moses had attended. Her farm was only a few miles up the road. Although famous for her primitive renderings of New England rural life, even she would have not used an outhouse as a subject. A single board, it had six holes in groups of three, and a mark showed where a wall had separated the boys from the girls. The holes were different sizes. "Little butt, regular butt, and big butt. All three sizes on each side," Jack said. He had the board hanging on the wall, each hole framing an old baseball glove. He got the remnant when the schoolhouse was being restored as an historic site; they didn't save the humble outhouse. "An old-timer told me that tourists got it wrong. They come up here, eat outside and shit inside. They got it backward," he said, laughing.

A collector came in then, looking for souvenir textiles, like a pillowcase with "Lake George, NY" stitched on it. Jack searched for something she'd like, but came up with nothing. "It's just something to look for," she says, "something to give me an excuse to stop." Another buyer nearby said, "You don't need an excuse to stop and see Jack."

Next a dealer came in, saying she was there to look at embroidered goods. Jack had called her. He brought out a heap of cloth; one was an uncut sheet of handkerchiefs promoting "Garfield for President." Jack named a price, and they started to haggle. The dealer went on about how she couldn't resell them and make money at that price and pointed out a stain in a handkerchief she was *sure* wouldn't wash out, while Jack pointed to designs on the doilies and scarves to bolster the price.

After they sealed a transaction, two elderly women came in. One announced she was looking for a nozzled gas can cap.

Jack seemed confused, "What do you need?"

"I got a gas can, and I need a nozzle like this." She had a nozzled cap in her hand.

"But you have one," Jack said.

"Do you want to see the can?" she asked. We walked out to the street, where a giant red Oldsmobile was parked, ancient but spotless. The woman's friend waited on the porch, eyes fixed to her toes as though expecting them to go somewhere without her. The gas can was in the trunk; the cap she had was too small.

Jack took her back inside, but I guessed he already knew he didn't have what she wanted. He tried to sell her any number of old cans to use for gas instead, but she stuck to her guns. "Come on, Jack. Let's find that cap," she said.

Finally Jack admitted he didn't have anything like what she needed and suggested she go buy a plastic can.

"I *know* I *could* do that," she said. She was a scavenger.

I suggested using a funnel instead of a nozzled cap, but she said that wouldn't work. Then she shifted gears. "Do you have any big bowls, like for making macaroni salad?"

"Those sell out really fast," Jack said. "I sell at least one a week. All I have is this, and it's probably too big." He held up a giant ceramic bowl.

"That's a washing bowl, Jack," she whined, then asked if there were any nice places for a picnic nearby. "I drove all the way out here. I might as well go have a picnic." Jack told her about a spot owned by the Battenkill Conservancy. Then she just as quickly left.

"She's a great old girl, but I had no idea what she was looking for, and I still don't," Jack said, grinning.

Jack told me condition in antiques was as important as location in real estate, and he showed me an old blue cupboard with several layers of paint, saying that for primitives, this was the ideal. However, with other antiques, good condition means perfection, and that's when people get carried away. "They want a new-looking toy in a new-looking box, but I'd rather see that it had been played with." Some antique dealers would call that "honest wear."

Jack was certainly against refinishing. On his porch sat a high chair, slathered in paint, probably lead paint, and not safe for use. For Jack, the paint was part of the charm, or the places where the paint was gone, to be exact. He loved the wear on the seat from all the "baby butts" and the bare spot on the foot rail. An entire family must have sat in the chair.

Once a buyer carried the chair into his shop, asked about the price, and then asked, "How hard do you think it will be to get that paint off?"

"Give me that. You don't get that," Jack claimed to have said, grabbing the chair out of her hands. How could she have contemplated erasing the signs of use? He took me inside to a wooden pencil box with "Donald Beaulier" written on top. "I'm glad Don put his name on there," Jack said, "I would have, too. But that's why I can't sell it." He put it down with a hint of sadness. Patina and honest wear aside, some things have to be pristine. He showed me an auction catalogue featuring a fine toy truck he had found. The description certified the provenance of such a fine example: "Recently picked out of the attic of an eighty-year-old man." When Jack did get something untouched by time and use, he knew how to maximize its value. However, he said other dealers sometimes refused to buy from him because their buyers want perfect merchandise. Jack thought they were missing the point. A tool collector he knew, Joe, one of the most knowledgeable in the area, had joined him in making presentations in schools, despite being legally blind. You'd think he'd be unable to judge the quality of a tool, but perhaps he is better equipped. Tool collectors certainly agree with Jack that a sign of use enhances the value of an item. Original, worn handles are critical on tools. Such signs of use are discernible even to those of us not accustomed to judging the world by touch. Likewise, tools are made for the hand, not the eye, and the pleasure of the heft and balance of axe or the comfortable proportions and palm-fit of a chisel handle can only be felt, not seen. The warmth of wood and coolness of metal, so visually alluring, has a tactile quality.

Not all dealers turned up their noses at Jack's less-than-perfect, well-used stuff. When his wife Mary dropped by to see if he'd had lunch, he said, "I've made my day already. Two dealers from New York City stopped by." Some days Jack could make a living simply through resale to a more lucrative market, by participation in the general motion of used goods. Like John Christman, Jack did not try to sell pure antiques to his upstate country market. Sitting down on his porch stoop, Jack brought out some pictures to tell one of his favorite stories, the recovery of a rare piece of Chippendale furniture from the nearby McClelland Mansion.

A religious group bought the mansion a few years ago, and they would conscientiously call Jack when they found something in the house or outbuildings and barns he might want. One day they were working on "the Nanny House," a servant's quarters that had been boarded up in the 1940s. Inside a built-in corner cabinet took up too much space, and they at first thought to cut it up for firewood but decided to call Jack just in case.

Jack wasn't sure how valuable it was, but he could tell it was an early piece. Jack had a coat of modern white paint dry-scraped down to the original dark blue milk paint underneath. He turned to a photograph to show me the finished cabinet. "You could see the tool marks on the solid panels. You could tell he was using a two-inch plane." The towering cabinet sat on a base with two wide doors and a glass-doored cupboard, all capped by a wide, complicated Greek Key crown molding. The restored paint was dusky and rich.

Jack then showed me a letter from Leigh Keno, of *Antiques Roadshow* fame; he eventually bought the cabinet and sold it at the Armory Show in New York City, what Jack called "the Superbowl of antiques," proudly saying, "If you get in the Armory Show, you've made it." Jack had never mentioned money at any time during the telling of the tale; for him, the thrill was all about saving a rare piece of Americana from the kindling box, a cabinet dating from 1790 to 1820 and likely made by famed Connecticut architect William Sprats.

Most of the dealers I have met are consumed with money, to be sure, and they have to be, because survival requires they jump on every opportunity, sniff out every profit. When Jack was swapping war stories with a customer who was also a dealer, the man told him about a pair of denims dating to the 1880s found in a mine that were cleaned and then sold to the Levi Strauss company for $46,000. The price was all that made the story retellable. Jack's stories were more complicated. He relished the details and the drama. He told me about two flags he once sold, one with only thirteen stars from before 1860, and the other from a Buffalo soldier Calvary unit, a black unit from the 1870s. Jack knew they were important, and he sold them to a sophisticated collector who would properly conserve them. He mailed them on two consecutive days, but they were stolen. In order to catch the thief, the buyer put a fake package on his porch and a surveillance camera. They caught a man who confessed to stealing the flags, but he said after their importance had been reported in the paper, he knew he'd never be able to sell them, so he burned them. What other business offers tales that include history, suspense, tragedy, and human folly, all at once?

These stories are another kind of provenance, and dealers collect them as well and give them out for free if you only ask—and have the time to linger. When I stepped into Sleepy Hollow Antiques in Coxsackie, New York, owner Bill was on the phone and painting a cupboard shabby chic white, but he hung up quickly to tend to me. Before long Bill was telling me stories. His most interesting sale, he claimed, was an oak partner's desk he found at an auction that had come from a courthouse and was made by the Sellew Company. Bill tried, and failed, to sell it to another dealer for $1,500, which would have doubled his money. "So I put it on eBay."

An executive from Sellew in New York City bought it, saying his great-grandfather had made the desk, and he sent a truck with "three teamsters" to get it who were also militaria collectors. Bill sold them some World War II German memorabilia; he had a photograph of them wearing helmets and holding rifles. They loaded the desk on truck, and all parties were satisfied. Bill later heard the desk was put on display in a museum at the company store on Fulton Street in New York.

Given the oblique way dealers find the right buyers for unique items, such stories are endless. One story I heard but can't attribute has the ability to keep me up at night. A dealer told me he was cleaning out a house for an estate sale, and he found the face of a black man in a jar of formaldehyde. "I just went down to the basement, and there it was." Such gruesome souvenirs were once taken at lynchings, though fingers or other appendages were more common.

"What did you do with it?" I asked, knowing how I'd answer. I'd call the police.

"I'm ashamed to say I sold it," he answered. "No matter what, there's a buyer."

In the final analysis, nothing about antique selling is certain, not the profit, context, or the things sold. All scavengers, everyone from yard sale operators to flea market vendors, know declaring "That's an *antique*" is a way of justifying a price. In some way the entire concept, as now defined, is a matter of personal interpretation. Some shops define antiques broadly, either because they've become indiscriminate like Gary Guarno or are just getting started in the business, such as a new dealer. One new dealer said, "I've only been open for three weeks. Most of what I have is from the '20s and '30s, but I'll be into real antiques soon. I'm doing well, though. People are buying their mothers' and grandmothers' things." She hadn't been in business long enough to get tired of listening to customers recount what someone in their family *once* owned. The others post signs that read: TEN DOLLAR CHARGE FOR LISTENING TO WHAT YOUR GRANDMOTHER HAD.

Like collectors, antique dealers start with humbler items and through buying and selling improve the overall quality of their goods. I found several dealers in New Lebanon, New York, quarantined in an abandoned motel that gave them no context, and instead made them look more like refugees than antique dealers. What they had to sell was even worse, mostly stuff you'd expect to see in a yard sale. They were obviously trying to become an antiques destination, as signs off the main road had steered me there, promising a concentration of shops. Nearby I found another castoff shop in a Cape Cod–style house, again lacking in context. Inside an older woman cheerily met me at the door, saying, "Help yourself to coffee in the kitchen and yell if you want to dicker on a price." She had thrown together an assortment of vases, salt and pepper shakers, single plates, and wooden boxes used for storing silverware or fine machine tools like calipers, but now being sold for the boxes themselves. The woman had one detail down pat, a radio tuned to a station playing swing, filling the air with a hint of what her goods failed to suggest.

Dealers have to keep their shops full, regardless of whether they stock true antiques, collectibles, imports, fakes. Someday the castoff shop might sport a better class of castoffs—and maybe not. Her shop might slip the other way, plunge into the wilderness of subsistence discards. Further up the road I ran into yet another dealer. What New Lebanon lacked in quality it made up for in quantity; in that way the sign had not lied. Wild Willy's enterprise, housed in an old ranch-style house, sported one of those red, white, and blue ANTIQUES flags many dealers use. The manufacturer of these banners is one of the more enterprising of those who try to capitalize on the used trade with a spin-off business, like Levi Strauss who recognized that gold miners needed sturdy trousers with riveted pockets that would not rip under the weight of gold.

Below the flag was a phony bomb made of sheet metal, with torpedo wings, painted red with white letters: "Bomb Them to Hell," a sentiment aimed at al Qaeda. In front of the house was a sheer tangle of metal, oranged by rain. As I walked through it, I saw a pile of wrenches, like a fossil bed of rusted femurs, nearly a hundred in all sizes, lying at the base of a farm machine, as though dropped there while working on it. Inside the living room sat a man, undoubtedly Wild Willy, and a woman, both smoking and surrounded by avalanching ashtrays. "I keep getting these colds," I heard the woman say to a customer, a computer beside her locked onto eBay. I saw hubcaps and other machine parts, ignoble housewares of all kinds, and some furniture, though all of it barnacled under other stuff. Despite his jingoistic display, this dealer's suburban-style house looked like it had been bombed instead. Likewise, despite his flag, Wild Willy's aspirations toward antiques dealing had turned the other way. His was not an antiques or collectibles store. He was a full-fledged seller of junk.

Chapter Nine

✤

In Search of the True Junk Shop

O NE OF THE BEST, MOST COMPREHENSIVE junk shops I have ever visited was Charley Hawk's. His melange was located outside of Athens, Ohio, in a hollow of the Appalachian foothills. Well-known to students from nearby Ohio University as a source of cheap furniture or household goods, Hawk's collection occupied an old farmhouse. In the surrounding barns and fields stuff outside was left to rust, such as metal bedsprings or shattered machinery. As though having fled a flood of junk, Hawk's little house sat on the side of the hill behind the former farm. The big farmhouse was organized, after a fashion. One room was devoted to tables of irons, toasters, and mixers, while another boasted small electric motors and parts of other little machines. What used to be a parlor contained what Hawk thought were his best pieces of furniture, arranged to avoid water damage from a hole in the roof. Upstairs, where I was never sure customers were supposed to go, the bedrooms were festooned with papers, clothes, dishes—anything lighter. Junkers don't waste energy carrying heavy items upstairs.

When I used to visit Hawk's, I would poke around upstairs for books. I had found a couple of early nineteenth-century volumes among the catalogues, cookbooks, newspapers, and magazines. Having paid Hawk fifty cents each, I sold them to a used book dealer for several dollars. As a graduate student, a few extra bucks were a real boon. One day I was pawing through a box and found an awl, a tool for marking wood or leather. Its pear-shaped, rosewood handle had been inlaid with a thin strip of maple and fit cozily in my palm. I had been working as a carpenter and was gathering tools however I could, and I wanted this one.

I carried it downstairs. Hawk was sitting at a desk, and when I showed him the awl, he stuck it in the desk top and gave it a squinting inspection. Clearly he hadn't seen it before. Nothing at Hawk's was priced—another sign of a true junk shop—and when I asked him how much he needed for the awl, he surprised me by saying five dollars.

"What about three dollars?" I asked, though that was more than I'd ever paid him for anything.

"I'd pay five dollars just so I could stick it in the wall and look at it for the rest of my life," Hawk answered, and I knew he didn't want to sell this elegant little tool. Sometimes not everything is for sale in a junk shop, unlike at most antique stores, where if you said you were a shoe collector, the dealers would sell you the shoes off their feet, for the right price. As far as I know, Hawk still has that awl.

The line between secondhand or junk shops and antique stores is increasingly blurry. Antiques and collectibles dealing has become so ubiquitous and all-encompassing, the most homely repository of discards now advertises its wares as antique because some probably are. In many ways the value of junk is collaborative, an agreement between seller and buyer. Junk buyers and junk sellers agree that discards have value, so the junker gathers them. What you agree to pay for an item determines its price—not a set wholesale/retail margin. In the same way, what claims you make for an item help set its value. Some even joke about it with signs advertising JUNQUE.

Like antique dealers, junk sellers often occupy locations where new retailing enterprises fail. A store sits empty for a time, accumulating the requisite grime and decay until the owner no longer can hope for a mainstream tenant. Then the junker moves in, and the store is reconfigured by the ensuing riot of refuse. Unlike antique dealers who will try to provide an appealing, pleasantly jumbled look reminiscent of a country store, or with more upscale dealers, a gallery, the junk shop might not even have an adequate sign. The sheer quantity of wares announces itself.

So, expanding like a gaseous substance, junk shops proliferate in abandoned car dealerships, down-on-the-heels shopping centers, and defunct downtown stores. They thrive in depressed areas, places where the bottom is in sight, or under their feet, like old mill towns in the

Northeast or the Rust Belt cities of the Midwest. Youngstown, Ohio, is a prime example of the petri dish needed for these hardscrabble merchants, and I used to worked for one there. Now fractured into many varieties, the used merchandise trade once broke neatly into junk and surplus. Junk shops thrived during World War II rationing; used goods were sometimes all that was to be had. However, after war production came to a skidding halt with the Japanese surrender, the government dumped military wares that might have a civilian use into the public market through Army and Navy surplus stores. These stores appealed to outdoor sports enthusiasts who snapped up tents, boots, and rain gear, all the same GI green, and after the flow of dented canteens and indestructible parkas dried up in the 1970s with the end of the Vietnam War, most of these shops morphed into sporting-goods stores. Their heyday long gone, they were once wonderful places, redolent of grease, canvas, and rubber, with surprises among their wares, such as military insignia and other curios.

World Supply in Youngstown began that way, but when Arthur Weisenthal took over the business from his father, he found a new secondhand bounty from which to pick and peddle. Youngstown had been built on iron and steel making, and when those industries closed, Arthur was there to resell the pallets, filing cabinets, desks, chairs, uniforms, chains, gears, coke shovels, and welding masks. The building still reflected its military surplus past with two bomb cases framing the door, one painted with WORLD and the other SUPPLY, but inside was a complete inventory of the useful jetsam of the industrial age. Not a true scavenger, as he was interested in very little that did not come in large lots, Arthur made no pretense of dealing in antiquities. His was a nuts-and-bolts business, and though some shopped his warehouse for the odd crate or old tool, his customers mostly wanted rope, chain, or corrugated metal. Because he had bought the contents of a window company, he also had rows of unframed insulated window glass, so in the 1970s World Supply was popular among those building passive solar-heated houses.

Descendant of the rag-picker and serving the same function in commerce as the crow does in the food chain, true generic junk sellers are still out there, but they are getting harder to find, as the robust secondhand culture is always reorganizing into new formats. Ask a junker, and he'll claim to be really into antiques, though auctioneer and antique dealer John Christman said most who claim to be selling antiques are actually in the used goods business. The market for pure antiquities is too narrow for many to make a living selling them. Standing behind a counter in their little antique store, where they also have candy and soda for sale, John's wife added, "You know when you walk into a real antique store. It takes your breath away, and you realize you can't afford anything there."

I have always been able to recognize the genuine junk shop with the same gasp of realization, not from price but from quantity. A well-established junk inventory is truly awesome, and instead of being impressed by price and rareness, I am stupefied by the sheer volume of stuff, by the fact I will never be able to poke through it all. So, when I rounded the bend on Route 372 near Greenwich, New York, I thought I had found one. From a distance I knew I had spotted either a junk shop or a building being demolished. A semicircle of dairy barns around a graveled lot were sentried by rows of doors and windows. As I pulled in I noted a faded sign on one barn: GERRY'S ANTIQUES, COLLECTIBLES, AND USED FURNITURE.

That last ingredient was key. Any junker who aspires to antique dealing but who must still advertise his wares by stepping down through collectibles and into the morass of "used furniture" has not quite made the leap. His curb-appeal selection was another tip-off: doors and windows. Not stick furniture or humpback traveling trunks, which an antique dealer might use; construction refuse scavenged from razed buildings was the best Gerry could do. Unlike an antique dealer, who will bring such attractions inside at day's end, Gerry left his outside, probably year-round. They were tied to the barn to discourage theft, a shackle of wire looped through the empty lockset holes.

I wandered the farm lot, looking for Gerry himself, and found no one, though each barn was wide open. While Gerry had the right context for an antique store, a country barn, he appeared to be the kind of junker who could not resist taking anything into his sanctuary. Inside the cow barn, stalls were stacked with old machinery, more windows, and hobbled wooden chairs. There was not an antique in sight, though rows of junk rested where placid cows once stood, attached to milkers. The walls still bore hay-dust webs, and rotten straw still covered the floor as though the herd had just left and castoffs had moved in.

The next building, about 12x20 feet, bore a for sale sign and was the only one that was closed. It was jacked up, on blocks, ready to be skidded onto a flatbed trailer. The building itself was for sale. Gerry would sell anything that could be moved. All around, the Battenkill River bottom stretched out, prime farmland in these foothills of Vermont's Green Mountains, and Gerry's fields were still cleared, still farmed, though undoubtedly not by this squire of junk. Gerry probably rented them to other farmers. Instead he harvested discards, the hayloft in the largest barn now a mound of used lumber, boxes splitting and spilling their contents, with a radial arm saw lying on its side on top of it all like a dying predator. The big bay doors were open on both sides of the big barn, and through them I finally saw someone, a man on a tractor pulling a wagon. He stopped, jumped off, and began shoveling dirt from the wagon. He seemed not to have noticed me. No one had come out of the house across the road or out of any of the barns.

The milkhouse bore Gerry's sign, so I figured it might be the central shop, and he might be sitting inside, like Charlie Witherbee in his corner office in his echoing, dim auction house. Peeking in the window, I expected to see a hoard of wares that might pass for antiques. Not only did I not find Gerry, nothing inside would have interested anyone but a junker—more of the same, as well as two empty display racks and a couple of inconsolable sofas.

A true junk shop, Gerry's place was both open and not open, and browsers need not be watched, as nothing was very valuable. Gerry was clearly a gatherer by compulsion and a seller by necessity, hoping to move enough of it to make room for more. I decided to come back on a weekend when Gerry would be more likely to be expecting customers. As I drove away, the man shoveling in the field watched me go down the road. Like other junk sellers I have met, if the man in the field was Gerry, he was instantly suspicious of anyone he didn't already know, especially a solitary guy poking around on a weekday. Junk collecting and selling is sometimes the last refuge of those who can't fit into another easily defined role in their communities; gathering and storing junk is a way of insulating themselves. Many junkers, at heart, are card-carrying misanthropes.

If you want used doors and windows, though, the best source is a specialist, the way all used merchandise is headed at this less-than-antique level. Architectural Parts Warehouse, in Albany, New York, is being replicated all over the country, in any town with a collateral of old buildings, the misfortune of watching them being torn down, and the good sense to try to save parts of them. At the Warehouse, you can find the finer pieces of Albany—the banisters, stained glass, and fireplace mantels of houses lost to urban renewal. House restorers use what some people would consider construction debris to replace what time and fashion have destroyed.

Each time I have gone to Architectural Parts Warehouse, it has been in a different location, finding better accommodations for its growing treasures. Once it was in an old brownstone on South Pearl. Jeff, a lanky, bearded volunteer, was scraping paint off a copper bay window roof when I walked in, looking for a baluster, a lathed post for the staircase of my house. Jeff sent me to the third floor after saying that it was nearly impossible to match the one in my hand. "Every set was different," he sighed. When I found the balusters, I could tell he was right; he had bundles of them, each set slightly different. Old houses were custom-made, unlike new tract houses.

The next time I went there, I found it boarded up. A phone book revealed the enterprise had moved to Lexington Avenue, closer to downtown. This time I was hauling goods to peddle. My neighbor had decided to modernize her perfectly intact Victorian house and had her external doors replaced with new ones, vinyl clad and prehung. She had put her four exquisite old doors, varnished oak with thick beveled glass, on the curb to be thrown away. The front door was especially decorative, with a scalloped-edged window and oak leaf carvings. These were in the back of my truck; I had no need for them, but I certainly didn't want them to go in the landfill (though probably another scavenger would have saved them). So I decided to see what I could get for them at the Warehouse.

I got a tax write-off of more than a thousand dollars. Started in 1974, the Architectural Parts Warehouse is the oldest, continuously operating not-for-profit architectural salvage business in the country, and they acquire their goods through donation only. Money from sales supports the Historic Albany Foundation, an advocate for the preservation of venerable buildings. Dave, who had been working there for only seven months, said the business got started when foundation members started picking up decorative doors, stained glass windows, moldings, and other "significant architectural elements" off the curb, and eventually they found a place to house them. As with other used goods merchants, the Warehouse inhabits an old business building, a former Buick dealership, with a small storefront opening onto a 10,000-square-foot warehouse in the back.

Dave said he believed the building had been used for another kind of business before that.

Dave said they discouraged what they call "inappropriate reuse," meaning they intend these materials to be used to restore old buildings, not to accent new ones. Likewise, they prefer their materials stay in Albany. As Dave said, "We don't want to sell a door and see it go to California to be used for a coffee table." However, when something "has been around a few months, we loosen up a bit," letting someone buy something for another use or for a cheaper price. Like all junkers, they are under the restraints of space and time; not enough room exists for everything. Dave added that someone was coming in later to buy four pocket doors to use in making a room divider/bookcase, but he was unable to hide a scowl.

These are idealistic junkers. They only salvage goods when there is no chance to preserve the whole building, getting people to donate the "salvage rights" on these doomed places. Now, though, they have to compete with antique dealers who have discovered the value of choice items, such as stained glass. Dave said plenty of for-profit dealers were selling high-end architectural parts. Still, it is a sign of the popularity of used goods that *everything* he now rescues would have been buried in a landfill only thirty years ago.

The warehouse displayed the humble and lavish in equal measure. The front room was taken up with fancy doorknobs, hinges, striker plates, and escutcheons on two tables, while doors, windows, and fireplace mantels lined the walls and led the way to the back, where they continued in the warehouse proper, filed in bins. Here were stores of modest hardware, pallets of roof tile, marble window sills, and iron window weights, and to one side, a huddled mass of sinks and toilets. Toilets? I wondered. Architecturally significant toilets?

I knew they took marble sinks, common before enameled iron ones were made; I had even brought one in, and Jeff had turned it down because of a crack I hadn't noticed. Dave explained how older toilets were shaped differently, with "recessed bases," and that some were "signed," meaning the basins sported an inked maker's mark tying them to the area, which was important to home restorers who wanted absolute local authenticity. Sensing my skepticism, Dave said if you looked at catalogues for new bathroom fixtures, "it's all retro, from the '20s and

'30s." People were most interested in toilets with overhead wooden tanks, though Dave said he has never seen one come in. I thought to tell him about a scavenger I knew who made oak toilet tanks into small tool chests, but I didn't. Dave wouldn't approve.

I also noticed some furniture for sale, which Dave explained had been brought in by members "either on consignment or donated because they didn't want to throw them away. We try to stay focused on architectural pieces; we could very easily become a used furniture store." The flow of secondhand goods is indiscriminate, and once you start to value discards, the stream turns your way, like water finding a fissure. Junk flows with the force of gravity, and it must it be resisted if you intend to specialize. If they left the gates open, the Warehouse would be indistinguishable from the many thrift shops and used furniture stores in Albany. These stores serve the economically depressed city community, not those restoring a stately Victorian home.

Generic used merchandise stores also take many forms, mostly based on their clientele or their own aspirations. Some are not purposeful or planned; they happen. Such was the case with a store in Ballston Spa, New York, with a charming 1960s name, "The Savings Scene," as though it, too, was left over from another endeavor in the old retail heart of the village. When I parked in front I saw a for sale sign on the building—actually two commercial buildings spliced together. The display window of the one on the right was shattered and repaired with red duct tape. Another sign, decorated with computer-generated frowning faces, said from now on the store would be open only on Wednesdays—and everything was 50 percent off.

The place was awash in banks of fluorescents. A night of rain had not abated by morning, and a white-haired woman inside warned me the floor was slick from roof leaks. Buckets everywhere were plopping and pinging. The walls were lined with rough lumber bins for categories of stuff: kitchen goods, knickknacks, socks, purses, and books. In the furniture part of the store, in the larger right-hand side, I found a lineup of naked lamps, a television in a maple "Colonial" console, a bookcase, and mismatched kitchen chairs that had been arranged behind the taped display window, the owner knowing any furniture has curb appeal. Signs on some things suggested uses; on a shelf of five-inch ceramic baskets, one read MAKE GOOD BALLOON WEIGHTS, I suppose for helium party balloons.

When I asked to speak to someone about the business, I was sent by the white-haired woman at the counter to the owner in the back. I had seen her before, at the Talk of the Town Auction. She had been making the left bids. Beverly Stanislowsky and her husband ran the auction house, and this was the repository of everything that had not passed muster with antique dealers and buyers at that more lucrative level.

I did not call Beverly's business a junk shop, choosing what I thought was a more polite term: a thrift store. Still she corrected me, saying a thrift store is "a consignment shop." Beverly's was a "next-to-new" store. Among used merchandise dealers, finer discriminations prevail. She said they sold "just about anything" and even sold food when they handled the closing of a grocery store. "Nothing gets thrown away," she said.

Beverly described her customers as being as varied as her merchandise, from business owners to welfare recipients. For instance, one winter they bought the contents of a clothing store, and what didn't sell at auction ended up at The Savings Scene. This included a rack of plain, terry-cloth dresses in three colors. Beverly priced them at $9.99 each, and they sold out quickly. On the first warm spring day she looked out the window during lunch hour and saw women from the local law offices and county courthouse all wearing the same dress. "I counted thirty of them on that one day," she said behind a grin.

Some buyers were much more discriminating, though. Few antique dealers came to the store; they saw everything at the auction before it landed there. However, collectors often visited. "Horses. I have one woman who just buys anything to do with horses or with horses on it," Beverly said. She and her husband were collectors, too (she collected music boxes and he gathered steins), and while many junkers get into the business through this specialized gathering impulse, Beverly said she couldn't remember how she had found herself in the secondhand business, though she had been buying and selling stuff for twenty years. Junk shops simply happen. Once you tap into the market, you must move its goods along quickly, such as in an auction. What doesn't move demands space. If you refuse to sell it cheaply, it will remain with you for a long time, joined by the next wave of the "next-to-new."

Despite its uncertainties, Beverly found the business interesting, though she added, "Mostly it's a matter of sheer survival." Business at the shop had slowed as the economy improved, she said. Perhaps more of her customers were poorer than she had suggested. Now the auction took up all of her time, she said, and they planned either to sell garden-variety junk "in big lots"—to another junker wholesale—or simply "stop taking it," which I knew might be impossible.

Before I left, a customer came in and spoke to the white-haired woman up front, who, in turn, called to the rear of the shop, "Beverly. Do you have any turtles?"

"Oh, there's turtles," Beverly answered. "Somewhere. On something."

Chapter Ten

✥

Secondhand Empires and Fiefdoms

W HATEVER BEVERLY STANISLOWSKY and her husband stopped selling would find another home easily enough, if not in a junk shop then in one of the classic, not-for-profit stores that continue to thrive, good economy or bad: the Goodwill and Salvation Army stores. Here used goods are marshaled to perform the good works of utility and charity. I have always been partial to Salvation Army stores because the organization once helped my grandfather out of a tough spot. Traveling the country looking for work during the Depression, Jake Leslie found a job and took a room with a man he had met on the road. The next day he awoke to find his roommate gone, along with Jake's clothes, watch, and money. The Salvation Army took Jake in, gave him some clothes, and fed him until he could earn enough to get back on his feet. Thereafter, during the holidays, Jake would put fifty cents in one of their bell ringer's kettles; my father continued the tradition when I was growing up. I have upped the ante to five dollars.

Although both Goodwill and Salvation Army stores are national used goods emporiums, they follow many of the first principles shared by their less altruistic brethren. First, they move into abandoned retail space. You'll find them in old stand-alone department stores, the ones built by independent store owners in the 1940s and then pushed out of business by Kmart and later Wal-Mart: in Ohio, the locally owned stores were called Valley View, Fairway, or Treasure Island. The Salvation Army in Glendale, New York, is in one of their yawning boxes, long and low with a roof over the double glass doors, the trademark red triangular sign where the old store sign would have been. Unlike other junk shops, the Salvation Army tries to imply they are simply another kind of department store. A truck was unloading when I arrived; I wandered over, past a brimming drop-off bin, and heard Chicago blues coming from the back, some melody on loss and redemption, perfectly apt where salvation and salvage are intertwined.

The parking lot was strewn with the detritus of dropped-off items, mostly bits of toys, like checkers, plastic parts from models, or doll accessories. The Salvation Army does not resell everything. They are large enough to discriminate, and as a nonprofit they do not need to wring every dime out of their goods. It's all donated, so every cent is profit. Likewise, they don't deal in damaged goods. Some things are beyond salvation, and lots of good junk probably gets set aside. If trash-pickers have found a way to interrupt the flow of rejects to the landfill, even these items will enter the secondhand economy. Still, signs warned that taking anything from the donation bins, or near them, is shoplifting and will be prosecuted. The Salvation Army is serious about getting first pick of the junk that comes into its orbit.

Inside the store, most dividers or counters from the former department store had been removed, and the gymnasium-sized space was a perfect geometry of rows of clothing, all clean and pressed. The clothes were organized by size and type, from skirts to blouses to trousers and from infants' to children's to adults'. I checked a few tags: $3.99 shirts and $7.99 trousers. Fair, but not quite junk prices. While clothing is the staple of any Salvation Army store, other goods get donated, and along the edges of the acre of garments were a display case for jewelry, everything priced at a dollar, and a housewares section, partially hidden behind the only room divider, in the back. There you could find $79 sofas, $35 mattresses and box springs, and $10 black-and-white televisions. I imagined this was probably the only place where you could still find one. The small household items were marshaled onto simple metal shelves, extending the exquisite order. One rack held a committee of identical busts of the Virgin Mary among recumbent ceramic cats and widemouthed jars plugged with corks. The only glimpse of disorder was behind the divider where the chairs and couches sat where they had been dropped, like a badly arranged hotel lobby frozen in the time of orange sofas, floral love seats, and spidery end tables.

In a tiny room at the back, barely noticeable from the front of the store, paperback books could be had for 80 percent of the cover price, though hardcovers were simply a dollar, and there was a smattering of everything and nothing: self-help, school texts, Kafka, and Gay Talese. That room also held bins of LPs, much of it music that will never be reissued on CD, and deservedly so.

The patrons of the Salvation Army store were harder to characterize, not having titles on their spines. I did notice a number of women between 50 and 80 years old wearing thickly made-up, Nefertiti eyes and hair dyed sulphurous. They were either eccentrics who found shopping at thrift store amusing, or people who did not go out in public often and had prepared for the occasion with the care of a mortician. When I arrived I had noticed a newer Lexus and a Mercedes parked on the side, and from the latter a young couple with a toddler got out, the child advocating for a gumball from a machine right inside the door. Why would such an affluent-looking family shop there?

THANKS FOR HELPING US HELP OTHERS, a sign read near the door. Here, the rhetoric of the store proclaimed, were good clean items for sale, well-organized so you might easily find and profitably use them, priced cheaply to enable you to own everything you'd like to own, or at least what you need, despite your economic fortunes. The floors had been mopped at least twice a week, and not a mote of dust marred the shelves.

Another sign read ALL SALES AS IS, WHERE IS, AND FINAL. No nonsense, no pussy-footing here. The Salvation Army sanctions no funny business about something not fitting when you get it home. You like it, buy it. Then take it with you and keep it. The clerks at the cash register seemed pretty severe too, a portly young man who looked like he'd like to smile, and a wan older woman who appeared to be keeping him from it. Both of them eyed me as I walked around with a notebook, trying to take notes behind the coffee pots. Maybe they thought I was from Goodwill or another competitor, recording prices so I could undercut them. Maybe I looked like a police officer, checking for stolen goods. Who knows what they had seen and expected to see? Finally the woman approached and asked if she could help me, and I said no, sensing she'd have no time or patience for questions. The store was busy, and each customer had to be monitored, served, and if necessary, saved. On my way out I saw a table stacked with brochures and job application forms. I thought to take one of each, but the acid eyes of the clerks stayed my hand.

If the world were run by the Salvation Army, we'd all have enough, just enough, of what we need, and we'd be supplied with it in a simple, efficient way. Commerce would be sensible and plain. Still, theirs is not a true junk shop. It is the outpost of an army on a mission to supply those in need. They do not gather with the same compulsion and joy of a real junker. Likewise it is not a junk shop because of their aspirations; they imitate a first-level department store. For them, buying used is not a matter of choice or ethics. On the contrary, their physical presence reveals they regard buying used as a bit disgraceful, holding onto the mainstream "new-is-better" doctrine. They not only want to provide for the poor, they want to dignify, even sanitize, the experience. The Salvation Army does not qualify as a genuine junk shop, finally, because of their attitude toward junk, though they function as one on many levels. However, they discount their wares based on the status of owning the same when new. They participate in the secondhand culture while holding their sanctified noses.

I'm not saying that individual workers at either Goodwill or the Salvation Army do not revel appropriately in the bounty of junk, quite to the contrary, but their overall attitude is a by-product of their corporate structure, while the used merchandise trade is an anathema to monoculture and the mass market. However, I wondered if there was a middle ground, a setting where used goods are sold as a form of charity, but where the entropy of the junk world is embraced. To find out I visited The Mission Thrift Store, also in Glendale, not three miles from the Salvation Army store. Clearly the traffic in donated used goods was busy enough to support independent competition.

At first glance, The Mission Thrift Store looked a lot like the Salvation Army, though housed in what had been a smaller specialty store, one for sewing supplies or paint and wallpaper. Likewise, its ambience was more relaxed, though not disorganized. I noted they had the same ratio of clothes to other goods—about four-to-one. In a back room I found what furniture they had to offer, older than the pieces at the Salvation Army, including a veneered, 1940s wardrobe, serviceable but splintered and as hulkingly ugly as Cheever's enormous radio. I found the place clean, but not sanitized.

I waited behind a few shoppers to talk to the clerk at the counter and read a sign that outlined the goods they wanted. Like the Salvation Army, they were choosy. For instance, they took a limited number of books because of the lack of storage space. Their book display was markedly different: three bookcases flanked by two overstuffed armchairs where people might sit to peruse a potential buy. Among their other stipulations, they wanted shoes that had "only been worn once or twice, basically new shoes." As I drew nearer to the head of the line, I saw a modern china cabinet showcasing a few attractive baubles, including a plaster-of-Paris head of a girl in a winged Dutch hat, exactly like the one that had hung in my grandmother's kitchen next to a Dutch boy, with a little pipe sticking out of his mouth. The tug of recognition drew me to it, and I was reminded of the appeal of the most modest used item when candied by some fond reminiscence. Although merely sentimental kitsch, I might have bought it had it been accompanied by its partner.

When my turn came, I began to ask a young woman at the counter questions; the counter was decorated with a bouquet of flowers with a sign saying "not for sale." Rather than answer, she called to a woman in an office to the right who came out and began reciting information about the store, as though quoting a brochure or company policy.

The second woman was middle-aged with narrowed, suspicious eyes, though with an earnest warmth underneath. Her hair was dyed a weak strawberry blonde, rising in billows above her brow, as carefully poised as the guard she had raised in reaction to my questions. She wouldn't give me her name, but in rapid succession she told me "The Mission Thrift Store is one of three run by a nondenominational Christian organization in the Schenectady County area." They dealt in "clothing, bric-a-brac, and furniture," she continued, and noted they had a "senior day" once a month when people over fifty could buy at half price. All of their merchandise, like at the Salvation Army, came from donations.

I could have learned all of this by reading store signs, so I quickly changed the subject. "Have you noticed that donations have dropped off now that yard sales are so popular?" I asked. She claimed to not have noticed any change, saying the Schenectady suburb of Glendale was too affluent for residents to care about selling castoffs, though I knew she was wrong, as Glendale was one of my favorite stomping grounds for yard sales. If the junk flow was not affected, at least the quality must be, though at a purely utilitarian shop like this, she'd be unlikely to notice, or so I surmised.

She said merchandise was donated "seasonally," and when I asked if she meant warm clothes were donated after winter, she said, "No, the seasons in people's lives—like when people in their seventies and eighties move into a condo and bring in stuff." She also claimed they didn't compete with the Salvation Army, wanting to draw a distinction. "Some people don't want their things sitting out in the rain," she said about their drop-off bins. She was implying the stuff the Salvation Army got was not as valuable as what their benefactors bestow on them. The Mission had a better class of junk.

However, she was as committed to a cause as the red-uniformed corps. She had been working there seven years. At first she had worked part-time, intending to quit after paying for her daughter's wedding, but after two years she quit her other job to work at The Mission Thrift full-time. "You don't make much, not as much as you would somewhere else, but I view my work as a kind of [Christian] service," she said, all aglow.

That led her back to what she most wanted to discuss, the religious rather than reuse function of The Mission. The organization runs a halfway house for substance abusers and a lunch program and crafts classes for elementary schools in the impoverished Hamilton Hill district of Schenectady. She said she kept a "prayer list" of customers needing divine intercession. She described one customer who had lung cancer and who now, after having a lung removed and after lots of prayer, no longer needed oxygen. She paused, letting this sink in, and I could tell she believed miracles were another offering of the store.

Not all of her customers were so needy. As with most junkers, she said they were indescribable, "all kinds," though she noticed some affluent mothers brought their children there to teach them about frugality. I recalled the young family with the Mercedes at the Salvation Army and wondered if that was why they were there. Buying used has a moral ingredient, avoiding waste of both natural resources and money, and I can imagine such a lesson for a child might be invaluable in our frenzied consumer culture where children are smothered in sales pitches. Everything designed to delight children is also an advertisement: amusement parks to promote movies to promote new toys. Finding joy in something outside of this ruthless, nonstop persuasion would be an epiphany, a moment of self-creation. "*I* like this toy," a child would think, "not because it's the newest thing or because I saw it on TV. I like it because of its shape, color, or because of how *I* imagine playing with it." Learning to want something because of what you bring to it, not what has been brought to you, is a sadly rare experience in retail culture and a great gift to children, even better than craft classes.

The clerk said the store "is like a community center." Elderly people came in as much to visit with the clerks and experience a little social interaction as to shop. Antique dealers stopped too. She said they "have a regular circuit they travel" between junk shops. A Vermont dealer had dropped by that same morning. When dealers bought something, she said, they usually tried to hide the fact they were dealers; for instance, one who bought a metal toy truck said he was buying it for his grandson. "But eventually it gets out that they're dealers."

The woman didn't seem to care if they were shopping The Mission— all were welcome. She even bragged about one dealer buying a Bit-O-Honey advertising sign there for sixty cents and then reselling it for $100, and she claimed another had found "a hanging Tiffany lamp for four or five dollars," but I'd heard what I had started to call The Tiffany Story so often I was starting to wonder whether it was an urban legend. So many unrecognized Tiffanys have been reported to me, I was surprised I hadn't turned up half a dozen myself.

"When antique dealers buy something, I listen to what they say so that they educate me," she said, and I realized she was as shrewd as she was pious. There was more behind those eyes than warmth. That's why they had the cabinet: to exhibit, and secure, the smaller items that they had learned were more valuable. "But sometimes we sell things, and we don't even know what they are until the person who buys them tells us," she added, smiling. We were both looking into the cabinet now, and I pointed out the little Dutch girl, explaining that my grandmother had owned one.

The woman said, "Isn't that cute? I sometimes think that's why people buy stuff, because they feel something about it; it means something to them, personally I mean." Finally. A charity junker who knew the personal poetics of buying used, how something can resonate for one buyer and have no appeal to another. At some level she shared the impulses that had caused Hawk to abandon his house to castoffs and build another nearby. Beyond what a thing might be worth or how it might be used, some objects offer stories. Antique dealers provide them through provenance. Junkers rely on buyers supplying them for themselves.

In addition to the bouquet of flowers, the counter was decorated with a plastic aquarium in which fake fish, suspended in a viscous solution, floated with the listlessness of a lava lamp. "They stole the last one," the clerk said, "so the manager put a sign on this one." On top of the aquarium a sheet of yellow tablet paper read PLEASE DON'T SHOPLIFT THIS. Who would shoplift at a junk shop besides kleptomaniacs? I was surprised the store would be so beset with thieves they would need such a sign. Obviously they don't have security cameras, mirrors, and guards, but they shouldn't need them to protect their humble wares. Perhaps stealing is the only option when you can't even afford to pay secondhand prices.

"The Salvation Army has a bigger problem than we do," she said. "This is like a community. People bring us cookies and brownies. You should see it at Christmas time. I'll bet that doesn't happen at a mall store." She was right, of course. The Salvation Army would not garner the same sense of local ownership and likely would have a bigger problem with theft. I had seen their signs, too. Nor would I expect people to bring holiday cookies to the clerks at The Gap. A store like The Mission belongs to those who shop there.

Beverly Stanislowsky had corrected me when I had called her shop a thrift shop, and while both The Mission and the Salvation Army use that label, the true thrift shop is a consignment shop, where the buyer can also be a seller. They usually have deliberately clever names: New to You, Second Time Around, Repeat Performance, or Past Perfect. Only hair stylists are more attracted to puns. All of these names tie their businesses to the new merchandise culture with a fragile, rhetorical thread.

I usually avoid these businesses in my own used shopping. Consignment shops sell goods owned by others, charging a seller's fee, a minimum of 10 percent. So when someone brings in an item to sell, the price charged reflects this extra cost and, like auctions with a buyer's premium, is inflated. Likewise, because the item is not owned by the shop, the clerk usually cannot dicker on the price, a staple feature of most used merchandise buying. Finally, consignment stores are often a suburban phenomenon, showing up like poor cousins in otherwise affluent shopping districts. No one is a worse judge of used merchandise than those who live in the new-is-better suburbs.

Still, treasures can be had in all venues, such as The Yankee Peddler, in the basement of a shopping center in Loudonville, New York, a suburb of Albany. Its basement location testified to the tenuous toehold of used merchandise in this upper-class residential area. It could never afford regular retail space. One room was given over to racks of clothing, with walls lined with shelves and cases of jewelry, pottery, and glassware including Wedgwood cups and saucers. Clearly the discards of upscale Loudonville are of a different sort. The other room featured a hodgepodge of furniture.

The sign on the door had also laid claim to antiques, but besides some older dishware and costume jewelry, the only thing that qualified was an overpriced oak chest of drawers. I stopped before a lathed wooden item, two balls connected by round shaft. I had seen them before in many yard sales and antique stores, and no one had ever been able to tell me what they were. It looked like what the sticker on it said, "wooden barbell," but it didn't weigh a pound. I asked the woman at the counter near the door, "Are you sure this is a barbell?"

"I don't know; you'd have to ask the owner," Jill said. She was the owner's daughter, and she told me her parents had been in the business since 1979. Her mother had learned the business by working at the store when it was owned by someone else. Jill liked working there because of the "interesting people" she met and the diversity of stuff they handled, which was, she said, 60 percent clothing, much of it on consignment.

All of their merchandise came from the neighborhood, she said, castoffs from the spacious center-hall Colonials and Italianate Revivals on the broad, tree-bowered streets of Loudonville. So much stuff came in, they never went out to look for merchandise at yard sales or auctions. This appeared to be one of the crucial differences between the junk shop and the antique store. While antique dealers actively seek out their wares, a pursuit that can be aggressive, junkers are more relaxed. They can gather goods almost passively, particularly if indiscriminate.

Like other junk sellers, Jill wouldn't characterize her customers in anything but the broadest terms, saying the shop was popular with both the "wealthy and not-so-wealthy, anyone who likes a bargain." Local college students patronized the Peddler, she said, as did the elderly "who like to come in and see stuff that reminds them of things." More than the simple principles of need and usefulness were in play at The Yankee Peddler. Jill said one of her elderly customers had remarked, "You spend the first half of your life getting stuff, and the second half getting rid of it," succinctly summing up the forces underlying the supply and demand of used goods. Most things made before manufacturers mastered planned obsolescence will outlast us, or outlast the needs that they once filled, and enter the secondhand market to serve again. New generations reap this bounty, either nostalgically as with antiques or from simple utility. An iron skillet might not be as easy to use as a newer, Teflon-coated one, but it will last forever. If the skillet is subsequently declared collectible, it will not only last, but it will be cherished for attributes that transcend a well-prepared omelet. Nothing gets thrown away, as Beverly Stanislowsky said.

Jill also said she liked meeting all the "crazy people" who like unusual stuff, then added, "I shouldn't say they are 'crazy'; they're colorful, open-minded." The strangest thing she ever sold was a "foot bath," which she described as a Jacuzzi for your feet. When I pointed to two ceramic pipes, framed and glued to a background of birch bark, someone's craft-class interpretation of a Native American peace pipe, she said, "Yeah, that's kind of strange, too. We'll probably have that for a long time." I also pointed to a pair of daguerreotypes on the wall behind her, and she said she didn't know who they were. I told her antique dealers called them "instant ancestors."

Jill had more than a passing knowledge of antique dealers, as they also frequented this shop. She said she usually didn't know they were dealers until they bought something, then some gloated over how much something was really worth. Her mother had become pretty knowledge-able about antiques but "sometimes things get by us." One dealer came in and bought a basket for a couple of dollars, then announced that it was Shaker-made and worth hundreds. "I wasn't so sure about that," Jill said, "but I didn't want to say it wasn't." Sometimes the dealers get aggressive, trying to get a better deal. One dealer was trying to get the price reduced on a clock. Jill wouldn't budge, but he kept pointing out its flaws. "Finally, after he kept pushing and pushing, I said, 'Look, you're going to have to back off.' He didn't even know he was being so pushy," she said. Though Jill was straining to be diplomatic, I could tell she had been hassled and swindled one too many times.

The Yankee Peddler was also targeted by shoplifters. Jill blamed it on not having a security system. "I try to watch," she said. "And some people think we are a pawnshop. Some kid will come in and say, 'This is my grandmother's jewelry. What will you give me for it?' and I say no thanks. The police want us to get names, addresses, and descriptions, but we don't want to get involved." She claimed to know if someone was selling stolen merchandise. "Black leather jackets, you know," she said. The shop owners would rather not buy something than risk buying something hot. Still, I wondered what she thought of me, a stranger in a brown leather jacket; had I been seen as up to no good? Had my question about wooden barbells been taken as a ruse to distract her while I pocketed something?

One time they even had a break-in. The thief came through the ceiling, from the beauty parlor above. If the ceiling tiles had not been removed, and the owners had not noticed that a little jewelry was missing, they might not have realized they had been burglarized. They don't know what else was stolen, as junk shops seldom keep inventory lists. They couldn't tell what else was stolen because there was simply too much junk.

Stuff that doesn't get claimed by the antique or collectible trade is so plentiful most junkers have to specialize, and that is the newest trend at this level of the secondhand culture. Likewise, if you get known as a good source for a type of item, buyers will find you; I've seldom bought something from a junker who didn't then tell me about one of his ilk who specializes in exactly that kind of item, whether it was a tool, clothing, or dishware. Specialists can also charge a bit more because those who seek them out really want or need what they have and are likely to not find it easily elsewhere. Specialist junkers rely on being able to corner the market on something, at least within a small, geographical area. Although mainstream marketers rue the popularity of junk and antiques, both markets share the basic tenets of capitalism. The used market is simply capitalism at its purest.

Specialists never fail to surprise me, as they will lock onto the most unlikely corner of the market and assemble astonishing collections. Sometimes they are accidental gatherings. I have seen a number of hubcap sellers on busy two-lanes, usually cross-country highways built before the interstate system. Homeowners find themselves on a busy road, perhaps on a tight curve or a bump that caused cars to shed hubcaps, and before long they have hundreds of them, gathered everywhere. One man on

New York State Route 29 now has an acre of them, hidden by fences and stacked like poker chips. He covers them with blue tarpaulins when he is not open for business. Still, if you lose a hubcap, he's the man to see.

Once, after crossing the Hudson River in the Adirondacks, Bob Miner and I were unable to recross the same bridge because of an accident in that lane, so we had to spin down the back roads looking for another way across. Seeing a yard sale sign in front of a pair of skeletal barns, I reflexively pulled over. This wasn't a true yard sale, though. This was a junker, one whose hand-painted sign designated as THE BIKE DOCTOR.

Two kinds of used merchandise are difficult to sell and easy to find: typewriters and bicycles. Typewriters have been rendered so thoroughly obsolete that tens of thousands languish in attics and basements. Bicycles, on the other hand, proliferate because their owners outgrow them, or technology renders them outmoded. Cyclists always want the newest, lightest models. The Bike Doctor's barns were surrounded by bicycles of all kinds and other wheeled apparatus: small farm machinery, lawn mowers, carts, and wheelbarrows. The doctor was a tanker-sized fellow, and while I walked around he talked to a guy loading two expensive-looking bicycles onto the rack of a mini-van. He undoubtedly repaired bikes as well.

"Can I help you with something?" the man asked as Bob and I started wandering through his assortment.

"We just stopped when we saw your sign," I said, "to see what you have for sale."

"Oh, I got stuff for sale. If you don't see what you need, just ask."

"Do you have any log-splitters?" I asked, remembering Bob had been searching for a used one.

"No . . . well, not in working order," the Bike Doctor said, and I imagined that deep inside his barns were any number of broken ones from which he someday intended to resurrect one or two working versions for sale. That is how such gatherings begin, with the often-vain hope that a critical mass of broken things will somehow produce an operational one. Unfortunately, the same part usually breaks on similar machines, so you are apt to never fulfill your aim.

The self-styled Bike Doctor limited the junk he collected to anything on small wheels. That was his angle; if it rolled on one, two, or more little wheels, he gathered it. This was the unifying principle behind his collection, and which prevented him from expanding to include cars and trucks, saving him from a general onslaught of castoffs. Obviously he was skilled at repairing machines and might easily have branched out. However, he had developed a sensible criteria for what he would fix.

The most natural category of specialization in the junk trade is furniture because if it is not deemed antique its value is dramatically lessened, yet it is easily reused. I guessed used furniture stores would prosper in depressed communities, as the sheer utility of a good used easy chair or kitchen table would appeal to those who cannot afford to either indulge in antiques or buy new furniture. Regardless of economic status, people need beds on which to sleep and chairs on which to sit, and commerce continues at an affordable level, a trade in unloved and unlovely pieces fifty or fewer years old that nevertheless can do more service.

So I went to Cohoes, New York, to D&S Used Furniture, which sat in an old gas station, now painted a neutral white, on a hilltop on Mohawk Street, before the road plunged into the old mill town, one of the most destitute in the Northeast. The city proper still bore streets full of early nineteenth-century, working class row houses, shoulder-to-shoulder, though in remarkably good shape as they were made of brick or stone. Clapboard structures of their stripe would have long sagged into demolition. The homes cartwheeled on steep streets around the Harmony Mill, an enormous high-Victorian brick building, as decorated as any old manse, with a slate mansard roof and Italianate cupola. On a covered walkway leading to the abandoned mill, a banner read: LOFT APARTMENTS AVAILABLE—RIVER VIEWS. I had read that a developer from New York City had purchased the mill and was turning it into lofts worth thousands a month. The depressed town in which it sat made it seem like a hare-brained scheme to me, though a noble exercise in reuse.

Up on the hill at D&S Used Furniture, I was struck by how orderly it was, as neat as a street of row houses. A woman was sitting at a counter, either D or S, I never learned which. The same gas station counter that had once offered candy bars was now filled with statuettes, a few old tins, and some jewelry. "I try to make it like you are walking into a house," she said, and each room did seem furnished: The back room had the feel of a dining room, with a table and chairs of the 1970s Mediterranean style, dark with thick, vase-like, fluted legs; an imitation painting on the wall of a helmeted conquistador; and a phony wagon-wheel chandelier overhead.

The anatomy of the store followed the function of a house; two old lift bays were set up like living rooms, with L-shaped couches and picture windows cut into the closed garage doors, imitating the setup of a typical suburban ranch house, though probably few D&S customers lived in them. The woman said they sold "to young couples just setting up" and to elderly people who, after moving into assisted-living homes, had sold their "big furniture" and needed smaller stuff, such as tables for their kitchens. "I told my husband that we have nicer stuff in here than we did when we were starting out," she joked, but with a kind of pride in the quality of her goods. Her husband had just walked in the door, a portly man whose roundness was broken only by the box of cigarettes protruding from the pocket of his tight green T-shirt.

D&S bought from estate sales, too, after the antique dealers and pickers had gotten what they wanted. They deliberately didn't deal in antiques, as they are "too competitive and there's too many shops." If they got something they recognized as antique, they simply put it in their shop and waited; eventually a dealer would show up to buy it. They didn't try to get more money for something older from a dealer, said her husband. "As long as I get my money out of it, they can get their money." The D&S was not the proper venue for capitalizing on the value of antiques, and so these more valued goods must continue in the pipeline; again, like water, secondhand goods must find their own levels.

The front office of the old gas station was dominated by a four-piece set of bedroom furniture, two big chests of drawers, and two smaller ones to be used as bedside stands. They had been painted white and trimmed with sugary gold oil paint. "That's all mahogany under there," she said.

"There's a vanity that went with that set, but she has it," he said, his thumb cocked in his wife's direction.

"If it is really all mahogany, I might scrape the paint off it," she said, showing her junker instinct for looking for the inner qualities of a castoff.

We'd been talking about a sign, one the woman said her husband had composed—IF IT'S GOOD ENOUGH TO GET OLD, IT'S GOOD ENOUGH TO SELL, which sounded to me like a fine, all-purpose junker credo. He explained that the sign was also meant as a commentary on new furniture, which, because of its particleboard construction, would probably not survive to enter the secondhand network. Most of what they sold was bought new in the 1970s, he said, suggesting stuff made then still had staying power. He admitted that some quality new furniture was still being produced, but it was too expensive for the ordinary person to buy—another sales pitch for buying used.

I examined the ugly painted bedroom set while he talked and pointed out that the drawers were constructed with dovetailed joinery, but I couldn't help noticing the inside of drawers of the larger chests were made of poplar, while those of the smaller chests were pine—and not dovetailed. Then it dawned on me, and the pieces separated in my mind: I saw different bases on the larger and smaller pieces. The only things that made this a bedroom suite were paint and the same brass and ceramic pulls—both added later.

When I called this to the owner's attention, he waved off the observation. It made no difference. The paint unified them, a kind of cosmetic provenance that allowed him to sell them as a "matching set." Moving from the cobbled-together suite, he pointed out a maple drop-leaf table with "captain's chairs." Such niceties, similar construction or history, do not matter as much at the junk level. "People buy new, and after a few years the chairs are all wobbly, but not those chairs." This stuff, he was insisting, had proven its value by surviving.

But these junkers were not uninterested in the kinds of curios you might find in an antique or collectibles shop. On the back wall he displayed a framed copy of the *Cohoes American* from the 1930s; "Nazi Terrorism Alarms Vatican," was the above-the-fold headline. "Cohoes hasn't had a newspaper in a long time," he said. "I just hung that there because I thought people would like to look at it." Beside it was a poster from the Cold War, a description of the old "duck and cover" drill. One of the precautions included the admonition to "Put one arm over face." He said he had fifteen of them; a local arsenal used to give them out. "A friend of mine is coming in to buy it to hang in his bar; I'll just frame another one." He then rifled through a drawer in a cupboard behind the counter and pulled out a plastic-slipcovered document, a fifty-stock share certificate from 1886 for the old Ohio Central Railroad.

The company, like many Midwestern railroads, has been sold and resold, combining with other short lines, escaping the fate of being dissolved completely and converted into walking and biking trails, but its physical remnants, such as the certificate, as exquisitely printed as a piece of paper money, are coveted, collected, bought, and sold. This junker, though, had found his in a drawer in a desk. "That has to be researched," he said, and I couldn't tell if he thought it was valuable or it simply had captured his interest. "I'll sell that to Sally Jessy Raphael," he added. "She's really into anything about railroads." He planned to send a photocopy of it to her. So he was just holding out for a good price, despite what he had said about selling antiques.

Chapter Eleven

❧

Specialty and Generic Junk

THE COUPLE AT D&S sent me to talk to another junker, simply called "Trink," whose shop was on Remsen Street, the main commercial street in downtown Cohoes. They seemed to like her and said when they went to estate sales and auctions, they'd pick up things for her. According to her card, Trink dealt exclusively in twentieth-century modern furniture, and it bore a drawing of a squarish couch on round, tapered dowel legs. It looked to me like another way to sell junk at a premium price: categorize it as something other than junk and make it a collectible because it has a category.

When I found Remsen, I saw how desperate the town had become. Almost all the stores, block after block, were vacant. A wallpaper store at one end and a pharmacy at the other anchored the street. The only stores between them without frosted or newspapered windows were two antique stores: a junk shop that was not open but had the enticing name of Good Stuff, Just Good Stuff; and Trink. Junkers had sensed the commercial vacuum in Cohoes. If, as I had been told, secondhand goods entered the market according to the seasons in people's lives, then secondhand stores popped up during the seasons in the lives of towns. Trink later flatly told me she was there only to take advantage of cheap rent.

When I parked in front of Trink's shop, what looked to be an old clothing store, she was in full and agitated negotiations with a fullback-sized antique dealer on the street. He had driven by and seen her unpacking a marble-topped, Eastlake lamp stand on the curb—not the kind of merchandise she advertised. As I soon found out, Trink's uncle had died and willed it to her; she planned to keep it, though the dealer left saying, "Don't sell it to anyone else but me," annoyed that she wouldn't part with it.

Trink was hands-down the loveliest junker I had ever met. Although I always err toward euphemism when describing the people I meet in this trade, they are often a coarse, haggard-looking bunch, with more tattoos than teeth. Trink looked like she'd be more at home in a nightclub than a country auction, and she carried herself with the alluring center of gravity only the very attractive possess. She was also savvy and had gone toe-to-toe with the big antique dealer as he tried to pry her loose from the stand. However, not only did Trink get rid of him, she had sold him a cabinet that didn't fit her niche market.

Trink's corner on castoffs was "retro" furniture, a word that speaks of the appeal of what I consider "ugly modern stuff." She sold tables, chairs, lamps, and sofas made by the great Modernist architects and designers, such as Charles and Ray Eames. After producing the sweeping and geometric buildings of the Bauhaus style, architects like the Eameses designed like-minded furniture. Though the furniture fit the experimental spaces they had created, when it was taken out of context and sold to the public as "the newest thing" in the 1950s and 1960s—when "new-is-better" was at its zenith—America's living rooms soon looked like they had been colonized by space labs housing miniature aliens.

Some of the furniture, though, is remarkably comfortable, as is the Eames chair, formed sheets of plywood mounted on pipe legs, amorphous but accommodating to the human body. Trink was quite proud of one she had just acquired, with its original varnished finish, having escaped the 1960s trend of painting furniture in order to make it appear newer. She admonished me to be careful when I started to sit down in it, as protective as any antique dealer would be of a handmade Windsor. Soon Trink and another woman and a man were sitting on chairs and couches near me— I admit, the furniture invites relaxation and lounging, decadent postures.

"I have an artist's heart," she said when I asked her why she got into the business. Trink, whose real name is Nadia Trinkala, found in this flavor of merchandise an essence of the last century, a style and optimism long gone and perhaps no longer possible, a naïve, sweeping futurism that germinated at the 1939 World's Fair with its Futurama exhibit, and that had to wait out a world war to flower into kidney-shaped coffee tables and hydra-like pole lamps.

Now castoffs, this era of used goods is hot in Soho, Trink said, and in California, where she used to live. We live in an age of irony, to be sure, and that fuels the market for genuinely ugly furnishings and kitsch. The fashionable gleefully surround themselves with a failed aesthetic. It is attractive because it was a stylistic dead end. "Retro," as it applies to used merchandise, has different connotations; retro toilets were from the years before high-Modernist designers, but retro in furnishings or clothing implies a sneering indifference to attractiveness. Again I was reminded of the young couple and their Mercedes at the Salvation Army, and imagined yet another motive for shopping there. For some in this sloppily defined post-modern era, even deigning to occupy a place, to furnish a home, is an act of high irony. Here used goods are more fashionable than any trend new merchandise marketeers and advertisers could devise. Trink and her associates are truly the bane of Madison Avenue.

Trink was not a retro collector, however. "I sell this stuff because I'm detached from it. I could sell clothes, but that would be too close to me." Her search for the quirkiest of Modernist goods had taken her everywhere, even to funeral homes, where she had bought candlesticks and torchier lamps. Some of these pieces had "removable religions," she said, laughing at her choice of words. The candlesticks would be adorned with a religious insignia, and "depending on who had died you could unscrew the Jesus stuff" and screw on something else, such as a Star of David. "Funeral homes are for all religions," she said.

The pair with Trink, either friends or helpers, had as much to say about the business as she did. The woman said, "Tell him how you got started in the business, by picking up furniture students threw out at the end of the year."

"That's not *true!*" Trink said. "I started out selling sofas. I'd buy any sofa and sell it to students. I figured they'd pay as high as sixty dollars for them, so I never paid more than forty." After Trink had a good supply, she would load them in a moving van and sell them in student housing areas at the beginning of the semester. When I suggested she could easily have gathered up the same sofas at the end of the year and sold them again, she said, "Who'd want them, with all the beer stains?" However, I'm sure she had found more than one she could resell. Eventually Trink must have noticed that students preferred the streamlined sofas from the

1950s and 1960s, and decided to specialize and offer accessories. Before long Trink was a full-blown dealer in these sardonic wares.

Now Trink saw this stuff as props, and she was hired as a decorator for businesses like coffee houses. Trink even rented out her display window to a couple who wanted to pose in fifties-style furniture for a photograph to grace their wedding announcement, the man reading a paper in a fat lounger, the woman at-the-ready in apron, a living tableau of those icons of domesticity. "This is my art," Trink said again, wistfully. For Trink, her merchandise were pieces of found art, and a customer's home was an installation. Pointing to a giant rollerskate silhouette, probably an old rink sign, filling the back wall, she said she used to deal more in items like that. Now she found everything from the 1950s and 1960s equally incongruent.

As a merchant, Trink was practical, too. She said she often found new uses for stuff. She pointed to a faux Victorian couch she was going to have re-covered with fake fur, claiming it would then make a "wonderful accent piece." "People say that reupholstering is expensive, but if you have an older couch, you have better springs and a stronger frame." Even if you weren't interested in decorating with an attitude, buying used was smart and economical. After all, as Trink said about new furniture, "We don't need more stuff. There's plenty of stuff already." Only a veteran junker would recognize the immense surplus our throw-away culture has created. Buying used only took more imagination.

However, it takes more than imagination to make a living as a used merchandise seller. I asked Trink how she coped with the serendipity of the trade. A new retail store orders merchandise from a central warehouse or a large manufacturer, and the price is generally predetermined. A junker never knows what she will have to sell from day to day, nor when it will sell, nor for how much. Leaning her head back, Trink said nothing about the business was certain; then, fingering her tangled, long blonde hair, she sighed with the resigned weariness of a beleaguered Scarlett O'Hara, "You just have to believe it's all gonna work out." Nadia Trinkala is the diva of discards.

Sometimes, though, from a buyer's perspective, only a generic junker will do. Buying used is all about the thrill of the hunt and involves what casinos call intermittent gratification. Every time you walk into a junk shop, you might find something you have always wanted or can't live without. It doesn't happen often, but like the addicted gambler, you know it happens often enough that each shop offers the hope this place is *the* place, this junk is the right kind of junk. Such possibilities keep the used goods consumer continually on the prowl, coming to a skidding halt when driving down the road and a building with a bulging mass of castoffs comes into view. Who knows what you'll find? Who knows when the next place will provide the bargain of the day, week, or lifetime?

Specialist junkers don't offer enough variety to keep such flickering hopes burning, and for that reason do not attract me in the way a generic junker does. For instance, you'd not generally bother to stop at the Auction Surplus Store in Corinth, New York, unless you were interested in secondhand sporting goods. They handled mountain bike parts, fishing tackle, ammunition, gun reloading and cleaning gear, taxidermy supplies such as forms for mounting antlers, and paper targets. One was a drawing of a deer with areas marked so you knew if you would have hit the heart, lungs, stomach, or intestines.

The clerk, a cheerful, round, bus-driver-in-training, with a tattoo of intertwining roses on her chubby arm, had been only working there for a couple of weeks, but her sister, who was a gunsmith, had been in the business for two years. Both businesses did not provide her with enough income, though, and her sister also worked part time as a security guard at Saratoga Springs Hospital. Her shop featured merchandise unsold at auctions and from failed retail stores, a path for used goods I had followed to The Savings Scene.

Auction Surplus was housed in a building the clerk said had been a store for more than a hundred years, and most recently had been a video store. There were no lights on in the building, and I wondered if they didn't have electricity and were only open during daylight hours. They hadn't changed the store much since its last incarnation, and the walls still bore signs for genres of videos, ADVENTURE AND ACTION or COMEDY, though bicycle forks and wheels now hung below them—yet another absurd non sequitur of the junk business.

The clerk had just said she hadn't made too many sales in the weeks she had been working there when an unnaturally thin woman with dark red hair walked in. She disappeared into the dim rows of sporting goods, then came back and asked for help. When both of them returned, the thin woman gave her some money and asked how long the store would be open. "Six o'clock," the clerk said.

"She'll be here in five minutes to pick it up," the woman said and left. The clerk walked to the back and returned pushing a rust-endowed mechanical lawn mower.

"Do you handle much old stuff like that?" I asked. I had walked around the store and had seen nothing but sporting goods.

"Not much. Most of the stuff we carry comes out of stores and already has a price, so I didn't know what to charge her."

"What did she pay for that?" I asked, and she said four dollars. Though they had few sales, when they did make one, it was an item you'd not expect to find there. Before I left a little girl arrived to push the mower down the sidewalk.

Given what the store generally handled, the buyer had been surprised to find the mower there, and though she hadn't been looking for it, bought it. No junk shop is without potential. Such are the pleasures of the quintessential junk shop, and I returned to Gerry's Antiques, Collectibles and Used Furniture, on a weekend as planned, in pursuit of them. I came into Greenwich on a different road, seeing a different part of town, and found yet another junk seller at the Greenwich Discount Center. His critical mass of stuff was crammed into an old mill along the Battenkill, and though the shop was closed, I could see an earnest collection clogging the place and blocking the windows. The riverbank behind the mill was as cluttered as the landing at Normandy with exhausted appliances and farm equipment, and the parking lot on the side was losing ground to the advance of his wares. However, the shop was closed; a sign on the door read: "I'm at the farm on Bristy Road on the way to Salem." He had a farm, too, and I realized Gerry had a rival junker in his midst, though it shouldn't have surprised me, as I had found junk to be so plentiful I now knew that no number of junkers in a given locale could possibly stanch the flow. The guy on Bristy Road and Gerry on his were as much competitors as colleagues.

Later, out at Gerry's graveled lot and circle of barns I saw a white-haired man stripped to the waist, skin the color of a well-used hickory handle, pants sidling over his hip bones. He was the same man I had seen shoveling the last time I was there.

As the man chain-smoked, he talked to a young man and woman about a twelve-pane glass door leaning against the hay barn. "You can cut two inches off the bottom, and it'll still be all right," he said, and the young man examined it, probably imagining the proportions of the door panels, top-to-bottom, once cut to size.

"How much do you want for it?" the man asked, and I thought, "Mistake number one: Ask what he *needs* for it."

"Fifty dollars," Gerry said, and the couple moved noticeably away from the door, looking for another, the young man's fingers finding his chin as though gripped by a sudden thought. However, the other doors were more weathered. "That's about the best I have," Gerry said. "The rest are good only for a shed or something." The white-haired junker intended to sell them the door they had first looked at, figuring he had a couple of live ones. Still, he couldn't bring himself to discredit all of his other doors; they were useful too but not *as* useful as the one in which they had expressed an interest.

As they thought it over, Gerry approached me, and I could tell from his purposeful stride that he expected me to need something. I needed a pretense. "Do you have any wooden storm windows?" I asked almost automatically because I had once scavenged for them when I was fixing up an old house. All I had seen at Gerry's were aluminum framed ones.

"I have lots of them on the other side of the barn," Gerry said, pointing to the milk barn, and he did, scores of them dominoed against each other. I looked them over, but I was actually more interested in the junk inside the barn. When I looked inside at this angle, I could see that large portions of the back side and roof were missing; barn swallows idly dived at my head. In one of the milking stalls I saw an iron counterweight, a piece of angled galvanized stove pipe, two oil cans, some wooden porch posts, a cluster of Aunt Jemima pancake syrup bottles, two splintered drawers from a chest, and a cache of broken dishes. Gerry had reached a crucial level in junk collecting. He was teetering between junk shop and junk pile.

I walked back to the parking area, but Gerry met me at the corner of the barn. "Find any you çan use?"

"I'll have to come back with a tape measure," I said, thinking fast. Gerry was thinking faster.

"I have a tape, if you have your measurements."

"That's just it. I need to come back with both."

"Ten dollars apiece," he said.

"Fair price," I replied, though they cost $2 at the Architectural Parts Warehouse. No sense starting to dicker when I didn't intend to buy, but I wondered why they were so high. Maybe he'd heard that scavengers were stripping these old wooden windows, filling the four or eight panes with mirrors, and selling them for as much as $300; if a junker hears a castoff is making money for someone else, he wants his piece.

Gerry had no dearth of business, though. On the other side of the barn with the storm windows I had seen a sign reading STOP IN, and people were; three cars in a row pulled over as I left. A yard full of generic junk is too compelling to pass up. The incomprehensible mass of a junk shop is like an archaeological site. Beneath the rubble of inconsequential trash might rest that rare piece of resonant junk, a forlorn but precious castoff whose story unexpectedly intersects with yours. Plenty of curious buyers were drawn to the mysterious contents of Gerry's barns. If he worked the crowd he'd make his day.

Junk selling does not have the drama and occasional thrills of the auction business, nor does it require the blind hustle and arcane knowledge of price lists of antique dealing. Gathering and selling junk is personal and must begin with an innate drive to acquire and save. A junker must first have a need, even a love, for junk; then, to satisfy a more rational side, he has to try to find a way to make money while satisfying that compulsion. I didn't need Gerry to explain to me how he got started in the junk business; all of the ingredients were there. He had space, access to discards, and the inner demand. The three had found each other, and the business was started by sheer momentum. As one barn after another had filled, Gerry began organizing and reorganizing, until he simply had to succumb, gracefully and with resignation, to the chaos of castoffs. Now he sells them, opening gaps in the collection and making room, always trying to make room for more.

Chapter Twelve

A Few Words about Pickers

THE MOTION OF GOODS in the used network is circuitous, guided by few controlling principles besides value, and even that mutates freely. However, you'd be tempted to think the network is roughly mappable, like a watershed which drains through a hundred tributaries, creeks and washes, but ends at the same ocean bay. By the same analogy, pickers are irrigation sluice gates; they interrupt and fine-tune the flow, keeping goods moving throughout the system to even more finely graduated, and fruitful, destinations.

I'd found pickers working in all parts of the network, from auctions downward, and as a tribe they defy all but the broadest generalizations. They certainly aren't getting rich by any stretch of the imagination. No picker I've met looked even vaguely well-off, judging by appearances, of course—but they do make a living, such as it is. As Gary Guarno, compulsive buyer and seller in Salem, New York, said, "They like the road. They see something here that they know a dealer wants three miles down the road, or three hundred, and they buy it here and sell it there and hopefully make a profit along the way. We're all pickers." In a sense, he was right.

Pickers often operate on the slimmest of profit margins. No antique dealer would give me a firm percentage as an expected profit margin, partially because it's nearly impossible to predict, and partially because they didn't want to reveal how much real room they had in a typical dicker. However, through comparing prices paid at auctions or yard sales with those asked in their shops, I could tell they try to double their money. They have to, because they always have so much tied up in inventory, they have to make that much on their sales just to keep afloat, and they are just as apt to break even.

Pickers, however, are gamblers on steeper odds. They have to know the network better than anyone else: where each dealer is, what the dealer most likes or collects, and where to find it. Moving stuff from one location to another is an investment in gas and wear and tear on their vehicles, though they are always buying and selling along the way. Gary Guarno said, "I look at what they have and sometimes buy something." He thought pickers performed a service by moving merchandise to people who either really wanted it or knew how to sell it. They sold at all levels and categories. Trink said pickers did not bring her much retro stuff. She did all her picking for herself, but when she was living in Los Angeles she was offered "truck after truck packed with furniture."

"That's a whole 'nother art," John Christman said of these travelers, shaking his head. They're on the move all day, and John claimed they hoped to make $200 or $300 at the end. "They pull in with a truck full of stuff and say, 'Okay, I want fifty for this and seventy-five for that,'" John said. A confident, knowledgeable picker can set a price, knowing if one dealer doesn't bite, the next guy down the street might. John knew lots of pickers and even worked as one himself, in a way. He would pick as an early bird, going to people's houses the day before they held a yard sale to get first dibs. John usually didn't sell to other dealers, only picking new merchandise for his shop.

One picker John knew ranked among the best. John was riding with him one day when he stopped at the The Pink Barn, a junk shop in Saratoga Springs that has since moved on, as junk shops sometimes do when cheaper locales beckon. There the picker bought some furniture, including "an ugly Italian piece" for a few dollars. He then drove straight to the main street in town, where high-end antique dealers, like Mark Lawson, had stores and galleries. "Watch this," the picker said, "I'm going to sell this for $300." And he did. The Pink Barn and the ritzy stores were only four blocks from each other, but the picker knew the market so well he was able to briefly tap it and come away with a fistful of dollars.

While John and I were talking, a picker came into his store on the Gordon Creek. He had reddish blond hair, and looked to be in his middle thirties. John could tell he was a picker right away, as I could, by how he acted. He glanced around, not with interest but as though he was pointing his eyes in multiple directions at once to catalogue what John stocked in order to pick appropriate things to sell him next time. All the while he eyed us, gauging whether John was finished talking to me so he could approach him.

John approached him instead. They spoke for a moment, then left the store. I followed a few steps behind. The picker opened the back door of a dirty maroon Ford Fiesta, and John reached in and began pulling out items and setting them on the top of the car. The picker talked rapidly, pointing to this or that, head bobbling in and out of his car window, while John silently unloaded the back seat. The man with the Fiesta did not seem to have the confidence of John's picker friend. He was a little too eager, I judged at a distance.

I went back into the store to give them room; a third party can change the dynamics of a dicker. A witness raises the stakes as the ego of a buyer or seller kicks in, neither wanting to appear having been bested. Inside, John's wife, Heidi, told me picker stories. Four or five antique dealers used to come to their store to sit around and one-up each other in swapping stories about their best finds. "There are no secrets in this business," Heidi said. "If you get a good buy, everyone knows about it sooner or later."

This competition heightened whenever a picker showed up. Out the door they'd go, *en masse*, their scavenger hearts aflutter with possibility. "Hey, this is my shop," Heidi would yell, "I get to go out there first!" but it would be too late. By the time she got to the picker, the other dealers would be already pulling stuff off the truck and working deals, and she couldn't even get a word in. Once a really attractive woman stuck her head in the door and asked if anyone was interested in buying stuff, and the dealers lounging around the store "rushed her." Heidi said they not only got to buy what they wanted, but they got to flirt with her, yet another contest, and I assume she had the advantage in haggling as a result.

Heidi said no matter who the picker was, the dealers would eventually come back into her store and immediately start lying about what they had paid for something. "'I bought this for five,' one would say, and another would chime in with, 'No way! You paid fifteen for that. I know because I heard you buy it.' They'd buy right beside each other and then lie about it later." Better dickering earned them both money and bragging rights.

The picker and John came inside the store and piling an armload of items on a tabletop, continued to dicker. John was driving a nail-hard bargain, and I could hear snatches, "Need for this . . . not the right kind . . . not going to get much for that . . . " Finally the picker front-pocketed some bills and left, and I walked over to John to see how he had fared.

"I thought pickers all drove trucks," I said.

"He sells smalls," John said, then he showed me what he had bought for $90. "He thought I only had ninety to spend, but after we closed the deal he saw I had a lot more on me." John had a few other angles on dickering. Bargaining on many items at once involved putting together a group of items for one price, taking items out or getting other items thrown in, producing fluid, algebraic shifts in value during which you had to keep a tally in your head, figuring how much each piece would fetch upon resale. After a dizzying combination of adding and subtracting goods from the pile, and even buying some stuff he didn't want for a couple of dollars, John was able to get a Victorian walnut stationery box for $45. After he removed a mirror on the top, which had been glued on by a former owner, and then oiled the dark wood, he was sure it would bring $125.

The stationery box alone would return his money. The rest of what he bought would sell as well, but not at as much of a profit: grocery store tins, some children's books, and some medical tracts with good plates. He paid $20 for eight tins and figured the picker paid $2 for each of them—making only a $4 profit on the lot, far from more than doubling his money, as John would easily do with the box. He said the trick to doing business with pickers was bargaining hard enough so the pickers don't think you are a pushover, but not so tough as to make them pass you by next time. You have to allow them to make enough money so they'll come back; dealers love to see pickers arrive, but have to deal with them tenderly. Pickers are not going to do business with you if they think they're being hustled.

John seemed to have a grudging admiration for pickers. A good picker had to have at least as much knowledge of the secondhand value system as an auctioneer or antique dealer, and maybe even a little more than some, given his precarious profits. "But someday he'll make a mistake,"

John said, and though the picker would never know it, he or she would hand-deliver a windfall.

Pickers who got their wares from lower in the distribution chain had the safest chance at making a profit, and some undoubtedly did make a fair living at it. I had heard of one legendary figure who only worked during the summer months, buying stuff at yard sales and even through want ads and reselling them to dealers. He was rumored to make as much as $5,000 a month, but hid the fact by wearing old clothes and driving a battered car. Most of the pickers I met seemed to hide their prosperity well. When I was lured to Fort Anne Antiques, I noticed the side yard was full, disappearing under a pile of weathered shutters and porch pillars. A man was sorting through them when a grizzled fellow pulled up in a truck suffering from too much innovation—at least three different-colored doors and fenders and a homemade bed—the original long gone. He had a load of tin architectural details, window lintels and decorative eaves, and before he could even begin his pitch the guy sorting was shaking his head. I can't imagine how you could be making much on demolition refuse—the humblest of castoffs—even if every dime a trash-picker makes is profit.

Regardless of what they sell, pickers have to be crafty to succeed, especially because they are trying to eke out a few bucks from the orbit of savvy dealers. Although pickers obviously study prices and even do research in libraries, much of what they learn is acquired experientially. For instance, a picker came into Jack's Outback and interrupted our conversation with, "Are old tricycles like that one out front worth much?" He was referring to one decorating Jack's deluged front steps.

"That one's not; it depends on condition," Jack said, then adding, "Don't I know you?" He had probably seen him at sales or even in his shop before.

"Buck," the picker answered and shot out his hand to shake. Buck was a stuttering redhead with narrow, dim eyes. His mouth wrestled every word. "I got a couple of tricycles."

"You want to sell them?" Jack said when he got his hand back.

"Well, I don't have them yet, but I will. This other guy has them."

"Bring them in when you get them. I'd like to see them," Jack said.

"The one is in good condition, and it's got these great pointy things, like it has rockets. It's blue and white with a white seat. It's all original, not like that one out there."

"Yeah, someone painted that one red." Jack had it on the porch only for curb appeal. "I'd like to see those trikes."

"Well, I might have them tomorrow, or today. The guy said he'd have them for me."

"I'm open today and tomorrow. I'd like to see them."

"They have these red, pointy rocket-things."

"Sound good. Bring them in." This bit of David Mamet dialogue continued for some time. The picker was putting Jack through this rigmarole to test his enthusiasm for tricycles. If Jack seemed keenly interested, he'd bring them by. If not, Jack would never see them.

Jack said he had a few pickers who stopped by regularly, and he sometimes bought from them. Another picker who visited Jack that same day also dealt to auctioneers. He had just been to an auction in Shushan, New York, and when Jack asked him how it had gone, he said the stuff was selling too high for dealers to buy; too many collectors were running up the prices. The picker had brought a two-sided Coke sign to sell and wanted the auctioneer to give him $75 for it. The auctioneer refused, countering with $55. "I started walking away, but he chased after me in the parking lot to offer $10 more. It went [in the auction] for $125. I'd feel better if he'd given me $75," the picker said, crossing his arms. He didn't mention how much he had paid for it, so I couldn't tell if he was working with a small profit margin or had only wanted a bigger slice of the ultimate price.

It can't be easy making money this way. A picker is competing against every other buyer on the yard sale or antique circuit and has to find a steal the others have walked by. One picker explained his technique for beating out the others. He watched the yard sale listings in the newspaper. If someone advertised a big item as part of a sale, something difficult to sell like a piano, he would show up at the house the evening before the sale expressing an interest in it.

He knew that people who wanted to get rid of such hard-to-sell items were eager to find a buyer and would let him look at it—and everything else at the sale—early. Once he showed up at a house at which a sale was to be held which included a pool table. An elderly woman answered the door, and he introduced himself, saying he had spotted the table in the ad. "I'd like to buy one for my son," he lied. The woman led him into the garage where everything they had for sale was stashed but said he had to wait until her husband came home from an errand to find out the price.

He glanced around the garage and spotted some desirable items, such as McCoy and Roseville art pottery from the 1920s, all priced from fifty cents to a dollar, collectibles that could fetch a hundred times that. When the husband came home, the picker began a long examination of the pool table, which was wedged behind a bunch of boxes. He measured it, checked the height, looked at the condition of the felt top, then sprang the question, "While I'm here, do you mind if I look at what else you have for sale?"

"No, go right ahead," the man said. The picker knew he'd agree to anything as long as he still thought he was going to get rid of his pool table.

The picker quickly bought all of the best stuff at the sale, then slipped the hook, "You know, I was really looking for an eight-foot table, and this one's only a six-footer." Then he left, having looted the yard sale of all its choicest items, the disappointed pool table owner none the wiser. The rest of us would show up early the next morning thinking we would find a deal and never know we'd been beaten to the punch.

Pickers don't care whom they buy from or sell to, or where, as long as they're buying and selling; they will even offer stuff to antique store customers, if the dealer isn't watching. They'd not be welcome back if caught. Once I dealt with a picker in the parking lot of an auction house. This auction was dealing in stuff from a closing lawn tractor and light equipment store, near Rochester, New York, so I showed up thinking I'd find a log splitter for Bob Miner. It would have to be cheap, though, and the merchandise from the store was all new, so my chances at a suitable bargain were slim. This was soon evident. The smallest of four log splitters went up on the block, but the bidding was keen, and it quickly outstripped the $100 I knew Bob would pay for one, ending at $450. I knew the others would go for much more.

One of the other bidders, who also had dropped out around $100, threaded his way through the crowd and stood by me. He said nothing as we watched the next log splitter being hawked. His eyes were slow and aproned by dark pouches deep enough to hide nickels.

"I got a log splitter in my truck," he soon whispered, running his hand through hair the color and texture of thread dipped in molasses. "I'll sell it to you for $100."

"Let's see it," I said, and we went to the parking lot. He was a picker, with a gray, green, and blue pickup heaped with stuff, all tied down with a web of rope. The log splitter was next to the tailgate, and I could tell right away it had been used hard and was the worse for it. The motor looked like it was seeping oil out of every gasket and seam.

I passed on the log splitter, but inside his cab, hanging on a gun rack, I saw a shotgun. It was an ancient muzzle-loader with two barrels and a pair of hammers—another item on Bob's wish list. He wanted one to decorate his post-and-beam country house.

"What's that gun like?" I said, pointing.

"Wanna buy it?" he asked quickly.

"I don't know. Let me see it," I said, trying to sound only mildly interested. The picker opened the passenger door, which shuddered and squealed, pulled the gun out barrel first, and handed it to me. I looked it over, pulling back the hammers and releasing them slowly with my finger on the double trigger, the way I'd been taught to safely cock and uncock a weapon. The gun was pretty beat up, but not corroded.

"What do you need for it?" I asked.

The man was watching my every move, trying to gauge whether the gun had hooked him a live one. "Sixty bucks," he offered.

"I have thirty."

"Real money comes in twenties," he said. I'd never heard that one before.

"Forty?"

"Okay," he said. "The gun guys won't buy it from me. They say it's not worth anything 'cause it won't fire." Then he stopped and screwed his face into a puzzlement. "Wait. Maybe it ain't legal to sell it to you."

Legal? I thought. What did he care about legalities? I knew there was nothing illegal about it. Most gun-control laws did not apply to purchasing black-powder guns, especially those made before 1900, which are considered simply collectibles. Absolutely no laws restricted the sale of black powder guns more than 100 years old that don't work, what collectors called a wall hanger. This old shotgun was less dangerous than your average umbrella. I sensed that the picker might not be so sure, so I played along.

"Do you know me?" I asked with half a wink.

"Nope."

"Do I know you?"

"Nope."

"If someone asked you to describe the person you sold this shotgun to, could you?"

"Well, I'd say you were pretty scrawny."

"That about all you'd remember?"

"Yeah, I guess."

"Then I'm guessing it's safe," I said and handed him $40. When I walked off, I looked back and saw Pennsylvania plates on his truck; he must have been on a long buying and selling trip, a real marathon. I wondered where he'd picked the old double-barrel, but I knew he'd either refuse to tell me or make something up. Unlike antique dealers who offer provenance whenever one is known, most pickers would rather you didn't know where they found their stuff. They are like the guy in the park who hides a pea under one of three walnut shells. You'd swear you can follow it, but the pea is always elsewhere. Pickers find stuff right under other people's noses and aren't interested in telling you where to look. Regardless of where it came from, Bob loved the gun.

Those who choose this part of the stream of castoffs must get started in equally serendipitous ways. Perhaps it all begins with a lucky find, something they know will fetch an easy profit, and like prospectors who glimpse gold or hear its rumor, they are driven to head out in search of more. Pickers are among the most itinerant of the scavenger tribe, preferring the ramble to the sedentary, aimless gathering of the junk hoarder. They are always questing by the seats of their pants, gleams in their eyes, sailing down the road in their crippled cars and half-gone pickups like beat poets in search of the next shining moment, to the place where a thing unloved or undervalued, or both, becomes valuable in their eyes. They then play matchmaker and deliver the choice find to those who will love it best or to a dealer who will, in turn, place a phone call and summon a collector who needs just that item, whose want-list will then be a little shorter and finer. Meanwhile the picker is out of the picture, off the radar, migrating on the circuit, finding the ripe fruit.

I decided to test all of this. Was it really possible to buy something at one antique store and sell it in another at a profit? If I hoped to succeed, the dealers would have to be farther apart than just a few miles. So I took a long drive east, ending up on the other side of Manchester Center,

Vermont. Actually, none of the names of places mentioned in this story are real, because I wouldn't want those with whom I bought and sold that day to think they had been exploited. Along a country road I found an antique store in a center-hall Colonial house, one of those classic New England farmsteads in which the house is attached to the barn through a train of woodsheds and mudrooms. Someone once told me the connected buildings allowed the farmer to feed his stock without having to go outside in the dead of winter, but I'm still unsure if that's true, because the building plan never caught on elsewhere, even in blizzard-prone Montana or the Dakotas.

I walked into the center foyer, greeted the man sitting in a stuffed wing chair in the left-hand parlor, and started looking at shelves cobbled onto the side of the staircase. They contained a trove of brass and copper stuff, candlesticks, bowls, and engraved serving trays. They were clearly old, with a genuine patina, not new like those I'd seen at Ebenezer II in West Stockbridge. I had just flipped over a tray to look for some kind of mark, when the dealer said, "If you like brass and copper, come with me out back."

We walked through the telescoping series of buildings into the backyard where a junker was loading brass and copper, mostly flashing and pipe, onto a flat-bed truck.

"This fellow likes brass and copper," the dealer said. "Pass him that big pot, Will."

"I could get maybe five dollars in scrap for that," Will said.

"Throw it over the side," the dealer said.

It was a really ancient, two-handled, three-gallon pot, wide at the base and narrow at the top, covered with rings of hammered floral and leaf decorations, all done by hand, each one different, as though the metalsmith was changing his mind each time he added another version of the motif. Aside from the arabesque decorations (I guessed the pot was Middle Eastern), I was also attracted to the later repairs. The pot was so old it had worn out, and a tinker had fixed the bottom with two pants pocket–size patches and then, when those no longer sufficed, had riveted on a whole new bottom. At the same time, the top rim had worn out, so a new lip had been crimped over it, held on with rivets. The repairs were ancient, too, so the age of the original pot had to be significant. The story of all those repairs, of the series of tinkers who rescued the worn pot, made the piece even more compelling.

"I'd take $20," the dealer said when he noted my eye-glowing appraisal.

"But that's a good heavy piece," the junker chipped in. "I could get good money in scrap on that." His comment was aimed at the dealer. He had obviously already cut a deal on a load of scrap, and the dealer was backing out on part of it when he sensed he could make a real sale.

I offered the dealer $10, and the junker kept complaining, "You might be able to use that pot for something." I don't know if he expected me to pass up the pot in deference to his wanting to scrap it, or if he expected the dealer to give him a cut. I eventually bought it for $15, but not until I had bundled the offer with a humped-back traveling trunk for another $25. The junker grumbled as he went back to loading his truck.

Now I had to see what I could make. I had passed several dealers whom I'd try on the way back. I drove for a half hour before I stopped at a store operated out of an extended garage. The dealer was sitting behind a showcase for jewelry and watches. "I have a couple things in my truck I'd like you to look at," I said, hoping that was the right opening line.

We walked out to my truck. "I have no idea what that is," said the dealer, putting on a pair of reading glasses and spinning the pot to look at the decorations. "You'll have to find someone who knows old brass." He clearly wasn't interested in my rescued pot. When I showed him the trunk in the bed, he said immediately, "What did you have to pay for that?" and I nearly fell for it. I had to stop myself from telling him. Such a simple trick: Ask a question, and people might answer it. He turned down the trunk, too, though, pointing out that part of the latch was missing—a fault I hadn't noticed.

Two stops later a dealer offered me $20 for the trunk and wouldn't budge. I'd have taken it if I could have made a profit on the pot, but he wasn't interested in it because of the patches. All of the dealers to whom I showed the pot considered condition above all other factors, even if the piece clearly had "old repairs." I had broken one of the cardinal rules of picking: Don't buy what you like; buy what you know someone else will like. I hadn't been thinking like someone planning to resell. Instead I had let the pot speak to me.

Finally I sold the trunk for $40. The missing latch kept me from doubling my money, but still I consider it a successful deal. All considered, though, I wasn't a wildly successful picker. I had spent $40 on a pot and a trunk and made $40 and was stuck with a banged-up pot. If you factored in my time, gas, and wear and tear on my truck, I had not really fared well at all. As a picker I'd be broke in no time. If I wanted to start out in the business, I would be better off grazing yard sales or flea markets and then peddling stuff up the line.

Luckily I didn't care. I loved that old tinkered pot and later found out it was either Pakistani or Indian, and perhaps centuries old. A picker would have done some research on it, developed a selling pitch, and then hit the road again. To be a picker, persistence is as important as luck, though with the latter you don't need as much of the former. It also helps to be a little hard-hearted, to have a mercenary attitude toward junk I could never muster. You can't get romantic about a piece of battered brass and expect to make money, too.

Chapter Thirteen

They Have It All Wrong

"IT'S THE HUNT," John Christman said about what kept him enthralled with the business. He said finding stuff was key; anything will eventually sell. For consumers, the hunt also magnifies their other compulsions and hobby-horses. This kismet of thing and place, of time and desire, simply cannot be bridled or manufactured. Still, some serious attempts have been made by mainstream, retail culture to codify this robust and eccentric commerce, and these too are part of the used goods continuum, though they lack significant features of the others.

One of the most successful spin-offs has been the production of price guides and other books that attempt, with the kind of hubris only print can embody, to calcify the business, to make it coherent. They might as well try to herd cats. The prices they set take only condition into consideration and ignore the unquantifiable, but powerful, factors of provenance, context. and personal significance. They also make any part of the trade seem finite, suggesting if an item in a discrete category is not listed in the book, it must not be valuable. What's more, all price guides must be updated after even a year. The predicted prices change, and tastes vary, more rapidly than print can represent accurately.

Another venture has proven more successful in capitalizing on our fascination with the old, albeit in a nonprofit context: Public Television's phenomenally popular *Antiques Roadshow*. Based on an original BBC version, the show takes the hunt to major metropolitan areas in search of the rare and historic to highlight in a few minutes of inspection by an antique or collectibles expert, accompanied by the usually delighted owner. These on-air appraisals culminate in a price projected at the bottom of the screen, accompanied by the travelling trunk logo of the show, and a tinkling, cartoon magic wand sound effect.

Part of the appeal of *Antiques Roadshow* is the educational component; in fact, each show includes an informative segment on a collectible or antique category. However, the human drama of surprise about rarity and value or disappointment over a fake provides the program's real currency. Likewise, the show has recruited a dynamic cadre of appraisers, such as the effusive and infectious Leigh and Leslie Keno who wax ecstatic over Early American furniture. The moment of truth for most segments is the sudden gasp, or onrush of tears, when the owner of a Native American artifact or piece of crude folk art learns its value. Like producers of game shows, those who choose which segments to air must factor in the level of emotional display with the beauty or importance of the thing discussed.

I perversely enjoy when an appraiser reveals to a proud owner that what is really sitting before them is a clever forgery, that Grandpa's story about receiving the blanket from Chief Joseph is no more true than his tales about having worked with Paul Bunyan. More than half of the time the people who bring in their heirlooms are hoping for an appraisal-as-windfall, and the chance to show off something left to them in a relative's will. "My great-aunt would be thrilled to hear that," they invariably exclaim when the watercolor proves to be worth tens of thousands. The disappointed ones are among my favorites, though, openly frowning when the appraiser breaks the news. I remember the murderous glower of one woman who was disabused of the notion that her silver tea service was made by Paul Revere in between headlong rides across the Massachusetts countryside. She had told the story to family and erstwhile friends for years, I guessed, and there she was, prized service on a carpeted table, face made-up for the camera, being shown a hollow braggart.

Usually the show tries not to humiliate its guests and belittle their heirlooms ("It's a copy, but a *good* copy"), however, and I similarly enjoy the happenstance that sends something worthy to the attention of the *Roadshow*. At least once every show, someone will bring in an object discovered at a yard sale, or found on the curb; one young girl said she and her mother regularly went to scrounge in the dump, which she sincerely vowed was her favorite activity. Scavengers of all sorts have their moments under the hot lights.

What effect has the show had on the general trade in castoffs? Colin Stair said that it has enhanced the public's awareness about antiques, though he thought the show stressed value over beauty or significance. When watching the show, Colin intuited an impatience on the part of the owners during the appraisal, as though they were thinking, "I don't want to know all of this. Just put down a dollar figure." "Sometimes I think they could just show the item and put up a dollar figure and people would still watch it," Colin said. That was what he had liked about working for Sotheby's: They stressed the beauty of their wares over value, as he clearly did. When I visited Colin's barn, he had lavished praise on a Scottish case clock, not tall and soaring like a Gothic spire, but stubby and wide. "He looks a squat, stout little man," Colin said, never once mentioning value. If Sotheby's had agreed to sell something, it was automatically valuable, so the appeal had to stretch into the aesthetic. Yet high prices are most often what get reported in the press. Cash has universal appeal.

"That's why I laugh at the TV shows, like *Antiques Roadshow*," Gary Guarno said. He claimed the values cited on the show are typically too high. "They're just estimates. Ask 'em to write a check and see what happens," he said, an eyebrow arched. He didn't watch the show anymore, complaining it gave customers false expectations about value. "'But I saw my chest on *Antiques Roadshow*,'" he said, imitating a customer's protesting whine. "'Yeah,' I say, 'but that was a real eighteenth-century chest.'" Like price guides, *Roadshow* estimates are only accurate if borne out in the market.

So while surely entertaining and educational, *Antiques Roadshow* has it all wrong. The show does all the hunting *for* the audience, and precious little of that. They simply move from city to city, and people come to them, lining up for hours for the chance to be on television with their heirloom or savvy find. It's like a talent show for used goods. Few actually go on to real fame, and some fakes get the hook. The appraisers always express delight over every fine example of this or that category of antique or collectible brought forth, but how many Colonial drop-front desks or miniature portraits can they present to us before we, and they, are stifling a collective yawn on each side of the screen?

Antiques Roadshow is a symptom of what futurist and economist Frances Cairncross has called the death of distance in his book by the same name. Broadly described, the concept maintains that information technology, in this case television, has erased the impact of regions, even the nation-state. Cairncross would predict new technologies would organize the scattered commerce in castoffs, and the anarchical essence of buyers and sellers would be marshaled into new paradigms. No longer separated by time and place, used goods would be amply and predictably available on the Web, in the same way *Antiques Roadshow* simply moves its lights and props to a new city and unerringly reaps another crop of heirlooms. Technology would shrink the distance between the object and the buyer, and the essential hunt would be an armchair enterprise.

Cairncross's theory would hold true if the anarchy of the used network, and the fact of distance, were not crucial aspects of its appeal. The Internet, itself a kind of anarchy of hyper-links, might provide the information forum that could centralize it all, and at a glance might seem to prove Cairncross prophetic. On-line auctions must succeed despite not having the advantages of setting and chance, assets not counterbalanced by the magnetism of the Web and its millions of transfixed eyeballs.

The original on-line auction, eBay, has a series of television advertisements that are more revealing than they are enticing. In one, a man with a metal detector is scanning a beach. The portrait is not flattering: He is unshaven, rumpled, and hollow-eyed, looking more like the stereotypical survivor in the desert than a treasure hunter or scavenger. He is poking along in a piteous way, when he looks up and sees a series of flashing neon signs with arrows pointing into the sand announcing "Civil War Cannonball" or "Diamond Ring," accompanied by a beckoning Vanna White look-alike. In another, a man watches a woman at a vending machine, where she retrieves a glistening sword. The machine, which looks like a soda cooler, is filled with goodies. "What are *you* looking for?" the voice-over asks.

If these ads are aimed at the scavenger population, they are missing by a country mile. First, while used consumers come in all shapes and sizes, what could eBay possibly be thinking by portraying customers as clueless, desperate, and ragged? Perhaps eBay was intending to suggest visually the kind of earnest need that inhabits some collectors, but the overall effect is debasing. More important, though, the advertising agency writers expose themselves as accustomed to selling mainstream culture and as completely out of touch with this target audience. Unable to think outside the mind-set that sells other goods as "easy, convenient, and reliable," they have used wholly inappropriate analogies, comparing the simplicity and surety of finding what you want on eBay with following neon signs and plunking money in a vending machine. No scavenger needs such simplicity, nor wants it. If anything, eBay might be opening up the used market to those who would buy there if things were as easily purchased as at a mall. Once initiated in the hunter and gatherer tribe, some will become full-fledged scavengers and leave their first-level consumer lives behind.

In a radio interview, Bob Hebler, an eBay executive, said the on-line auction strives to be accessible, to allow anybody to buy or sell. He understood the allure of castoffs, though, saying buyers are "looking for something they reflect on from their past." However, when asked what he thought was the strangest thing ever sold on eBay, he cited a mother who tried to sell her advice, an answer he had probably prepared because Mother's Day was approaching. When pushed, he said someone had once sold a car with a jet engine and cited Enron items, like company manuals—nothing that suggested introspection.

Hebler further noted the auction was a "reflection of pop culture," hinting at how collectibles dominate the site, and tossed off another buzz phrase, calling it a "people's marketplace." Traditionally, such a claim would be redundant; the marketplace has always belonged to the people gathered there. Corporate culture and its marketplace have tried to supplant this, but it still survives, though Hebler should look to flea markets and antique shows if he wants to see the real thing. Marketplaces are destinations, and getting there should be an adventure. The trouble with naming eBay a marketplace, despite how it economically functions as one, is there is no there, there, as Gertrude Stein said.

The eBay Web site has a comprehensive list of categories, from antiques through cameras, coins, dolls and bears, home and garden, motorcycles and "everything else." Sorting is one thing computers do best, and in theory eBay could provide consumers with infinite categories and subcategories, if the demand should surface; they already claim to have "millions of items . . . across thousands of categories." The Web site also lists its foreign "branches": Argentina, Australia, Austria, Belgium, Brazil, Canada, France, Germany, Japan, Korea, Mexico, Netherlands, New Zealand, Singapore, Spain, Sweden, Ireland, Italy, Switzerland, and the United Kingdom. They probably can't wait to get connected to China, where they could double their market. After all, their stated mission is "to help practically anyone trade practically anything on earth."

Founded in September of 1995, eBay has rapidly acquired 42.5 million registered users—a phenomenon to be sure, but still only a small fraction of the uncountable participants in the used market. Over time they have developed rules in reaction to the kinds of things people have tried to sell, now posted on the SafeHarbor page, which outlines the Rules and Safety Overview—the guts of the organization, the protections for buyer and seller. It includes an escrow program to allow a purchase to be received and approved before payment is sent, Authentication Services, and a Dispute Resolution service. It makes the entire process appear to be so regulated as to be seamless and wrinkle-free.

Of course this elaborate apparatus is unnecessary in hands-on used commerce, or at a real auction. As Gary Guarno said, it's hard to tell from a picture, especially one digitalized and sent through cyberspace, what makes something valuable. Some who take these photographs are hapless amateurs. For instance, I saw a photograph of an Arts and Crafts Morris rocker for sale in Arkansas sitting forlorn outside in a yard full of scavenged materials; you could see heaps of junk in the background. When at an auction preview, despite the house's attempts to highlight, every object is there in all three dimensions, including its heft and feel. How can a photograph approximate the presence of an object? Likewise, if a beginning collector could be fooled in-the-round, imagine how many mistakes he could make on-line. Dispute resolution is also unimaginable when you are dealing in real time and space. A seller's reputation in the community is at stake, and he or she can't simply disappear into cyber-anonymity. Those in the used goods trade expect people to be responsible for their own actions, a rather old-fashioned idea, it seems.

SafeHarbor includes three other classifications: prohibited, questionable, and potentially infringing. The bricks-and-mortar secondhand network does not shrink from many of the things in these categories. So while any number of interest groups and legalities prohibit alcohol, animals and wildlife products, counterfeit items, plants and seeds, firearms, lockpicking devices, and of course stolen merchandise, from crossing the e-auction block, I have seen nearly all of those things freely traded among unwired scavengers. Likewise almost everything on eBay's questionable list is sold in the open air, from artifacts and autographed items to food, weapons, and knives. Buyers and sellers in real time need not be so squeamish; the transaction is not witnessed by millions. This broadest-standard-for-public-distaste approach to selling used goods takes much of the edge off its renegade nature. Under offensive material not allowed on eBay, I found the Web site noted: "Examples of items that will generally be removed: Items that bear symbols of the Nazis, the SS, or the KKK, including authentic German WWII memorabilia that bears such marks." The two guys who bought the Nazi flag at the Stanislowsky auction could not have been on-line sellers after all.

I wrote to eBay requesting an interview, but company officials never responded, so the next best thing was an introduction by Pierre Omidyar, founder of the company, to *The Official eBay Guide to Buying, Selling and Collecting Just About Anything.* He was a software engineer, not a collector, but the spirit of the business was also shaped by his wife Pam, who collected Pez candy dispensers, those little plastic tubes each topped with a different head, usually a cartoon figure, whose mouth would emit a sugary candy disc. They are one of the first pop-culture collectibles and are often cited as one of the oddest compulsions. I had seen an extensive collection of them in the airport gallery.

Omidyar started the Web site so his wife could meet and trade with other Pez collectors, and the phenomenon that transpired was unexpected. According to Omidyar, the popularity of trading and selling on-line was "more of a happy accident than a grand business design." By the next February he began charging people to use the site to cover expenses, and by August had to quit his other job and hire staff to help maintain what had become eBay.

Omidyar lushly described how eBay gives people a place to meet others like themselves and provides them with a community, but he had it all wrong, as wrong as the television ad. The e-community, much vaunted by those who design and promote it, is actually a shallow and lonely place. People who use this medium to interact with the world understand this, and long ago coined the term "face time" for actually meeting and talking to a real fellow human, underscoring the stark facelessness of reaching out to people from the bright unreality of a computer screen. Used goods merchants might glean the Internet for a deal, but the Internet will never substitute for the give-and-take of an in-person transaction.

Most used buyers and sellers agreed with postmodern junk maven Trink, who disparaged selling on the Internet as "too much of an office job." Beverly Stanislowsky thought eBay was overrated as a place to sell; you might look up a particular item and find "300 of them for sale." A worldwide market available to everyone can easily become glutted, and besides, collectors and sellers "like the face-to-face part of it." The only effect of the Internet Beverly had noticed on her "next-to-new" business was that people now came to her in search of stuff they believed would bring a profit on eBay, particularly advertising items, even if "only 10, 15, 20 years old." If anything, the on-line auction had improved her business. Likewise, pickers had discovered eBay, and used it to sell some of what they gathered at yard sales or another low-end venue rather than run it through a real auction or peddle it to stores.

Auctions did not appear to have been much affected, though you'd assume Internet sales are in direct competition. Rather than compete with Internet auctions, auctioneer Dean Doin used the potential price of an item on eBay to endorse the price he was verbally pitching; "You can get twice that on eBay," he'd say when coaxing an advance. Mike Smith used the Internet to list the contents of his next sale and to answer queries. Colin Stair had his own Web site, but to enhance his traditional print auction catalogue, not replace it. Colin said the Internet had "taken a bit of a bite out of the auction business," though he was starting an auction house despite it. He also thought the Internet gave people "a little bit of knowledge about prices, and you know what they say about having a little bit of knowledge. . . ." The Internet gave people "instant access to that little bit of information." Like *Antiques Roadshow*, the Internet usually only misled customers Colin then had to disappoint with a real-world appraisal. "Sure, Madam, a desk like yours sold for $23,000, but yours is oak, not mahogany, and so on," Colin said, to show how when he filled in the missing information, the results were usually disheartening for the seller.

Like Stanislowsky, Gary Guarno thought eBay was too big. Too much competition, either in an antiques town or on the Web, has a diminishing effect. The eBay company would make lots of money, he said, but the money to be made by dealers there was minimal. "There are millions of items for sale, and the chance of your stuff being seen is less all the time." However, Gary said you could once sell almost anything on eBay, as their slogan asserted, even big items. Shipping was not a huge deterrent. The benefits, however, were mostly collateral. Gary once sold an ornate brass National cash register to someone in Ohio who picked it up en route to a sale in New England. The money was not as important as the exposure, though. Now the dealer knows where Gary and his hotel storehouse are and will probably stop the next time he is out East. For Guarno, eBay was free advertising.

Jack Metzger said eBay was okay for small items, but you couldn't sell furniture, at least the kind of furniture he liked to sell: genuine primitives. Jack put his hand on a wall cabinet, the finish a layering of paint as coarse as the encrusted sides of an amphora brought up from the Aegean. "You can't show all the great layers of paint, the old hardware, the inside." He swung open the door and it let out a satisfying squawk. Some things can't be reduced to the digital. They are still best experienced with our five built-in analog receptors. If you doubt this, browse eBay and, without reading the write-ups, simply page through the photographs, and try to find one that is arresting, in the same way you might browse an auction preview, waiting for that inchoate connection. Even if you stop and enlarge each of the photographs, the simple truth is professionals are seldom behind the camera. They don't know how to control angle and light to capture some nonvisual quality. The pictures are merely snapshots, and in them even a great antique has that "smile-for-the-camera" awkwardness so common in our family albums. Stripped of context, these castoffs look as orphaned and desperate as eBay's televised scavenger.

"At first they said it would be the best thing to ever happen to the antiques business, but it's not working out," Jack said, while in truth the business has been a roaring success, though in unusual ways. One of my enterprising friends, Norman, caught on to how eBay worked very quickly and made some early wins as seller. A musician, Norman had an eye for the unusual find at the $1 bargain bin at a used record store. He would then list the same CD on eBay and sell it for six or seven dollars. Like any auctioneer, he learned that inviting competition for a price was part of ensuring the price would rise, which is an especially good gamble if you had virtually nothing invested in what you were selling. The nearly worthless CDs actually appeared to be valuable by virtue of being listed on eBay. Similarly, once Norm went to a music store to price used electric

keyboards. He saw that almost all of the used sound equipment and instruments sported "Sold" signs. The store owner told him a guy had
been buying a couple of used pieces each week; finally they asked him
what he was doing with this random equipment, and he said he was
selling it for a profit on eBay. So they hired him, and within weeks he sold
almost every used item in the store.

Norman admitted those stories came from the early days of eBay.
Now, he said, it was getting much harder to make easy money because
the site had become saturated with goods and the prices were dropping.
Auctioneers do not compete directly with each other, as they invariably
do on eBay. Imagine putting three or more auctioneers in the same room
with the same items for sale and asking them to compete not only against
the room but against each other. The virtual auction house is getting to
be a cluttered, clamoring place.

CDs are easy to sell because shipping costs are minimal, and eBay
is certainly efficient for smaller items, but it has yet to kill distance entirely when dealing heavier items. The company recognizes this and has
attempted to compete through "eBay Local Trading," where buyers
can geographically limit their search and "shop for more difficult-to-
ship items such as automobiles, furniture, or appliances." But doesn't
that defeat the purpose of eBay if it aims "to help practically anyone
trade practically anything on earth"? Most of the appeal of eBay is its
ubiquity and long reach.

If distance cannot be entirely defeated by the Internet, how will eBay
replicate, or compete with, the thrill of the hunt and the inherent, price-
less inefficiency of the used goods market? Although undoubtedly here
to stay, I predict eBay's popularity will plateau and settle into a pop-cultural
swap meet once people realize immediate gratification is beside the
point in buying used and is only a mainstream, new retail gestalt. The
want-it/buy-it crowd will continue to enjoy eBay, but they have never
been players in the overall used network.

The eBay world is about money and acquisitiveness, not about community; bright promises by company executives about the people's
marketplace aside. The process does not build human connectedness.
People don't actually meet each other in a backroads junk shop and develop
those oblique relationships that serve to broaden and enrich the trade,
nor does eBay commerce revitalize little towns, generating corollary

businesses such as coffee shops, restaurants, and inns—other places where humans must interact. In the real marketplace of the people, you must physically search for something that entices you, take the time to rummage and roam to find that object so fine and sweet it can't be improved by dipping it in chocolate. In the e-marketplace, you only have to scroll.

What does eBay offer us in its place? We get the icy clarity of the computer screen, throbbing with advertisements, to which we are as rigidly fixed, like Alex in *A Clockwork Orange*, having our neurons rearranged so that we are vulnerable to the cannonade of pop-ups offering magazine subscriptions and automatic upgrades. If we don't find what we want on one page of the eBay labyrinth, we can go down or up or click back to next-to-nowhere-at-all. We are given the world as a mediated experience, counted, sorted, digitized, and simplified as a series of yes and no choices. And nothing so pleases the mentally lazy as a set of polarities, gross generalizations that provide a simple-minded spectrum onto which the used network has been awkwardly, ineptly marshaled. While eBay has not quite resulted in the death of distance, it certainly threatens our sense of adventure.

The good folks in San Jose who started eBay did not aim for such negative outcomes. On the contrary, all signs indicate they only planned to wed a new technology to one of the oldest of human endeavors, with uneven success and some deleterious side effects. However, they don't seriously impinge on the used trade. The only venue that might feel the weight of on-line sales are newspaper want ads.

As old as newspapers themselves—they can be found on Colonial broadsheets—want ads have always been a source of used goods, and are essential to people who are looking for other services and commodities, such as real estate or jobs. These other categories are perhaps best suited to want ads; people who sell unwanted stuff through the newspaper are usually unfamiliar with the network, or they wouldn't pay to advertise. Because of this, I don't look for many bargains in the papers. People who sell their used appliances or furniture through want ads have a false sense of the value of their castoffs and usually list a price that reflects the cost of the item when new. And nothing could be more irrelevant than the comparable price of something new when valuing used goods.

Sellers usually indicate in want ads whether a price is firm or if they will entertain a dicker with the initials OBO (or best offer). At least the latter offers a hint the owner knows he or she can't expect more than the used network is prepared to pay. People who hold pat to a price should be prepared to hold on to their castoffs. I have also noticed the occasional antique dealer will list a few items, hoping to use the disguise of a casual seller to off-load some white elephant. Antique dealers will likewise scan these ads for the rare find, for someone who is selling something without knowing its real value; one or two have reported making real killings through want ad purchases.

Newspaper used selling at least preserves the questing side of the trade; most deals are cash-and-carry. One of the few times I have used want ads, besides to find work or places to live, was to buy a woodstove. I wanted a potbellied stove for my barn wood shop, telling myself it would be ideal because you can burn coal as well as wood in one. In truth, I liked the looks of a potbellied stove and didn't care if it was more or less efficient than other kinds of stoves. Newer, boxy stoves were more popular and easy to find. As usual, I had cornered myself into wanting something unusual and probably only available used.

I tried a few likely junkers, then one day picked up the *Penny Saver*, a weekly want ad newspaper. I get a vague thrill from scanning want ads, because the stacked ads do carry the whiff of promise and discovery. I flipped past the dozen pages devoted to campers and automobiles until I reached the page of miscellaneous goods. Remarkably, four ads listed woodstoves. One ad listed three stoves, including one potbelly. A collector of stoves? A savvy hoarder? I called for directions to his house.

I never found out how the man had accumulated his stash of stoves, but I could surmise why: He was a scavenger. He lived on an island in the middle of the Hudson River, a long spit of sand reachable by a bridge. A main house sat up on a raised foundation, the better to tiptoe over floods, and several outbuildings, deserted mobile homes, and other shacks lay along the sandbar as though washed up from some doomed settlement in the north. A wiry man with a fulsome collection of dark tattoos met me at the end of the road and led me to one of the mobile homes where the woodburners were cached.

Inside what had been the living room, sitting under a long window where a sofa might rest, were two boxy stoves. I summarily looked them over, but I wanted a potbellied one, so he led me to a bedroom. There it was. I was charmed by its diminutive size, with its perky, half-bushel cavity for wood, and by the baroque decorations and stout little feet. Old woodburners were often dolled up to offset the fact that having a hunk of blackened iron in the middle of the room was not a decorator asset. The stove had a name, too. I'm a sucker for nineteenth-century machines with names—"The Pippin." Perfect. It made the stove even more spunky, and I was reminded of John Steinbeck's seldom-read political satire, *The Short Reign of Pippin IV*, in which a meek amateur astronomer is crowned King of France. I knew The Pippin and I were going home together.

The man immediately said, "I have to have $300 for that little beauty. Firm." Obviously he valued The Pippin more than the others, because he had taken the time to paint it with stove black; the others were a little rusty. The potbelly was even in a separate room, the junker's attempt to sequester and ennoble it. I had stumbled onto a fellow scavenger who, like Charley Hawk, would hold out for his price out of sheer admiration for the plucky stove.

Sensing I'd have no chance at dickering, I decided to at least salvage a certain amount of bargaining dignity. I had brought along a flashlight, so I unscrewed the lens end, exposing the bulb, set the flashlight like a candle inside the woodstove, and closed the door. Then I walked around the stove, looking for light. Another scavenger had told me this was a good way to check the tightness of the seams in a used stove. It was solid. I turned the damper knobs and checked the hinges on the door. All of these inspections were really cursory. I already knew I was buying it. It was too late for me; the stove was exactly what I wanted. I paid him and left with the potbelly riding like a serene Buddha in the back of my pickup.

The potbelly was not exactly ideal. The burn cavity was a little small for a standard size log, so I had to cut ten-inch firewood. And I never burned coal in it, as I had planned. However, sitting in my barn on a base made of scavenged paving slate, it provided all the heat I needed. I eventually found out that it worked best when burning scrap wood. The best fuel could be had free at the local lumberyard, discarded oak and maple pallets that I cut up with a power saw I had picked up at an auction for $10. The dry, cured hardwood pallets burned hot and clean, and left a clean stovepipe at the end of the winter. When I sold the house and barn, I thought to replace the stove with a newer, boxy one and take the potbelly with me, but The Pippin looked so at home there I left it for the next owner.

In finding my woodstove, want ads functioned in ways familiar to me from my other scavenging forays. However, the ads are controlled by people supposedly outside the network—a newspaper staff—and I wondered how they viewed the business. Did they share any of the same impulses and interests of auctioneers or junkers? To find out, I visited the advertising department of the local paper, the *Saratogian*.

I had to wait in the main reception area to talk to Cindy, the woman who actually took the ads, who was sitting behind a counter. To the left lay a wing of closed offices, sequestered to keep the newsroom out of the public orbit and away from the taint of the moneymaking arm of the operation.

Cindy was busy citing rates to a tall, blonde woman wearing a full-length leather coat that hung off her shoulders in severe columns. I tried to imagine what she might be selling, and decided on a luxury SUV, but I was only stereotyping in the same way eBay was in its television advertisement. She could be selling anything in the back of the business section of the *Saratogian*. I glanced around the office, sound-whitened with trilling phones and ticking keyboards, and noticed a slogan on the wall: THE MAN WHO STOPS ADVERTISING TO SAVE MONEY IS LIKE THE MAN WHO STOPS THE CLOCK TO SAVE TIME—UNKNOWN.

Finally I got to talk with Cindy. At first she wanted to refer me to the Classifieds Manager, and I noted right away the difference in rhetoric. I had asked for the Want Ads Editor. This arm of the paper was "managed," not edited, indicating the *Saratogian* thought these few pages were only a way to earn money, and not, as I had naïvely thought, reporting on the availability of goods and services. Likewise, they were concerned with classification; in that way they were truly the predecessors of eBay. I had thought of them through the lens of wanting something. Did they think to disentangle themselves from the sinews of need, desire, and pursuit? If you are looking through the classifieds and go to the few gray inches given to miscellaneous items, you have no idea what you might see there. However, you probably have some vague notion of what would provoke you to reach for the telephone and set up a rendezvous. While a paper's advertisement staff might try to categorize their listings to reach the most applicable slice of their readership, they can't accurately anticipate all who search them. The irrational, willy-nilliness of used merchandising stymies the efforts of either eBay or newspapers to route it.

After I described why I was interested in the classifieds, Cindy brightened up and eagerly answered my questions. She said peoples' biggest mistake was in making ads too generic, "not very descriptive," though she added, "This Friday we have a very descriptive one going in; it's an antique." She was clearly impressed by the words assigned to the castoff, and I surmised they were drafted by a knowledgeable dealer or collector. I had learned, as I moved down the castoff food chain, that descriptive language became less elaborate, less particular. That something was "old" or "unusual" usually sufficed on the lower links.

In a want ad, the language is at its most skeletal, reduced to a handful of trip wires. These might include brand names if the seller is a rookie (except in selling appliances or cars), always contain abbreviated specifications (dbl bed, 4.5 hp), and when selling furniture the listing will always cite the kind of wood. Aside from cars, age is rarely mentioned, though something might earn the descriptor "antique," which I have found to be a caution flag. Unless the seller is a dealer, a want ad seller will list something as "antique" because he or she thinks it is worth more than the value of its basic usefulness.

Sometimes the reason for the sale also will be noted, the most common being moving. This is an excellent selling word, even better than almost new or exc. cond., because it signals the seller is jettisoning otherwise desirable goods out of necessity. An ad that cites a price is also a better bet than one with only a phone number, because in the latter the seller knows he or she is asking a higher price that might keep you from calling.

Cindy said the most common items sold in want ads are real estate, automobiles, household appliances, and furniture. The business has "a 75–80 percent success/response rate," so people know "it works, so they stick with it." The *Saratogian* is a local paper, so the merchandise is guaranteed to be within reach, not anywhere in the world, as on eBay. However, a want ad placed with the *Saratogian* also appeared in the *Troy Record*, a daily in nearby Troy, New York, and in three free weeklies. They also had a Web site, and listed want ads on-line, directly competing with eBay. The ads were priced on a sliding scale, depending on the asking price, and by the line and word. Stuff under $50 could be advertised for free, which eBay would never do. Cindy interrupted our conversation to take a phone call for a free advertisement from someone giving away a dog.

Want ads work. A friend of mine recently bought a car from a guy who said he has sold 220 cars out of his front yard through drive-by traffic and want ads. They are so good at selling things, an entire class of newspapers are almost exclusively supported by them. There's one in every community, and you probably have never given a second thought to it. When it is delivered to your mailbox, you might simply toss it. They go by predictable names: *Want-ad Digest, Classified Chronicle,* the *Trading Post.* These weeklies carry a little local news and announcements and have largely replaced small town newspapers, but they are seeded with hundreds of tiny ads for everything imaginable.

One of these, the *Penny Saver,* where I had found The Pippin, is published in seven other editions in small towns around Albany, New York, by the Capital Region Weekly Newspapers. Their headquarters is on Pierce Road in Clifton Park. Clifton Park is a by-now-classic suburban nowhere, a mirage of a place of the kind lambasted in James Howard Kunstler's *The Geography of Nowhere.* It is a region in which the activities of human existence are segregated into living areas, working areas, shopping areas, entertainment areas, and so forth, what Kunstler calls pods to emphasize their inhuman-ness. When I went looking for the want ad newspaper office, I expected to find it close to the retail pod, so business owners might drop by to place a display ad, but I drove straight through the mall/shopping center area and didn't spot it, nor a Pierce Road.

I pulled over at a convenience store and inside asked the clerk if he knew where Pierce Road was hidden. He ran the road name through his mental catalogue of those in his suburban sphere of influence, but came up blank. Then a customer came in for cigarettes, so we asked him.

"I should know where it is, but I'm not quite sure. Follow me back to the depot. A guy there will know," he said.

I followed him up the road to a corrugated metal warehouse at the end of a rutted gravel lane. Was this the depot? Where was this guy taking me? We went in through a side door, and inside the mostly empty building I saw a delivery truck with the name of a uniform supply company on it. They were a delivery service. Of course they knew where all the roads were in this cul-de-sac hell.

My guide took me upstairs to the dispatcher's office, and together, by checking routing charts, they found Pierce Road. I thanked them and left, struck, as I often am, by the casual kindnesses often available from working people.

Pierce Road was in another exclusionary pod, an industrial park, where I would never have casually ventured. I expected the office to be like those of the want ad circular for which I once briefly worked in Warren, Ohio, in an upstairs, downtown office, reeking of rubber cement. The only other employee was my boss, the editor, a grumbling old guy who wore a suit coat and tie at all times, even though no one ever saw him as he worked over the light tables, a razor knife in one hand, cigarette in the other. I'd been hired to do layout, but he soon let me go when he realized he didn't really need help. I expected the *Penny Saver* to not be much more than a one- or two-person operation.

So I was more than a little surprised when I found the *Penny Saver* was housed in a flat-roofed, faceless corporate building, with the requisite shrubbery and designated parking, surrounded by other equally severe business headquarters. They had an antechamber bigger than at some daily papers and a pair of receptionists. One was prepared to answer my questions, though she sighed between each of her sentences as though annoyed or very tired.

Like the woman at The Mission Thrift Store, the receptionist began with a litany of company facts, how it had acquired a number of older weekly papers, and as a composite had been growing, and becoming more popular, because they kept their rates under those of the dailies. Behind her I could see the blank flanks of cubicles, behind which probably sat people who could give me some insight on the business. I was stuck on the other side of the counter, though.

So I asked the receptionist a question that could not be answered with company statistics, "What is the strangest thing you've ever sold in a want ad?" A frown of thought crossed her weary features, then she called out to the back, "Hey, what would you say is the strangest thing we've sold?"

A woman had just stepped out of the cubicles to go to a photocopier and another followed behind her. They looked at each other with that colluding glance of people to whom the same thought has occurred.

"The ironing board," the one at the copier said.

"Yeah, an ironing board was advertised for lots of weeks," said the older woman. She walked toward me. "It must have been a *special* ironing board."

"No, wait!" the woman at the copier said, "what about the Fat—" and then choked on laughter.

"The Fat-ass Eliminator!" the older woman said, and they both laughed harder.

"The Fat-ass Eliminator?" I asked over the head of the receptionist.

"Some guy had a patent on an exercise machine, and was trying to sell them through us," the older woman said with a wave to suggest he hadn't been very successful. Her name was Donna. The receptionist explained why I had asked the question.

"I never buy retail," Donna offered immediately. "There's no need to. That's why retail stores are in trouble." She was referring, I assumed, to the mall in the retail pod of Clifton Park that was now largely empty—and home to Acorn Auctions. Donna also spent time shopping on eBay. "I've bought a car, car parts, oh lots." However, she believed the want ad business and the on-line auction "co-existed" and didn't directly compete.

"This is a topic close to my heart. I've been in this business for fourteen years," Donna continued, "and I've seen it, stuff turning over and over again." She was either a manager or editor; I never found out which. "Never buy a new television!" she said to the receptionist, who looked at her with a tinge of surprise.

"Never?" the receptionist asked, almost to herself.

"Never!" Donna answered. "There are loads of televisions. They're everywhere. People will call and say, 'I'm moving. I'm not taking my televisions. I'm going to Florida. I'm not going to need my winter clothes, my shovels, my snow blowers.' I see it all the time. Where does all that stuff go?"

I could have talked to Donna all day; I love meeting ebullient fellow scavengers and was frankly surprised to meet such a well-versed, wholly committed member of the tribe in this mainstream setting. It's ultimately not about how someone partakes of the bountiful secondhand culture or what he or she is seeking; it's a mindset, a matter of the heart.

Donna just as quickly swung back to her fascination with the e-used world: "I spend a lot of time on Dumpster diver Web sites. Just type 'frugal' on a Google search, and you'll get them. That's where I live." Donna talked until she reached the door. Although she was on her way to lunch, she simply couldn't quit expressing the thrill she got from gleaning the material world.

The strongest, most fruitful connection between want ads and the rest of the used goods network was not in what they sold, but in the other sales they advertised. Any Thursday's paper will be well-stocked with them, as people choose that day to announce their weekend yard sales. Cindy at the *Saratogian* said they were an integral part of the used trade by advertising these intensely local sales. eBay would simply never compete with the reality on the ground. Selling anything in the world (except for the restricted and prohibited) to anyone in the world (with a computer and a credit card and an Internet connection) can't replace the sheer joy of tearing across the countryside, yard sale listing and road map at your side, on the prowl for bargains, or replace the adventure of attending one of the true market gatherings, a flea market or antique show. This is a nomadic business, one not easily confined to the computer screen and larger than even cyberspace.

Chapter Fourteen

❧

The People's Marketplace

ONE ASPECT OF THIS TRADE has been positively influenced by the Internet: the promotion of antique shows. Prior to Web sites dedicated to them, word of mouth was the best way to discover these gatherings. I've been going to shows for twenty-five years, and although they have been advertised in newspapers and with circulars posted in public places, I've learned about most of those I've attended through the advice of a fellow traveler.

I'll be at a show, and someone, either a buyer or seller, will tell me, always with a kind of pride, about an even better show held elsewhere. Although my informant is being helpful, the subtext of the comment is that he or she is more firmly plugged into the system and knows where the best buys are. "You think this is a good sale?" often prefaces the tip-off. You then learn the sale you've never visited is bigger, cheaper, and more varied and simply not to be missed. It reminds me of the accounts of European explorers in the Americas. Down the river were a remarkable lands, with marvels to behold, the people they first encountered promised. The cities of gold were elsewhere, but always within reach.

A scavenger's Eldorado is not some burnished mirage, however; it is a landscape of booths and table-displays, limitless acres of castoffs offered for your approval. It's not unlike an auction preview, except generally much larger, and with the benefit of asking prices already determined. You needn't wait to bid; you can have it right now. You can negotiate a price without the competition of a room of buyers. Although hundreds of buyers are cruising these tables, maybe you've been more observant, better informed, or luckier. Hope springs from the sheer multitude of stuff. You might snatch what others have overlooked.

Antique shows are rarer than flea markets, but more predictable. They are usually held once or twice a year, and dealers on the circuit have their calendars marked, and spaces reserved, for years in advance. For instance, the annual antique show in Round Lake, New York, has been evolving over time, as such shows will. I picked up a brochure a few days before it occurred in late June, a bookmark-sized slip decorated with a woman clad in the fulsome fashions of the Victorian era, hair piled on top of her head. Rather than posing stylishly, though, she was walking determinedly, goods stuffed under her arms and what looked like a lampshade in her hand.

Antique shows begin with some local organization sponsoring them. Eventually they grow too big to be easily controlled or managed, and the Round Lake Antique Show was one of them. After twenty-nine years, the sale had been turned over to a company handling trade shows: Allman Productions. When more than 250 dealers and 10,000 visitors descend upon a village of less than a thousand, someone has to take the reins. Sponsored by the Women's Round Lake Improvement Society, the show was the main town library fundraiser and consistently well advertised; I saw vehicles with license plates ranging from Maine to Florida.

The village of Round Lake is a made-to-order setting for selling antiques, especially Victorian-era stuff. Founded in 1866, the village began as a Methodist religious revival camp, part of the Burnt-Over Region, so-called because of the religious fervor that swept the nation after the Civil War, and spawned zealous, utopian settlements throughout the Northeast. In Round Lake, the pious built Victorian cottages as miniatures of the grand mansions typical of the times. Round Lakers also put up an auditorium for lectures and a hotel for less permanent visitors, which today is a bed-and-breakfast called Inn Cognito. Once beside a genuinely round lake, the village is now cut off from its shores by Route 9, a four-lane highway.

Round Lake clearly turned over its annual sale to Allman because of parking. The cottages are built close together on narrow streets, providing little room for vendors, so the sale was held in the public green, a park built on land on which vernal pools form but which dries up in the summer. Still, on sale days the village swiftly became impassable.

Enterprising locals charged $3 to $5 to park on their lawns, depending on the proximity to the action. Those who didn't stuck NO PARKING signs in front of their houses. Leaving your vehicle in the parking lot of an empty grocery store a mile away and riding a shuttle into the village was another option.

I turned off the main road, following one of several signs promising parking, and found all the side streets turned to dirt after a block or two. The makeshift lots had full signs when I got there. Although the sale had only been open for an hour, the village was already overrun. I wondered how the old-time evangelists would have reacted to their summer enclave being remade in this worldly way. I imagined them wishing they could reclaim carnal form so they could banish the merchants from their sanctified ground.

The show radiated out from a central point, where the main street cut through the long, narrow town park. Each seller had open-sided tents that were white and uniform in size, so I suspect they were rented from Allman. They were staggered about the center, as though unsure how to organize themselves. Eventually two or more must have decided to get in line, and avenues radiated away, five in all. Mixed in were food vendors, some loudly hawking their drinks or snacks, adding a carnival ambience. The tents would come in handy on this hot June day, humid and soupy, already spitting moisture, not rain but a kind of 100 percent humidity, the air full to bursting.

Why would antique dealers go to shows? What advantages did it bring and how did these gatherings function in the overall network? I noticed the prices many of the dealers asked for their goods were higher than normal. So you might conclude these sales were less advantageous for the buyer. In fact, dealers with shops will bring their best stuff to a show, and the prices reflect that. They do this for a convergence of reasons. First, they want to attract attention to their setup, because they know buyers can't possibly take in every item in every tent. They know a bright Red Fox Oil sign, an eye-catching hall tree with beveled mirror and fancy carvings, or a shiny display of fiestaware or lusterware, will suck you off the walkway. The concentration of buyers also encourages dealers to trot out the more valuable and unusual pieces in their stock, because the law of averages dictates that a one-of-a-kind piece is more apt to find a matching buyer among thousands of roving eyes. Likewise, dealers will bring their fancy stock and unique pieces out of simple pride. All of the other dealers will saunter through, and you want to be known as a quality dealer. Finally, a show is a chance to advertise. While dealers will pass out business cards and hang signs naming their stores, they will also try to impress buyers with their offerings so the buyers might be tempted to stop in if they are ever in the area.

Another class of dealers have prices that are generally more reasonable: show dealers. These sellers don't have stores, and they do the bulk of their business on the road. Paul Ferrara, one of the best refinishers I have ever met—his work restoring desperate pieces of furniture was admired universally by dealers who knew him—spent all year gathering and fixing pieces predominantly for shows, picking up stuff other people didn't want at auctions and yard sales. The little barn behind Paul's house was always packed with pieces in various stages of resurrection, and a shed nearby held finished work. He sold year-round to dealers or collectors he knew well, but the bulk of his sales were at shows from May to October.

Paul was a furniture magician, and I'd know his work anywhere, recognizing how he applied his finishes and the touches he added. For instance, Paul stripped the burlap covering from old traveling trunks, the kind used by *Antiques Roadshow* as its logo, then stained and varnished the wood beneath. If the brass-plated tin hardware was too worn or rusted, he painted it with gloss black lacquer. If the inner lining was stained or ripped, he used floral wallpaper to replace it. Paul was not the only person who reworked trunks in this way, but if you compared one he had fixed next to another's work, I'd be able to pick out Paul's. He knew just how far to go to make something look refreshed without ruining what those in the trade call its character. Paul wouldn't sand away every scratch or fill every crack. I saw plenty of traveling trunks in Round Lake, usually set out in front of the tent openings to catch the eye, and one or two of them were undoubtedly Paul's work. He sold as often to dealers at the shows as to regular customers.

Paul drove a three-quarter-ton van rather than a pickup, as do most of the dealers who come to shows. Vans are better suited to picking and hauling, and the van can become their living quarters. Some bring along campers or RVs for the same reason; all are more comfortable than sleeping in the bed of a pickup. Some of the vehicles are decked out with sinks, hot plates, and other accoutrements. They are ideal because they can be crammed full of goods, emptied, then lived in for the weekend. Dealers could reload their stuff at night and head to a motel, then set up again the next day, but most don't—that would only be extra work and expense. They stay put for the entire weekend. At night the vehicles parked behind the tents are alight with lanterns while camp stoves heat the evening's repast, to supplement fried dough and hot dogs grazed on during the day. The Round Lake show was a temporary village within a village, and when the workday was done, the sellers visited each other, old compatriots from other encampments. They played cards, watched a movie if someone had a VCR and a DC/AC inverter to run it off a car battery, and swapped stories from the day, exaggerating how well they had done, bumping up selling prices in order to acquire a patina of shrewdness. Over the years many had made friendships that they renewed each season.

When sellers socialize, they also do a little research. One way dealers learn what to hunt for is by asking other people what they've been selling. Goods sell in cycles in shows—something becomes hot for a month or more, and dealers share that information, more or less. Sometimes they will even take advantage of someone's ideas about how to sell something. For instance, Paul Ferrara hadn't invented a way to refurbish old trunks, but he did devise a use for old treadle sewing machines. Foot-powered sewing machines were ornate affairs, with hardwood cabinets, sets of carved-front drawers with teardrop-shaped brass pulls, and frilly iron stands. The machines themselves were usually painted black, highlighted with gold filigree, and when not in use covered with a wooden box, itself decorated with moldings and carvings. They'd be among the fanciest objects in a nineteenth-century home.

Electric-powered sewing machines created tens of thousands of idle treadle ones. Unlike other relics, such as oil lamps, which could be wired and refitted, these machines were simply obsolete. They were pushed into attics, cellars, or barns. Something so ornate was difficult to discard outright. For many years they have floated around the used network, being bought and sold, but no one could figure out another use for the dolled-up machines. Even I once bought one for a couple of dollars. It sat for years, presenting its carnival finery to me whenever I passed it in the barn; I eventually resold it in a yard sale.

The best anyone seemed to be able to do with old sewing machines was to turn them into plant stands, and somehow covering the hole left by removing the machine. The plant stand or planter is the use of last resort for used merchandise. You know a seller is really stretching when he or she suggests, "That would make a nice plant stand." I've seen people try to sell anything with a flat surface with that line: lifeguard chairs, typewriter stands, enameled gas stoves, and even a rusted iron bed for which the junker built a wooden box to fit inside. He had one on display in his front yard, full of impatiens. "It's a flower bed," he said with bow.

Paul Ferrara had more imagination than that. He studied those old sewing machines, then figured out a practical and attractive use for them. The problem with taking out the machines and reusing the fancy stands was that the little drawers were too far apart. Something always looked liked it was missing once the machine no longer sat between them. So Paul removed everything but the drawers and the curliqued iron legs and moved those closer. Then he built a small wooden top from either maple or oak and, using his secret stain formulas, made it match the drawers.

What was left was an attractive end table with four to six little drawers. Paul signed and numbered each table under the top, and they sold at shows as fast as he could make them—for more than $200 apiece. So he started to specialize in them, going to yard sales to buy up as many as he could. The last time I asked, Paul said he had made and sold almost two hundred of them; however, as he expected, they had caught on so well another restorer had taken note of them when on reconnaissance at a show. Thousands of sewing machines are in circulation, so they'll barely cut into each other's markets. I haven't seen the other guy's tables, but I'll bet they're not as fine as Paul's. Still, such ideas cannot remain monopolized in the show world.

At Round Lake I marched down one of the main avenues, flanked by big tents full of furniture; I would have thought dealers who specialized in similar goods would have tried to avoid each other, but perhaps they enjoyed talking with close colleagues. The dealers at the show were more insistent than usual; they were here to dicker and sell and wanted to make their table rent and expenses. Only then could they relax in their chairs beside the open side doors of their vans, coolers at the elbow.

I stopped to look at a dining room table, one with a fifth swinging leg underneath, called a gate-leg, to support additional leaves. I checked the gate-leg, which is often cracked from misuse. "You won't find one with that many leaves," a dealer rushed out to say.

Of the seven leaves in the long table, I could tell only one was an original. The others had been made, skillfully but recently. The finish was not well matched to the original top so it couldn't have been the work of Paul Ferrara. I also never knew him to make them.

"They're all original," the dealer said, a wholehearted lie. "You in the market for a dining table?"

"Not really, but this sure is a nice one," I said, lying as well, and moving on.

At the next booth where I lingered, looking at a small chest that had been "scalped"—refinished so thoroughly it looked almost new—a man seated nearby craned his neck in an awkward confrontational way and growled, "You can go ahead and walk this whole sale and you won't find another one of those." What was the problem? Had someone come by and insulted the piece or laughed at the price, which was high at $450?

"I'm sure you're right," I said, backing away. He'd have to lighten up if he was going to make his day.

When I'm floating through a sale, I often note themes or patterns. Sellers will bring items they know will sell at a particular place. This year wooden toolboxes seemed popular. Old toolboxes have multiple appeals: They were handmade, no two are alike, and they were usually made by the carpenters who would use them so they often contain some clever joinery—a kind of advertising—and were always made of fancy hardwood leftovers. Finally, wooden toolboxes usually have lots of little drawers, divided compartments, and a hinged top that reveals sliding trays—all very appealing to people who collect things and need places to put them.

One toolbox caught my flitting eye. It was in a tent occupied by a couple from Potsdam, New York. The chest was finely made of oak and ash, two woods that imitate each other yet contrast through the direction of the grain—the former straight, the latter often curled. Then the carpenter put one slim drawer made of cherry in the face of the chest.

"I'm a sucker for old tool chests," I said as the dealers approached, and the woman immediately began pointing out features: the hand-planed top, beveled on the edges and a secret bottom drawer that looked like part of the base, but pulled out if you knew where the notch was on the bottom. She knew the key selling points of this chest, and of every other item under their tent, and was prepared to recite them.

"Why do you think he used cherry for that one thin drawer?" I asked.

"I was surprised by that drawer when I refinished it," the man said. "I suppose he wanted it to stand out."

The couple had just returned to the sale circuit after a long hiatus, now that they had retired. They had spent their regular working lives in the grocery business. Their other life in the used network began right after they were married. The woman's mother had given them an old dry sink—a stand for a water pitcher and basin. The man was stripping off the paint, planning to put a hole in the top to hold a potted plant, when he fell in love with the refinished wood and couldn't bring himself to cut into it. Moved by this newfound passion, they invested $50 in the antique business by buying another piece he could refinish and sell. They made a profit and bought another and another, always putting the money back into antiques. Now they had an antique store stocked entirely with goods bought with the successive profits from their initial $50.

The couple said all of the real wheeling and dealing at an antique show took place before the sale began, early in the morning when everyone arrived. "They'll buy something right off the top of your van," the woman said. "They'll see you have something they want and follow you to your spot." She liked Round Lake because you didn't have to compete for that spot. At some sales dealers had to line up early in the morning and, Oklahoma-land-rush style, sprint in and stake out places to put up their tents. At Round Lake they were predetermined.

I left the retired grocers and made my foray into the depths of the sale. It's easy to get lost or overwhelmed at an antique sale; the real competition is not for space but for attention, as dealers will do anything to get you to veer off the makeshift boulevard and spend a few precious seconds among their wares. Some try strange offerings to stop you in your tracks. For instance, a Round Lake booth offered the only complete zebra skin rug I have ever seen. Try finding that on eBay. Another had a sign announcing a rarity, THE CHEESE CASE FROM THE LAST SURVIVING GENERAL STORE IN NEW HAMPSHIRE, essentially a square glass cover atop a circular platform to display a hunk of cheese—an attempt to use setting and provenance to sell something otherwise unremarkable when taken out of its quaint context. Curb appeal in an antique show takes on some rather outlandish qualities.

Antique shows are not limited to antique dealers; the market is open to all. I saw junkers selling heaps of doorknobs and architectural details, cabinetmakers selling repros, an artist who painted new duck decoys and other resemblances of a quaint past, and even a discordant display of welded metal planters and lawn furniture. I had seen them at other sales, so the seller must have found antique sales fruitful. With such variety, it's difficult to adjust your attention, so I find having a quest of sorts useful when at a sale, something to narrow my searchlights. This time I decided it would be a gold, six-sided, open-faced Elgin pocket watch. While I looked for the watch, I knew other compelling things would catch my eye.

You don't really need such a fine-tuned object for your search, but I really wanted to find that exact watch because I had once owned, and lost, one. My father had several pocket watches, each once owned by an ancestor, and when I was sixteen he gave me one, which I carried for three years. I kept it in the watch pocket of my pants, the shallow little pouch above the right pocket of most classic denims. To safeguard it I attached it to my belt with a braided, black leather watch fob. The watch needed winding every day, but it was accurate, thin, and simple. It had belonged to my father's father, so it gave me a direct handhold with my paternal ancestors.

Then one afternoon I pulled on the fob to check the time, and the watch was gone. The constant rubbing of denim on leather had weakened the strap, and the watch had somehow slipped out of my pocket. I checked the inside of my car and retraced my steps that day, but I never found the watch. I have always assumed someone else had spotted it—anything gold is certainly an eye-grabber—and someday it would enter the used goods market. I'd actually be satisfied with one similar to it, if I could find it. Ideally, the watch should have a diamond shape engraved on the back, a place for the owner's initials, and that decoration should be slightly worn away. Then I would know the original had finally come back to me.

It's a long shot, I know, and I've asked lots of dealers about them. They've all seen a hexagonal Elgin but never currently have one on hand. The elusive nature of the watch keeps me enticed. And having it as a quest makes me look at small things. The big things will always catch your eye, like the loud guest at a party, but it takes a different level of attention to pick out the quiet, but interesting, stranger in the corner. At a sale the unnoticed treasures are more apt to be in locked, glass-topped trays. While I could still scan the booths for interesting tool chests and other larger stuff, when I saw tables of trays I was drawn in, not by the dealer's hype but by my own internal discrimination.

Trays are filled with anything less than ten inches long. In a sense, trays of smalls are like antique shops in miniature, and a booth full of them is a Lilliputian antique sale. A tray might contain these things and more in communal chaos: corkscrews, political buttons, pocket knives, straight razors, calipers, Christmas ornaments, locks, brooches, dice, rings, military medals, marbles, lighters, compasses, glass stoppers, folding rulers, nutcrackers, musketballs, thermometers, skeleton keys, crucifixes, playing cards, fossils, beads, derringers, police badges, cufflinks, cigar bands, nail clippers, baby spoons, and watches. Some dealers who specialize in small things will segregate stuff into categories and have separate trays for them, so in looking for a pocket watch all I had to do was find the watch tray. However, most dealers have miscellaneous trays, so you have to have patience to pick through what's there.

As the day warmed at the Round Lake sale, I stopped more often to take advantage of the shade of the tents. I then found out they trapped hot, moist air, and became suffocating. I watched as the dealers moved their chairs out from under their canopies, then, when customers shied from the humid enclaves, began moving goods to the edges to draw people at least to the margins. One dealer put a table on the edge of his tent, and his curb appeal worked for me. Although my eye first caught a golden figurine, I soon saw his display trays. What's more, I could tell he had unusual stuff because of the meso-American pots and terracotta figurines on shelves above them.

The trays contained small artifacts, many dating from ancient Rome and Greece. "Do you have many Greek coins?" I asked, and the man reached under a table and pulled out tray after tray of ancient artifacts. I was thinking about my friend Mike Sham's quest for a Greek coin from the Athens city-state, one featuring Minerva's owl.

"I've had them," he said when I described what I was looking for; everyone had said the same thing about my sought-after watch. "If you find one, it's going to cost you," he added, also a common response. In some ways, it's a mistake to say what you are looking for at a show, because if you admit something has been hard to find even in a mass gathering, you are helping to raise the price in the mind of the seller. It's like being a bad bluffer in poker. If you can't keep a face on, don't bluff.

I'm always a little leery of classical antiquities dealers, because, like Asian antiques, I'm uncertain what I should be seeing. To test him I pointed to the gold figurine, something I assumed was a replica because it was simply sitting in a ziplock bag and not inside a locked case. "What's the provenance on that?" I asked.

"It's a repro; I wish it was real," he said. His quickness in admitting this thickened my trust in his claims for the tiny stamped coins and other bits of the ancient world. The fake had done its work, though. It had attracted me, and I had ended up spending more time in his booth than I had in many of the others.

Antique shows are regional, but some attract sellers and buyers with a broader net. Held three times a year, the antique sale in Brimfield, Massachusetts, just east of Springfield, is arguably the largest in the country, though a sale in Atlantic City makes louder claims to the title, and the monthly sale in Atlanta, Georgia, is a close rival. However, by dint of its popularity, the depth of its offerings in antiques-laden New England, and its fame, I'd give the bragging rights to Brimfield.

The sale actually consists of twenty shows held simultaneously on either side of a one-mile stretch of land along Route 20, the old east–west corridor from Massachusetts to New York before the interstates were built. Most are timed to be open from Tuesday to Sunday on one week in May, July, and September, and together they attract an advertised guesstimate of five thousand dealers. If anyone knows of a bigger sale, I wouldn't want to go to it. This show can fatigue even the toughest scavenger.

The toll collector at the Massachusetts Turnpike booth was so weary of telling people how to get to Brimfield she had taped a handwritten set of directions to the side of her booth. Once off the pike, though, the country roads were not as well engineered for heavy traffic, and jams, either at the beginning or end of the day, were easy to predict. Junk shops, yard sales, and even a flea market were all poised along Route 20, flags flying and signs prominently propped, trying to siphon off the Brimfield-bound. However, all of the vehicles in front and behind mine were single-mindedly negotiating the turns, heading east to the great gathering.

Brimfield, once an agricultural town, sits in a level river valley. I could easily see the congestion and hubbub up ahead, so I pulled into the first parking lot I saw; it cost $4. I could hoof it. I came prepared for it, with good walking shoes and a backpack for gear and to hold a possible buy.

When I handed the attendant a $10 bill, he gave me back a one, then waited, as deadpan as Buster Keaton, just a whiff of a smile under the shade of his straw hat.

"I'll take a few more of those," I said, sensing a gag.

"Just seeing if you were paying attention," he said in a dragging, high-Boston accent. In many ways his little joke characterized the entire Brimfield sale. In a gathering this huge you have to pay attention if you want a deal or want to avoid getting taken by someone. In fact, close attention is your greatest collateral as a buyer and seller.

I started up the broad berm, passing kiosks with free copies of the newspaper, *New England Antiques,* which was using the sale, and its concentrated population, as a chance to increase its circulation and offering an especially thick edition as enticement. I didn't grab one, though, because I'd have to carry it and traveling light is important in this campaign. Strategies varied. Some people were outfitted with puffed-up walking shoes and broad sun hats. Others were pulling children's wagons or pushing carts with wire-sided baskets, and a few even had motorized carts. Some were riding bicycles, the better to scan the entire sale quickly, though they were a bit of a menace when you rounded a corner of a booth and met one coming the other way, brakes squealing and front wheel wavering to find a path around you. Fast and light was the rule of the day, reconnoitering with speed and acuity.

The parking lots were more expensive the closer I got, and they were mostly full, even though it was early and a Thursday, the least attended day of the event. From a distance I could see tents pitched to the horizon, looking like an encampment of Genghis Khan and his hordes. If a band of horsemen had ridden through the aisles, a roiling cloud of dust rising from the hooves of their steeds, I would not have been startled. The closer I got, the more the gigantism of the enterprise struck me, and I admit to a tremor of anticipation. This was an awesome gathering of the scavenger tribe, an endless unfolding of possibilities. This was a place where I could truly get lost.

I reminded myself to slow up, to not look ahead to the rest of the sale but be in one place at one time. You can find anything at Brimfield, from iceboxes to branding irons, if you have the time to canvass for it, the attention span of a prowling cat, and the proper shoe leather. The hugeness of the sale was mirrored in the size of the displays of each dealer, I noted once I plunged in at the very first row. The tents were larger than I'd seen at any sale, as spacious as many antique stores, accompanied by large vans and RVs from as far away as Florida, Georgia, Indiana, and Tennessee. This was a national event, and dealers had assured me it was not uncommon for them to sell $20,000 to $30,000 worth of stuff in four or five days, so it was worth the trip, especially if you were already on the summer circuit.

The dealers also seemed to specialize even more. There were the familiar large tents full of furniture, but another giant tent sheltered only nautical equipment: floats, buoys, big brass ships' gauges, oars, and nets. I supposed that dealer sold lots of stuff to seafood restaurants or oceanfront inns, but how many of these entrepreneurs were apt to file through the sale? A dealer of lamps and light fixtures was set up across from him, most from the great age of electrification at the end of the nineteenth century, next to a seller of stuffed animals and hides. A full alligator skin was draped over two sawhorses. Passing through this menagerie I found a few crafters, a fellow who made folk art carvings and paintings, and another who had found a use for wooden shoe molds, an item as easily found and as compellingly useless as treadle sewing machines. His use was not much more inventive than plant stands: He made coat racks by screwing the wooden shoe shapes, toes pointed up, to a slab of barn wood. I didn't see many people examining them, but he must sell a few. Specialists would tend to do better at a gargantuan sale like Brimfield, because the sheer number of browsers can produce enough buyers interested in their nooks.

Curiously enough, I never saw any dealers I knew, and I wondered if those here were exclusively show dealers—at least I had hoped to see Paul and Millie Ferrara. They had told me they had a space reserved annually on the grounds of an apple farm, and when I found the farm I started looking for Paul's white van. When I couldn't find it, I asked a couple of West Virginia dealers who specialized in old tools if they knew where the Ferraras were.

"Oh yeah, that's Paul's stuff right there," the woman said, pointing to a closed tent, the flaps tied down. "He sets up on Tuesday night, sells on Wednesday, and then goes home on Thursday." Paul sold only to the dealers and early birds on Tuesday and Wednesday, then took a day off to marshal his strength for the weekend. He would be back Friday through Sunday. I had picked the one day on which he took a break from the field.

"I'll tell him someone was looking for him," the woman said, "see if he can guess. I'll tell him it was a woman just to get him going," she laughed. "We set up beside each other every year; we have lots of fun together." Aside from not having to compete for position, having reserved spaces year after year had the corollary advantage of engendering a comfortable camaraderie with your neighbors. Paul Ferrara had cited not wanting to lose his spot at Brimfield as one of the reasons he had not retired or scaled back his participation in the trade. The West Virginia dealers were obviously charged with guarding the Ferraras' wares until Paul and Millie returned.

I left the Ferraras' friends and tried to plot a systematic tour of the sale, though it was a vain attempt, finally. Running through a sale this size was like following a scent in the woods. I would be lucky if I could keep track of which direction the road lay so I could get out of one part of the show and walk to the next. Soon I saw a guy handing out flyers for the Atlantic City show. I overheard his pitch: "We're the biggest in the country. A thousand dealers." That was hardly the biggest sale: If his estimate was accurate, the Atlantic City sale was only one fifth as large as Brimfield. The fact he was canvassing Brimfield was another sign the New Jersey gathering did not live up to his claims. He had a two-foot stack of flyers that he was dragging behind him in a little wheeled basket. He might not even have enough flyers to go around.

I decided to once again focus on my Elgin search and immediately saw a booth with lots of cases; as I approached I saw they contained mostly costume jewelry. The tent was staffed by a cherubic young girl who was modeling as much of the jewelry as she could at once. The big fake pearl earrings and matching necklace looked even more oversized on her miniature features. At another tent, two women, jewelry dealers from Boston, worked on me for a full fifteen minutes, even after I learned that they did not have a watch like the one I wanted. They kept me at the booth, though; one asked me a string of personal questions, such as where I was from, and what I did to make a living, remarking along the way "You must think I'm awfully nosy," while the other tried to sell me a number of watches, such as a railroad watch and a key-wind watch the size of a quarter with a gem-encrusted key. I left with her card.

Another dealer was handling silver, so I checked to see if he had any watches, and I overheard a conversation he was having with what was undoubtedly another dealer. He was arguing that he'd had to pay at least $10 an ounce for all of the samovars, serving trays, and flatware in his tent. "So that's 48 ounces, so it's $480," he said with an edginess suggesting they had been haggling for quite awhile. The other dealer listened to him with his arms crossed over his chest and an expression stuck between neutral and a scowl. One dealer will give another a break on price, but the silver dealer had just sunk to what he considered his basement, and the other man wasn't buying it. Eventually they parted. No deal.

Lou, a dealer who was selling lots of new reproduction samurai swords and knives, the latter kept in small cases that drew me into his tent, said antique sales throughout the country were in a state of transition. Once sales like Brimfield were attended by those who dealt exclusively in antiques, but over the years he had seen vendors with flea market–style goods, generic used and surplus stuff with no provenance and scant age, take over some of the sites. Obviously no one screens sellers to ensure what they will bring fits the reputation of the venue. Lou said 70 percent of the stuff he saw at some sales fell outside what you'd expect to see at a gathering of antique dealers. Like the line between junk shops and antique stores, this distinction was also blurring.

I had noticed that trend during my wanderings at Brimfield. As a rule, the vendors farthest from the road were selling the cheapest, less precious stuff. It made a kind of sense: Those who had been attending the sale the longest, when it was wholly an antique show, would have staked out the spots nearest the road—the best because even if someone did not steer off in your direction, you still got all of the walk-by traffic on the main drag. As you moved down the row, the goods got less distinctive. One Brimfield dealer at the tail end of a lane had a ring of tables covered with smalls. "Everything is $4," he chanted to those poking through them, and buyers were incredulous. "Everything?" one woman asked, holding a flower pot. She put the pot under her arm and picked up another one. What a brilliant idea. Almost nothing on the tables was worth $4, as he mostly had 1960s and 1970s dishes and bric-a-brac. However, if something seized someone with nostalgia or a private significance, few would hesitate to drop less than a $5 bill to get it. It also encouraged browsers, because they thought the seller had to have missed some mark on a vase or a stamp on a cast-iron bank that proved it was worth much more. At $4 such a mistake is a windfall; and despite how savvy, how thorough and knowledgeable, the seller has made that mistake at least once, and will again, they gambled.

Another transition, one I had noticed elsewhere in the used network, was the influx of imported goods, such as a crude box I saw in a wide tent, sitting on a camel saddle with a tag that promised it would make a good footstool.

"That box has a story to tell," a man seated at a table several feet away said, who asked me to read aloud the price on the tag—$145. "I can cut off the 45," he added quickly.

I had been only casually inspecting the box—opening and closing the top—so I wondered why he was so eager to dicker, and dicker so deeply. "What can you tell me about it?"

"Not much, except it's real old. It's probably Afghani, or maybe Chinese." I could tell he didn't know much about the box. However, he'd have to provide more provenance than "maybe Chinese" if he expected to get nearly a hundred for it.

"Asian imports are tough to judge," I said.

He agreed, then added, "I could go $90 if that helps you out." I thanked him for his time and left, suspicious that he had been duped by someone else on the box. At first I had thought it was an American primitive. Maybe he was eager to recoup his losses and shed the dubious piece.

I sallied out into the masses, the heat of the day soaring and percolating with the odors of popcorn and fried sausage sandwiches. One dealer of ceramic gin bottles, imports from Holland, was basking in the heat and attracting attention by sitting shirtless in a battered red and blue amusement park ride capsule and wearing a straw hat on which plastic flowers sprouted as though an invasive species. When I stopped to take his picture, he said, "People have been doing that all day. I'm famous." He lounged back in the capsule as though in a bathtub and smiled. Not everyone was so relaxed, though. Lots of children were at the sale, and by early afternoon many were demonstrating their impatience with their junk-enthralled parents. One young boy was whining like a French ambulance and straining on the end of his mother's arm. "It's fun, David. It's like a treasure hunt," she cooed, but to little effect.

I stopped to talk at length with a Florida dealer of jewelry, as much because he looked friendly with his straw hat, lip-covering moustache, and long ponytail as because his tent, an awning sprouting from the side of his van, looked cool and inviting. He also had lots of display cases. He had been going to sales for twenty years and had occupied the same spot at Brimfield for the last twelve. "You get repeat customers if you stay in the same spot." People come back and look for you there every year. For that reason, he paid the show organizer the $340 annual fee.

The dealer didn't attend some of the other shows, but he wouldn't miss Brimfield. He boycotted the Atlantic City sale, though he admitted it might have changed since the old organizer was gone. The vendor said he stopped going after the organizer had refused to give a refund to a friend who had reserved a spot, but couldn't go because her father died that week. I remembered the man I had seen with the cart full of flyers and guessed he represented the new organizers. He was probably trying to rebuild goodwill among the tribe; maybe someday Atlantic City would host the biggest antique show.

The Florida dealer did go to the monthly show in Atlanta, undoubtedly because it was close to where he lived, but he said it was not as good for jewelry as Brimfield. He also liked Brimfield because of the old friends he found there every year. "We hang out and drink beer," he said, and a group of them would go out for dinner. I could tell he also liked Brimfield because of the sheer volume of business. He had set up folding chairs for us, and we were comfortably chatting in a corner of his tent. However, we were serially interrupted by customers with questions. As I was saying goodbye, yet another a customer stepped in with a question about an ornate silver fruit knife. The dealer examined it with a jeweler's loupe, and then said, "I think it's American." She next handed him a cameo. They appeared to know each other; she was probably one of his repeat customers. I waved and left.

I am convinced that having radically different merchandise is crucial to attracting buyers at a major sale like Brimfield. I practically sailed by dealers with predictable stuff, but I stopped at a Michigan dealer right near the road.

I spiraled into the Michigan dealer's tent because the walls were lined with trays full of rarities and curios: compasses, knives, cudgels, daguerreotypes, tarnished flintlock pistols, and trade hatchets—as much like a museum, or an traveling Victorian collector's cabinet, as any I'd seen. The entire package, though probably not as deliberate as it seemed, was alluring. The tent was dark and dusky, like entering a hidden storeroom of castoffs up to two hundred years old and inhabited by an attendant with a long, gray beard.

It was difficult to concentrate, and my quest for a pocket watch evaporated as my eyes lapped up the sight of such a fascinating, one-of-a-kind assemblage, all arranged geometrically in wooden-framed glass-topped trays, the contents so skillfully wedged in they could hang from the side of his tent without anything shifting to the bottom. While my headlong survey of Brimfield ground to a halt, and I slowly picked through the dealer's display, I overheard him showing a man, who I later learned was a nineteenth-century photograph collector, a tattered cardboard photograph album, the kind in which snapshots fit into little pasted-in corners. I drifted over and stood nearby.

"Here he is, again," he said, and pointed to a picture of a black woman dressed in an evening gown and striking a back-arching, mock-elegant pose. He flipped to the front of the album and a thin, similar-looking African-American man was staring back at me. At first I thought they must have been brother and sister, but then it sunk in. The seller had bought the album in a box lot at an auction outside of Chicago, and after analyzing the sequence of pictures he had deduced it had once belonged to a black entertainer from the 1930s, a female impersonator who had practiced his craft in the clubs on the South Side.

The album was a frank look at a slice of American life that wouldn't have been chronicled if the man hadn't been an amateur photographer. Besides pictures of himself, he had some of his fellow entertainers, strippers, comedians, and jazz and blues musicians. A few, the vendor said, were later famous. I was impressed with how much the dealer was able to read into the collection of photographs, the way he made the anonymous man come to life.

The dealer hoped to have enough time to study the album more completely, perhaps finding an expert who could help him with identification. However, I knew he would give up the opportunity if the photograph collector could be persuaded to take up the quest. The collector was suitably impressed with the album, but it was outside of his collecting interest. He turned his attention to a few daguerreotypes in the cases on the tent walls.

I started to ask the dealer about a case with a brace of ancient dueling pistols, but we were continually interrupted, so I moved on and returned in the afternoon when the sale was perceptibly waning.

"So what do you collect?" the dealer asked as soon as I came back. I mentioned a few things that appealed to me, and he brought out some examples from deep in his cases. All were of the finest sort; for instance, when I mentioned that I liked compasses, he set two eighteenth-century compasses on top of his counter, with sun-dials built in. "All of the paper is original," he said about the North-South-East-West quadrant printed on the bottom.

"What do you collect?" I responded, not wanting to get into a dicker over the compasses. They were each priced at close to a thousand dollars.

"I don't collect anything, but I only buy things I wouldn't mind keeping." If he only stocked things that he found compelling, then he could put a high price on them and be content to keep them if no one bit. He only dealt in smalls, so no one thing would take up enough room to demand he discount it. No wonder I had found his tent mesmerizing. I was entering a collection stamped by his personality and unified by his own passion.

Although it might seem counterintuitive, don't go to an antique sale looking for a bargain. The simplest of economic principles would seem to suggest that a large gathering of sellers would produce competition and subsequent discounts. However, secondhand culture undermines most assumptions of this sort. A show is a beauty contest in which the contestants are innumerable, and the judges never get to see them all. It is also not unlike a county fair, where proud owners bring their finest crop of castoffs. It is part camping trip, part reunion. Selling happens as a by-product.

Does a sale have to be the biggest to be the most impressive, the most thrilling? Size can be counterproductive. For the local economy, more buyers and sellers is a boon, producing its own lucrative by-products; at Brimfield I even saw impromptu packing and shipping services set up to help customers spirit away their finds to distant places. Other mainstream business, such as gas stations, restaurants, hotels, and other service businesses, surely benefited from the centrifugal movement of money around one otherwise drowsy town. All the way there and back I noticed a keen awareness on the part of all businesses that they were in the path of a great migration.

However, dealers were less sanguine about their swelling ranks. "You can get too big," Gary Guarno said about the Brimfield show. He used to go to the Atlanta show, too, where he made thousands each day. Then the owner added a huge building, and the extra competition reached the threshold of diminishing returns. "If a show gets too big, it can kill you," Gary said. In contrast to the centralized, bigger-is-better new retail world, the biggest do not gobble up the smaller competition. Likewise, Paul and Millie Ferrara actually preferred another sale later in the summer, the Madison/Bouckville sale in upstate New York. Part of the appeal was it was smaller and more manageable. Coincidentally, it, too, was on old Route 20, hundreds of miles and another state away.

As traditional downtowns have been replaced by suburban retail developments, the old national byways have been bypassed by a half century of super-highway building. In many parts of the country these towns and roads, relics themselves, are secondhand versions of our culture. While they are now being revisited and reused, larger corporations are not moving into these off-the-beaten-track areas; instead, many hundreds of micro-businesses arrive, with not more than a van's worth of merchandise. Together they make up a whole larger than the sum of its parts—each the philosophical descendant of the pack peddler and the traveling huckster. They have reinvented the vital, traditional marketplace, one that is even more mobile than ever before.

Chapter Fifteen

❧

Flea Markets

I T'S HARD TO KNOW WHICH CAME FIRST, the antique show or the flea market, as both operate on the itinerant marketplace model and like junk shops and antique stores have begun to spill into each other. Whenever possible, flea marketeers will try to pass off whatever has joined their cavalcades as antique or collectible. One major difference between the flea market and antique show is frequency. An antique show might be held, at most, three times a year, while flea markets are held monthly or even weekly. Having a sale this often in one place leads to a slow degradation of the market, or at least to the transition to surplus that the Brimfield dealer had noted.

The heyday of the flea market was perhaps twenty years ago, but they are still flourishing in the rural expanses. The used goods that most flea markets offer are not rarified enough to draw customers from afar, as will a nationally known antique sale. Perhaps because of this, flea markets are not quite as popular in the Northeast, where the trade in antiques is paramount. Called swap-meets on the West Coast, flea markets there have been adopted by the Mexican-American and Asian-American communities as surrogates for the open-air markets with which they are familiar and have been turned into farmers' markets as well as castoff delivery systems. Likewise, Florida hosts huge swap meets to handle the household goods of the elderly who move there, and then pass on. However, flea markets are at their most viable and vigorous in the Midwest and South.

I began going to flea markets in the 1970s, and my favorite was Michelangelo's, a sprawling blanket of junk near Coitsville, Pennsylvania, a real excursion for my beat-up Buick, a car I was never comfortable driving more than thirty miles in one direction. Nevertheless, on the third Sunday of the month, late spring to early fall, I would check the fluids, hoses, belts, and tires, add some oil if the lifters were ticking in the six-cylinder engine, and take the long two-lane country road to the market.

This was before flea markets became entrenched establishments, and they were truly transient affairs. Eventually, once their popularity was full-blown, flea market organizers built giant pole barns to house permanent booths, charging more for spaces inside than outside because a seller inside did not need to schlep wares to and fro. Even after these fortified positions were in place, such as the market in West Middlesex, Pennsylvania, where a huge building could be seen from Interstate 80, FLEA MARKET written in twelve-foot letters on the roof, I continued to attend them. However, I preferred those vendors who set up outside. They were much more likely to offer bargains and unusual finds, as their stuff was usually fresher to sale and had to be boxed and trucked at the end of the day.

Michelangelo's was the Ur–flea market, the seminal gathering of junk, set in an enormous dusty hayfield, one that undoubtedly a farmer had abandoned to this new crop, this new source of revenue, a homemade billboard the only investment. I'd park in self-described rows as orderly as corn on either side of the lane from the road, then walk the rest of the way to the middle of the field where the tables sat. These were quick and impromptu setups. Unlike antique shows, they seldom had tents, and some didn't even have tables, just blankets spread on the ground held down at the corners by the heaviest items or stones picked up nearby. Others would simply set boxes on the ground, and not bother to unpack them, or put prices on anything in them. These boxes would often contain construction hardware and tools, and I loved pawing through the oily boxes looking for something I could use. Dickering with these vendors was quick and to the point. I'd hold up something and ask the guy in charge, "What do you want for this?" He would cite a price, a dollar for a wrench or screwdriver, for instance. If you offered fifty cents, he would either shake his head and look away or wince—there had to be some sign of resistance—and split the difference with you. Everything was so cheap very little ceremony attended the haggle.

I had already discovered yard sales, though, so nothing could be cheap enough for me. My budget didn't allow me to be more than a nickel-and-dime scavenger. I went only to Michelangelo's because of the concentration of stuff and because you were more apt to find something unusual or really useful there. Flea marketeers make a profit by gleaning curbsides, garage sales, and estate sales and bringing the choicest finds to your attention. Attending a flea market is simply a shortcut to what it might take many weekends to locate by simply plundering yard sales.

I'm sure I must have picked up lots of interesting stuff at Michelangelo's, though I was usually on the hunt for books, as they were always as cheaply bought there as at a yard sale. Flea marketeers, and antique dealers, don't usually have the depth of knowledge necessary to price used books accurately, and when they have to buy them as part of a larger lot of merchandise, they try to move them cheaply. There are few things heavier to lug around than boxes of books. My best modern first editions, from Steinbeck's *Of Mice and Men* to Evelyn Waugh's *Brideshead Revisited*, have come from flea markets, books left in boxes under a table coated in dull carving knives, souvenir ashtrays, wooden poodles, glass shoes, manicure sets, ceramic toothpick cups, and dinner plates printed with a 1958 calendar.

Other than books, the best finds I ever made at Michelangelo's were much more expensive than I normally could afford, but they are still with me. One was a small kitchen table, with one leaf, and a battered coat of celery-green paint. It was solid oak, though, so I paid $10 (the seller had asked $15), and, once refinished, it has served as a kitchen table, plant table, and computer table in the more than twenty places I have lived over the last two decades. It now needs refinishing again, but I might simply allow the next inheritor to refurbish it. I certainly got my $10 worth of use out of it.

The other find was a barber's cabinet. As much as I like toolboxes, I'm also fond of little wall cabinets, likely because they are handy for keeping some of the stuff I collect. I remember agonizing over this one, though, the first of the half dozen I now have. Unlike the kitchen table, I didn't really need it and wouldn't have normally spent the few dollars the man wanted for it, a guy who specialized in ceramic figurines. I didn't ask, but he probably trash-picked the thirty-inch-tall, sixteen-inch-wide cabinet when a barber remodeled and thought those who bought his figurines might be drawn to the cabinet as a display case.

I think the cabinet reminded me of the old downtown barbershops to which my father used to take me when I was a child, when he stopped cutting my hair himself. I was fascinated by the barber's tools, and I became familiar with them through their sounds: the distant airplane growl of the electric clippers, the sound of hair oils being slapped on his hands, and the decisive rasp and click of the scissors. All came from inside two cabinets on either side of the mirror; I could hear him open and close them, but I got to see them only when he turned me toward the mirror to show me his handiwork. When I opened the cabinet at Michelangelo's and closed it, I heard again that satisfying click of a chrome, Art Deco spring-loaded latch.

So I bought the cabinet, though I have never been able to figure out a satisfying use for it. The shelves were sagging, the curved wood veneer was cracked, and the finish was grimy with decades of cigarette smoke. Not until many years later did I finally give the cabinet the attention it deserved, but only after it had served for years in many different capacities: whatnot cabinet, stationery supply storage, wineglass cupboard, and spice rack. If something should be refinished, I'm better off doing it immediately before it starts being used. However, as many uses as the cabinet has found, it has never been fully adaptive to one of them. The Art Deco design was so unlike anything else I usually scavenge that it never looked right except when hanging above a 1939 RCA floor model cabinet radio I had saved from my grandmother's attic. What's more, the oval glass in the door was too small to make it a very effective display case; you could never see more than about a quarter of what was inside.

Flea markets yield those kinds of finds, useful items that need lots of work, like the green kitchen table, or white elephants that never seem to settle into your life, like the barber's cabinet—now sitting in the back of a closet, waiting for my next idea about its use. Flea markets are also a place where the market appeal of a category of castoff is given a trial run. The former Valley View Department Store in Brookfield, Ohio, stretched for a tenth of mile and housed both an antique mall and a flea market, with a clear line of demarcation between them. The antique mall was delineated in rows, with signs identifying Avenues A through L. The avenues ended at a bank of glass display cases, and on the other side was the flea market, with some more-or-less permanent marketeers and others who came and went. The transition from art pottery and fiestaware to knit toilet paper roll covers and "collectible" dining table placemats was stark when physically reinforced. Also, the antique mall side was void of actual merchants; the avenues were broken up into booths overseen by a pair of über-dealers who sat at the front. However, the flea market side was full of marketeers, each eager to tell you why what they had was useful or valuable.

Flea marketeers will provide a rationale for why their goods are worth buying, because it's not apparent at first glance. The market is a kind of testing ground for used merchandise, a place where proto-collectibles, things not coveted enough to be scarfed up by antique dealers, find their niche market. For instance, at the Valley View market I saw a guy standing within a ring of tables covered with wooden wine crates full of eight-track tapes. The dealer, who proudly sported a T-shirt printed with the cover from a Buffalo Springfield album, told me the cumbersome tapes, infamous for easily tangling and garbling, were collected by people who restored muscle cars from the 1960s and 1970s, Pontiac GTOs with 427–cubic-inch engines and Mach V Ford Mustangs with four-barrel carburetors. In a bid for absolute authenticity, the owners of these growl-ing gasaholics wanted tapes to play in their factory-equipped stereos and eagerly snapped up Steppenwolf or Cream tapes long set aside for cassettes and now compact discs. I found it humbling that the medium for the sound track of my youth was on its way to becoming as quaint as wax cylinder recordings.

So that's the flea marketeer's gamble: Hope that what you have will eventually become collectible or at least worth more than you paid for it and might someday migrate into the antique business. Research is seldom useful, and what is worth $20 one season might fall out of favor and be hard to give away a year later. For instance, in the 1980s, beer cans were the hottest flea market collectible. The collecting craze got increasingly more complicated as beer companies fed it by issuing special editions of beer cans, either with older designs or featuring professional athletes. Before long a beer can collector could look for hundreds of varieties.

There's no accounting for what will flip a collector's switch, but be-cause I never caught the beer can bug, I was able to judge it objectively, albeit a bit cynically, from the outside. From a scavenger's perspective, beer can collectors were a real boon. The collectors craved genuine garbage: beverage packaging. Taking a cue from other aspects of the trade trafficking in retail residue, the trash-pickers went into overdrive and soon flea market vendors had ancient beer cans for sale, salvaged from

God knows where, and began pricing them according to condition and rarity. An entire class of collectible was created overnight. Cans with detachable pull tabs were worth more than those with tabs that remained attached. Actual tin cans opened by church keys were even more valuable. Eventually, cans in the finest condition were those that had been drained by punching a small hole in the bottom, leaving the top untouched and opened with the collector in mind. Still other arcania must have applied to can collecting that I never learned.

Before long, early beer cans surfaced; it was inevitable. These oldest cans had cone-shaped tops, in imitation of bottles, with screw tops. Where did these cans come from? How did something designed to be imminently discarded survive the decades to reemerge when finally most valuable? You can always count on the ability of scavengers to root out even the most humble castoff when a need arises for it. I heard a variety of tales about their sources. Old cans had been found inside a demolished wall, tossed in by workers who built it. They were discovered in a barn, in the back of the grain bin. They were stacked in the back of a closed grocery, old stock that was never sold or discarded. Now their time had come, and they had found their way, with the magnetism possessed by junk, to the place where they were prized.

Slowly this collecting craze abated. Maybe the market became glutted. Maybe people found the multiplication of types of cans being produced or uncovered too daunting to collect, or if collected, to display. Perhaps people grew bored, and the cans once again simply became what they always had been, empty containers with little to recommend them but as representations of a moment in retail history. The cans never entered the antiques trade, not even the oldest, and perhaps that contributed to their waning. Only flea marketeers bolstered the interest in it; the appeal did not ascend the food chain. Perhaps someday a few collections will be uncovered in boxes in a basement, and the fad will enjoy a resurgence. In the meantime the market has drained away.

Some new retailers have recognized that "collectible" is a self-defined concept, and like Ty Warner of Beanie Babies fame, companies like the Franklin Mint, which makes "limited edition" replicas of classic cars or plates featuring pictures of pop stars, also feed flea markets. If people indeed do collect the output of these companies—and they must because the Franklin Mint puts out a steady stream of advertisements for the next "rarity"—flea markets are natural for such quests. Flea marketeers do not require price guidebooks for a category of merchandise. They price what they have on a trial-and-error basis or based on whatever rumors of value are on the circuit. If people are buying dinner plates with the portraits of characters from *The Wizard of Oz*, marketeers will find them. Companies might make five hundred or a half million of them, and if a market develops, someone will cart them to the nearest flea market.

Flea marketeers sell anything, for sure, but they must have an eye for the offbeat or for marginal memorabilia. Because the stuff they sell generally doesn't have the collateral of great age, it has to offer another feature. Newer tourist trinkets are a common item in flea markets. These are some of the most curious of castoffs, because their entire reason for being owned is that the purchaser wanted to buy something to preserve an experience, to tangibly capture a moment spent in a place, without considering any other intrinsic values of the object. So if the vacation has been to the beach, a napkin holder made from scallop shells appears to be the perfect artifact, or if the trip involved a tour of historical battlefields, a pot-metal cannon will make the perfect paperweight, though you've never truly needed to weight down paper.

Once home, and after a number of years, a winnowing spring cleaning turns up more tourist clutter than you ever can remember buying and out goes a parade of kitsch to the yard sale or curb, followed by a vow never to accumulate such useless junk again. These items do not ever disappear, of course, though you are able to purge them from *your* life. Scavenged and washed up into the secondhand network, they end up on a flea market table, among dozens of fellow refugees from cross-country trips and forays into the Grand Canyon. Now they are valuable because of—or despite—their homely attributes. You have to fall in love with someone else's souvenir for personal reasons. Perhaps more than any other arm of the used delta, the things run aground on the banks of a flea market are the most uncertain of value.

If what flea marketeers sell is so ephemerally valuable, so risky and volatile, how then do they make a living at what they do? They don't. Most marketeers are engaged in the trade as a sideline; they are top-of-the-line, part-time scavengers. "We don't need to do this," a man told me at Stan's Flea Market. He and his wife had a tent crammed with stuff. He complained she had too many smalls, and he had a 25-foot box truck equally full. He'd pull about half the stuff off, and then they'd sit at a table with a parasol, smoking cigarettes. "It's something to do on the weekend. We do it for the people we meet."

Stan's was north of Saratoga Springs, on Route 9, the old two-lane highway from New York City to the Adirondacks. The market was set up on the grounds of what had been some sort of amusement park, using some of the buildings that persisted: a decrepit relic of a miniature gingerbread house, a wannabe South Seas thatched hut, and a collapsing building flanked by silos topped with conical roofs, like the towers on a Camelot castle. Other buildings were so far gone they were not used by the marketeers, and they stood, roofs sunken in by rain or falling trees, in the midst of an outcropping of pipe-framed tents. It looked for all the world like a ruined village occupied by marauders.

It was hard to tell exactly what the place had been used for, but it certainly felt like it had been abandoned in the 1970s. Not long after, the used merchandise peddlers moved into the vacuum, organized by someone named Stan. The only other transformation of the site was the billboard-sized sign, over which another sign had been nailed, STAN'S FLEA MARKET. I could still see the old sign underneath, a truncated FOR . . . Had it been a theme park called the "Enchanted FORest" or "Sherwood FORest"?

On the Saturday I visited, many of the marketeers had their tents or shacks walled in with plastic drop cloths, as a driving mid-morning rain had all but closed the Saturday and Sunday gathering. All of the open-air merchants, itinerants without shelter, had covered their tables with the plastic drop cloths, held in place with large yellow alligator clamps. I peeked through the flaps of a couple of tents and was surprised to see they were full of merchandise, though the sellers were gone, perhaps for the entire day, having pulled out by 11:00 A.M. in face of the torrents and the subsequent dearth of customers. Nothing much here was so precious it was worth guarding or packing and then unloading again if Sunday proved drier.

By afternoon the weather cleared, and only eight marketeers were there; normally there would be fifty or more. I slogged across near-ankle-deep water in the field to reach peddlers still holding out against the elements. One had installed himself in a pavilion made of slab wood, the rounded side cuts of logs left over from milling lumber. The open-sided building was topped with a conical roof, a fanciful touch from the days of Robin Hood. It appeared to be an ideal shelter for someone selling trays of smalls.

The marketeer was named Rick, and he specialized in jewelry. Like many flea market denizens, he had a full-time job. He owned and operated something he called a food-o-rama, a hybrid grocery store and restaurant, and had started a used goods sideline after running a weekly flea market at his store. One of the regular sellers handled jewelry, and Rick noticed he made about $300 to $400 a day, a roaring success by flea-market standards. Anyone who did that well at Stan's, even on a sunny day, would be prosperous indeed.

One day the man confided in Rick that he had cancer, asking whether the grocery store owner wanted to buy him out, and so Rick took a chance and bought a warehouse full of jewelry. When Rick got inside, he discovered it had been burglarized and ransacked; he found a pile of jewelry on the warehouse floor that he had to shovel into the back of a truck. "It took me two years to sort it all out," he said.

Now Rick also ran a wholesale auction for castoffs of a newer variety, stuff left over from failed businesses or that simply didn't sell. He was offering some of that merchandise at Stan's too, mostly cheap toys. "I figure if I sell $100 of that stuff," he said, "and a couple of these," passing his hand over the jewelry trays, "I'll do okay." It was unlikely, I thought. The tattered pavilion had gaping holes in the roof. He was sopping up water from the counters, and the black velvet display trays were juicy with rain.

"New York state sucks," Rick said about its offering of flea markets, declaring the Midwest as much better. I concurred. "I have to drive an hour and a half to get here," he said; his home was in the middle of the state, near the Finger Lakes. Rick even disparaged the quality of the marketeers he met, saying "the old guys," meaning those who had the best spots by dint of having been the longest attendees, "were basically antique dealers." Here he pointed toward the main alley of tents at Stan's, those that were closed. Most of the others he called "junk sellers," who "sell dishes and stuff." I expected to see such a range of merchandise at a flea market, so I wasn't sure what point he was making. Where did he situate himself between those two poles?

Rick's jewelry and toys were essentially surplus, new but discarded stock, so perhaps that's the category of goods he expected to see at flea

markets. He pointed out other smalls he sold, claiming to have thousands
of items like them. They included cigarette lighters, pocketknives, and
political buttons—one boosting Franklin D. Roosevelt for governor. If
you are a collector of political buttons, you'd really have to know your
field well to buy at a flea market. A marketeer once told me nearly every
significant political button ever made has been reproduced in the thousands. Reputable companies mark the back with "copy," but you can't
trust all the buttons to have not been made by counterfeiters. Rick's
Roosevelt button was pretty badly rusted, so it was likely authentic, and
he said, "If that was in better shape it would be worth $100." However,
scratches and rust can be artificially added, too.

These things were in display cases, so they weren't rusting more in
the day's rain. I poked through the rest; Rick had what at first I
thought was a selection of coins. As I looked more closely, I saw one
penny was soldered to the head of a nail so you could fasten it to the
floor and, as a tag read, "watch the fun." Another copper piece had a
pair of breasts on one side and buttocks on the other (head and tails).
It opened up to reveal a cigarette lighter inside. I supposed Rick could
have been characterized as neither an antique dealer or junker, but as a
novelty peddler.

Rick pulled out red plastic tubs from under the counter to show me
more jewelry, in ziplock plastic bags. "That's a platinum pin," he said,
holding up a bag to what light there was on this gray day. "Did you
ever see abalone pearls?" he added, pronouncing it as if it rhymed with
Stallone. "If they are out in the sun, they melt." He had several bags of
them, big yellow, brown, or black teardrops.

I asked Rick about one of the few kinds of collectible jewelry I knew
about. "Do you have any Old Pawn turquoise?" Made of turquoise and
coin silver, Old Pawn is authentic Native American jewelry. The pieces
were made for personal use rather than for trade. It is so-called because
it usually entered the wider market through pawn shops and is the most
highly prized of all turquoise jewelry.

"Somewhere," Rick said, and he dug through another tub, coming
up with bags of earrings set with unworked nuggets of turquoise. I realized
he didn't know what I'd ask for. I reminded myself to find out if abalone
actually produced multi-colored pearls the size of scallions and whether
they melted in the sun.

Chain-smoking through his grizzled beard, Rick said, "I used to go around to yard sales to find stuff, but now I have too much. I'm forty-three now, and I'd like to sell out and retire. I wish I could find a reputable auctioneer," he added, "and that's not easy."

"What do you mean by reputable?" I asked. I wondered why he didn't just run his stock through his own auction at the food-o-rama.

"Someone who would really advertise this stuff, and sell it." Surely Rick knew that there wasn't enough interest in surplus jewelry and smalls on which any auctioneer could hang a whole auction. Likewise, no one would meticulously list individual pieces or types of gemstone and costume jewelry in a catalogue or flyer, let alone photograph more than a sample. A veteran auctioneer would know the regular buyers would be bored at a sale dominated by jewelry, and that it would be nearly impossible, no matter how much advertising, to pack a house with jewelry buyers.

The rain picked up again, and Rick began moving jewelry out of the way of the gaps in the roof. As I turned to trot through the rain to my truck, I called out, "How'd you get so lucky to get the pavilion?"

"I don't know!" he said with a big grin.

One of the reasons that flea markets might be past their nadir is many marketeers aspire to the status of antique seller, wanting potentially greater profit margins and status. A row of shacks sided with graying wood outside of Meissner's Auction house in Lebanon, New York, made a grand promise with a weathered sign MANY ANTIQUE DEALERS IN ONE LOCATION, but they were permanent flea marketeers. Inside the row of buildings were tables of undistinguished and indistinguishable dishware. At first I thought the building had been a closed motel, but the inside walls were unfinished, and the ceiling was so sloped I couldn't stand up in the back. Whatever had been planned here had been abandoned, so of course junkers had siphoned into it. Perhaps the place had originally housed antique dealers, but the quality of goods had eroded with the slow deterioration of the half-completed shacks.

The hovels were so dismal one marketeer had moved his stuff onto makeshift plywood-and-crate tables outside in the autumn sunshine. He was talking to a neighboring seller who was offering homemade, cut-out and varnished plywood silhouettes of moose. While I am convinced, as Trink said, that we don't need more stuff, that we have enough stuff, I am absolutely certain the world does not need more plywood silhouettes of animals, cowboys leaning against the wall, and women bent over, bloomers to the open air. Still, his neighbor was excitedly giving him advice on how he might sell his four-foot moose. In truth, most of the stuff both of them had to sell was pretty desperate.

They did have some examples of one kind of dishware I had been seeing steadily filtering into the flea market arena: blue and white plates, bowls, cups, saucers, and serving dishes featuring Currier & Ives prints. Because of the quaint subjects of the prints—Currier & Ives intended them to elicit nostalgia when they were first etched in the nineteenth century—you might be fooled into thinking the plates were antique or at least worthy of collecting. However, if you are over thirty, you'd know they were not so old; they had been given away as a premium by the old A&P supermarket chain in the 1960s.

My mother very deliberately gathered a full set of those dishes, a piece at a time, whenever she bought groceries. It was a terrific deal. You got a set number of dishes at a greatly reduced price with an order of groceries, and I was always interested as a child to see which print a different type of dish bore. Dinner plates were decorated with horse-drawn wagons and plows, while children in flying scarves skated on the bottom of the soup bowls. My mother got them all, every gravy boat, meat platter, and dessert plate, and we used them exclusively for years, until enough had been broken to coerce my father into replacing them with a set bought at a department store. I know a box full of the surviving pieces resides in my mother's attic.

Now the old promotional giveaway dishes were resurfacing in the used merchandise system. One dealer at the New Lebanon flea market had a cup and saucer for sale, with a card noting: "Have 61 pieces." I saw a single plate priced for $30, probably fifty times what it had cost my grandmother. Since our family had eaten off them every day throughout the 1960s, you might expect me to be moved to buy them, that such familiarity would add another layer of nostalgia to the covered bridges and steamboats depicted on them. Instead, in seeing the print on the dinner plate, I remembered every long, tedious dinner I had to endure as a child, my plate still partially full of boiled potatoes, a staple in almost every meal, and my least favorite food. I would push the tasteless white pulp around on my plate under the disapproving eyes of my parents, trying to wear them away through friction, occasionally dispensing with a partial forkful. The designs reminded me how I longed to see them, on a clean plate, the loathsome potatoes gone.

So every memory trigger is not so useful to the used seller. While others might have a better association with the plates, one that would bring the impossible prices some of these marketeers had optimistically pinned to them, all I had to recall was the impatience of a child wanting to bolt from the dinner table. My best remembrance of that first super-market chain was its fragrant "Eight o' Clock" coffee that you ground right in the store, which was my job whenever I went there with my mother. As it was, the musty smell of the dismal shanties, many of them vacant, prevented my further exploring them.

Many flea markets come grafted to an auction house, as though after each auction, when those truly antique items had been trucked away by dealers, the lesser quality fruits could not bear traveling very far from the tree. The White House in Niskayuna, New York, was a permanent second-hand goods emporium over a periodic auction in the basement. Above ground space in the former toy store was rented by people who sold collectibles and junk. When I was there, only a few of the stalls were staffed; one seller was explaining to a customer that, while the building was called the White House Antique Market, "It's really a flea market." She had just sold a fine example of that kind of goods: a doll's-head facial tissue dispenser. Tissue sprouted from the top of the head, along with multi-colored hair. It was proof positive that the White House was an epicenter of used kitsch of an indeterminate age—the kind of stuff re-covering drug addicts make to ease their pangs in rehab. The buyer was one half of an equally unorthodox couple. They were dressed in a post-industrial, post-punk fashion, with hair dyed the color of lollipops, and wearing long coats with hand-painted designs on the backs. "Isn't it cute?" the young woman said to another customer, the head cradled in her black-fingernailed hands, her voice lifting with purest pleasure. There truly is a buyer for anything.

Such stuff might be the trademark of flea markets, but the buyers and sellers are not immune from the other forces in play, such as provenance. In another booth at the White House, I saw a homemade cabbage slicer, a cobbled-together affair some tinkerer who really liked sauerkraut had made from tin cans—a protective shield over the blade still bore the design from the tomato can from which it was fashioned. The seller wanted $15 for the crotchety old device.

I had seen the slicer before; it had been offered in a general merchandise Talk of the Town auction. The dealer, an effeminate man on the cusp of middle age, was hovering nearby, so I asked him where he had found it to see what he'd say. "I don't know if it works. I just like how it looks. It came from a place in Ballston Spa," he said. That's where the Talk of the Town auction was held, so the guy hadn't lied. Instead he had kept his response ambiguous to suggest the item had come from a house or perhaps a business. He knew that provenance still mattered, even at this level, even one ever so slight.

Unlike antique shows, which grow over the years and become annual institutions, flea markets rise and fall, a kind of junk regime that takes over a place, then wanes. And like any regime, flea markets have a tough time getting started, and sometimes have to make strange allies with surplus new goods sellers and others marginal to the trade in used stuff, in order to establish a base. Some, like the enormous Trader Jack's Flea Market outside of Pittsburgh, Pennsylvania, will undoubtedly last for decades, but even Michelangelo's is long gone, and an established flea market in Austintown, Ohio, had vaporized before I tried to attend it a few years later. Flea markets require a critical mass of marketeers in order to be maintained, and when they start to slip, the markets suffer a quiet death of inattention.

A flea market was trying to get established in a pole barn used as a hall by a fraternal organization south of Whitehall, New York, just across the border from Rutland, Vermont. When I arrived at mid-Saturday, when any flea market should be in high gear, I found only a hodgepodge of dealers at four-by-eight-foot foldout tables arranged in rows. Most of the tables were empty, unrented. The sale had a grill/kitchen setup, with coffee and bottled water for a dollar. One hulking marketeer was demolishing a hamburger at a nearby table. Above his head hung an electric bingo board. The hall was used for other money-making ventures on the other days of the week.

The prospects for this flea market getting a foothold in Whitehall were dim. Not only had it not attracted many sellers or buyers, but the genuine used sellers were staying away, for the most part. I gave the small sale the once-over and saw two women sitting with a table of homemade muffins and cookies, the products of their best recipes being largely ignored by the handful of shoppers; a crafter offering, but not selling, beaded whatnots; and a gemstone dealer with pails of polished stones, also looking pretty lonesome. MAKE ME AN OFFER—CLOSE OUT SALE, read a sign at his table. I thought back to Rick at Stan's who was also looking to get out of the jewelry and bauble business, and then to the Florida dealer of antique jewelry at Brimfield who was doing a proverbial land-office business, and then to the display cases of museum quality adornments at the Hughes auction. It seemed that jewelry certainly gets harder to sell as it moves down the food chain. Part of the intrinsic value of jewelry is a degree of rarity, so when it sheds that quality, much of its appeal evaporates. Simple adornment can carry a castoff only so far.

All of the buying traffic, what there was, had migrated to the other end of the hall where a team of true flea marketeers was roosting. They had taken advantage of the mostly empty space and had spread out to four tables. Two of them had signs taped to the front: 25 CENTS EVERY-THING ON THIS TABLE. A dozen or more customers were orbiting the table, probably more than had sniffed at the baked goods or fingered the polished stones. Here people were prying open paperback novels and out-of-date textbooks and fondling a true junk cornucopia tumbling out of a cardboard box rather than a horn-shaped basket: curious bottles barely cleaned from the dump from which they had been obviously dug, brass bottle openers, a ceramic elephant, hand-painted terra-cotta flower pots, bell jars without bases, lids of casserole dishes, a Matchbox car, a clutch of magnets, and a tower of decorated cookie tins. Any of these, if you could find a use for them, or needed one, was worth a quarter.

The marketeers in charge of this installation were sitting at the other tables, covered with a few better items, all unpriced. I always find that a bit of a disappointment, whether at a flea market or a yard sale. First, it is usually a sign that the seller is probably going to want a high price for something if you ask. In fact, if prices were stuck on the items, you'd probably examine a couple, catch on that things were overpriced, and move on to another table. What's more, I like to ponder a piece and its price together, privately, to make the connection between whatever value has been placed on it and its appeal to me, prior to working myself toward a dicker. Not having a price also suggests the seller might ask you to make an offer, always a risky maneuver because then the dickering is going the other way.

One other verified marketeer sat nearby, further accounting for the huddle of buyers at this end of the hall. He had a small arsenal of fishing rods and reels, a cigar box of lures, and another box full of knives. He also had spread to more tables and had the middle one dedicated to long cardboard boxes, filled with index card files. These were postcards, alphabetized by town, so Bennington, Vermont; the Bronx; and Boston were in the Bs.

When the marketeer saw me looking at them, he moved a stack of albums with even more cards so I could pick through them more easily. I was looking for one made from an old photograph of a house I used to own in Ballston Spa, New York. Not long after I had moved in, a woman in her nineties, Gladys, who had been born in the house and lived in another next door, had given me the photo, keeping the postcard that had been made from it for herself. It showed two sleighs sitting in front of the house, herself a baby in the back seat of one. Written in her shaking hand, in pencil, at the bottom, was "Coldest Winter on Record, 1904," but that was not all she wanted me to know about the past. Gladys explained who was in the picture, pointed out the trees that still stood nearby, then only saplings, and told me the matched horses were named Jack and Jill. Gladys had wanted the picture to tie me to the history of the house, which was partially her history, her life, so that something of her would remain there.

I had the photograph matted and framed, and when I sold the house I gave it to the new owners, along with a written description of everything Gladys had said about it. She had died three years before. Ever since I had looked for a copy of the postcard for myself, but I had looked in vain. This marketeer didn't have one either. They had been locally produced for only a short period of time.

I turned my attention to people selling cheap, new merchandise and collectibles. Like the antiques trade, these were mostly imports from Asia; however, these goods don't pretend to be old—just "collectible." Here the attraction for the buyers was beyond me, so I talked to one who was looking over ceramic figures. "They're going to be worth real money if you hang onto them," said a woman so thin she looked like a crane peering into the water as she looked down at the goods on the table.

"I've been trying to get my son-in-law interested in collecting Franklin Mint, but he doesn't get it." And honestly, I don't either, though I didn't say so to her; she seemed so confident. Of course if you hang onto anything long enough, several generations, for instance, it will become rare and valuable. However, I hoped that she didn't expect to see much of a return on her investment in marginally accurate ceramic renditions of W. C. Fields or Bruce Lee.

The nearby table of cheap toys wouldn't appeal to this optimistic collector, nor would a table full of cotton handkerchiefs that were large enough for a man with a long ponytail to advertise them as "scarves." Something told me he was new to the market. With a hopeful smile, a sense of expectancy in his posture, the man was leaning forward, catching the eye of everyone who passed nearby. A sign hanging from the table edge read $10 A PIECE, $25 FOR THREE. He certainly priced his merchandise like a rookie.

A woman from another table walked over to him. "Ten dollars?!" she said between breaths, "for common handkerchiefs?"

The seller smiled at her helplessly.

The woman picked up a handkerchief by a corner as though it was toxic and crowed, "That's outrageous!"

I was secretly glorying in the woman's spunk and brashness, as that was certainly not a flea market price, but I also pitied the man. He had undoubtedly just gotten started in the flea market business and didn't have a clue about pricing. Stuff has to be visibly set at bargain pricing, a fundamental principle he had violated. The man probably bought them from some wholesaler, a real sharpie who sold him, along with the scarves, the idea that he could resell them for this fabulous price.

The man held up a scarf for her appraisal; it bore a badly printed likeness of Janis Joplin. "These are unusual," he said, as though the dead rock star's image proved it.

"They are common," she fired back, not letting up. "You can get them everywhere! That's a *stupid* price." She stalked off to her table, and he sat back down behind his many-colored offerings, doubt washing over his face, and what I imagined had been visions of big profits dimming.

Another newer collectible marketeer was doing a bit better, however; it was not impossible to make money on such dubious rarities. This marketeer had a sensible mixture of items, some miscellaneous used goods at modest prices and a grander display of "collectible, limited edition" plates made to commemorate people, mostly those celebrated in popular culture or the broadest version of history. They were also manufactured "collectibles."

"I guess I'll take that one," a woman said at his table. She pointed to a plate with John Wayne wearing his trademark white Stetson.

The vendor smiled ripely and nodded his appreciation. "You know what I like about him?" he asked as he wrapped the plate. "He was a good, humble actor. He wasn't on drugs or anything. These stars today are all druggies and snobs." The man handed the wrapped plate to the woman, whose head was bobbing as she handed over her money. Next a guy picked up a leather tool pouch out of the pile of miscellaneous goods, and the vendor said, "Three dollars. You got a good eye. That's worth maybe $25." He was doing a steadier business than most at the sale and keeping up a steady banter, praising his customers for their taste and "good buys." The guy with the scarves could learn a thing or two from him; rather than tout your merchandise, give the customers what they want—the feeling of having gotten a bargain.

His booth was the exception, though. The Whitehall flea market had a desperate, holding-on-by-its-fingernails aura. Unlike antique shows, which can be off the beaten tracks and still thrive, flea markets are so regularly staged they have to be nearer to the highway to attract sellers and buyers who might pull over on impulse to browse. Antique shows are magnets, while flea markets are siphons. Being closer to the main thoroughfare might not even have helped this market, though. It would be a hard venue to fill, if it wasn't full on a July day when the outside market scene is in full flower. The marketeers seemed to know the place was doomed; the boxes in which they had carried their goods were under the table, and some were only half unpacked, as if they were ready to hustle out of the hall as soon as the trickle of patrons ceased in another hour or so.

Flea markets may have passed their zenith. They have became too big, too popular, and reached that diminished-return point. This infusion of new, surplus goods, especially cheap tools and leather goods, has irreparably altered the nature and texture of these markets. They are simply less interesting than they once were. Buyers have also moved on to other venues, discovering the cheaper sources of many marketeers' offerings. I have not found it surprising that as flea markets have come and gone, yard sales have steadily increased, and perhaps these mini-markets, this anarchical assemblage of buyers and sellers, better fits the natural flow of used goods. Flea markets have become too regular, too stationary, and too predictable. Yard sales defy place by being held everywhere.

Chapter Sixteen

✿

The World's Largest

Yard sales defy the power of place and make up the largest outdoor market existing nowhere and everywhere simultaneously. Sometimes they are choreographed and form sales with far more possibility than any flea market: town-wide yard sales. One of the reasons flea markets appear to have waned is the preeminence of these headstrong replacements. Some of them have become annual festivals rivaling the Fourth of July. Unlike a flea market or antique show, those who live in a host town bear the direct responsibility for its success through its citizens' voluntary participation, though a village board or other functionaries are usually charged with promoting it. While flea marketeers flock to these sales, too, the core is formed by people who unload their basements and attics onto their porches and yards.

When I attend town-wide yard sales, I make a point of being under full sail by 8:30 in the morning; by 10:30 on sale day the traffic in a little village can be as orderly as a stampede. Then it is best to find a central place to park, shoulder a daypack, and hike the neighborhoods. If you buy something too large for a pack, or too heavy, most people are happy to put a sold sign on it and set it aside—at least that is the proper etiquette. However, some understand curb appeal and will leave something eye-catching, like a handsome set of armchairs or an oak sideboard, sitting in plain view even though it's already sold. For the buyer, though, nothing is so disappointing as to stop at a sale because of its curb appeal and to find all the best stuff sold. Likewise, it is also disheartening to find the goods on display are overpriced, the surplus from an antique show dealer's stock who has rented the yard and is masquerading as the owner of a split-level ranch behind it.

These town-wide sales can be great adventures if you can discern quickly between the ringers and real yard owner/sellers. Like other organized sales, though, they can grow too big and die the death of the overpopular. Warrensburg, New York, boasts that its annual village-wide scavenging bonanza is "The World's Largest Yard Sale." I decided to attend and see what being the largest meant to buyers and sellers.

Warrensburg sits on two streets that meet at a scissored intersection, one residential, the other commercial, with nineteenth-century buildings made of three-foot-thick blocks of local sandstone signaling the kind of permanence and future-thinking a growing town would have exuded in the early part of that century, years before it would find itself within the Adirondack "blue line," a demarcation that would declare the surrounding countryside "forever wild." The town would then be mired in wilderness, with severe restrictions on its ability to develop beyond those streets already laid out.

Even the residential area spoke of a prosperous past with mountain foothills crowned by frilly Victorian houses telescoping into annexes. Many had equally decorous carriage houses that enterprising owners had turned into antique stores of varying quality and aimed at tourists. Every year, though, at the end of September, another kind of wildness prevails, when businesses and residents set up shop on the street and rent space to fellow marketeers.

I scouted out the town a day before the sale, getting a sense where the traffic would be at its worst, as I lived within an hour of Warrensburg and had this advantage over people who traveled long distances to reach it. I noted that a shuttle service was set up at the south end of town, so I surmised that most attendees would approach from that direction. If I wanted to get into town unencumbered, I'd best not take the most obvious route, the Warrensburg exit on Interstate 87. Instead, on Saturday of sale weekend, I approached Warrensburg from the old two-lane road. Although I was five miles away, I was already seeing yard sales, cars pulled over on the wide berm, and people walking in the direction of town. Surely you can get closer to Warrensburg than this, I thought and kept driving, passing up some impromptu parking lots in yards and fields where you could park all day for $5. Even when I had gone to Cooperstown, New York, for Induction Day at the Baseball Hall of Fame I could park closer than that, I thought.

I never got closer than two miles to Warrensburg; there the berm was packed with parked cars and the road was jammed with traffic exiting the interstate and trying to merge. I parked on the curb and walked a few hundred yards toward town, but turned back. There had to be another way into Warrensburg, I figured, some back door on country lanes, so I got back in my pickup and headed south to the Prospect Diner in Lake George.

I took a counter seat in the classic stainless steel dining car and studied a Gazetteer, a book of topographical maps, of New York State over coffee. These books are essential for the used goods buyer, especially the cruising yard saler, and DeLorme Mapping has published them for thirty-one states. With one of these, there is no such thing as not being able to get there from here; I saw a couple of alternate routes into Warrensburg, ones the long-distance, nomadic used merchants couldn't possibly know.

The only drawback with DeLorme maps is they are drawn by optimists. Their cartographers mark even the narrowest dirt roads, even old logging roads that couldn't even be traversed now by Humvees; even some railroad grades are drawn in as roads. Unless you are paying close attention to the legend, and even then treating some paths with a jaundiced eye, you can't be sure of whether a route is for real. Dotted lines are suspect, that's for sure, so I should have known better, but one more cup at the Prospect, and I was on my way.

I headed farther south to Fourth Lake and then took Old Stage Road. The Gazetteer showed it would cross Potash Mountain Road, and afterwards was known as Viele Pond Road which ended at Cross Road, which led to Alden Avenue on the southwestern tip of Warrensburg. I'd go past some mountains called "The Three Sisters" and of course Viele Pond. Simple enough, or so I thought. However, this is the Adirondacks, a genuine wilderness and not a place to merrily skip off in the woods without preparations or a clue about what truly lay ahead, and I should have known that too, with or without the map.

I found Old Stage Road, but the only road that crossed it that might have been Potash Mountain Road was unmarked; I stopped to check the map and a guy in a giant Pontiac came around the corner and nearly rear-ended me. He turned left and went up Potash. With no more information than before, I kept going on what I assumed was Viele Pond Road, and except for three cantering horseback riders, I never passed another person.

Right after spotting an END OF COUNTY MAINTENANCE sign, the road turned dirt and gravel and then into a joint-jarring, north country washboard lane. Emboldened after passing a couple of hunting camps—though at twenty-five miles an hour—and full of Gazetteer confidence, I continued on even after another sign warned LIMITED ACCESS: ROAD OPEN ONLY MAY–NOVEMBER. It's September, I reasoned. It's open.

A wide one-lane funneled into a lane barely car-wide, then only two tracks with a weedy center brushing the underside of my truck. The road started to spiral and go uphill, each level reached by cutting my truck around a horseshoe bend. On one I paused, as part of the road had washed away down a sheer cliff face, and I had to drive so close to the mountainside I could not have opened my door; the ground felt loose and tentative under my wheels. That I had long ago shifted into four-wheel drive did little to bolster what sense of daring and adventure was left me.

Then, to my left, I spotted water, one of those anomalous high-altitude Adirondack ponds, a bowl scooped by the retreating glaciers and now spring fed. It must have been Viele Pond, for which the road was named, and I then realized why it was no longer called "Old Stage Road." The old stage could never have made it this far. The road widened there a bit, probably a parking curb for those who fished Viele, so I made a baroque, twelve-point turn and picked my way back down the hill, defeated, but not foolhardy enough to continue. Later, when I checked the map, I found that the pond was more than two-thirds of the way to Warrensburg; I had almost made it.

I tried another route, one more promising. I went farther south to Lake Luzerne, where I could take Route 1 to Stony Creek and then to Warrensburg. I wasn't quite sure where Route 1 was, but I was guessing it was the road that crossed a bridge over The Cataract, where Lake Luzerne empties into the Hudson River, so when I got to the bridge I stopped at an antique store there, the Village Variety Store. The owners, a man and woman, confirmed for me that it was the back way into Warrensburg, but they disagreed on how far it was. She said eight miles, and he said fifteen. I guessed they seldom went that way. While I was there,

I checked for hand-forged stuff for Jack in Cambridge, but the man said this was their last weekend to be open before closing for the winter. Most of the older stuff in their store had already sold. The dealers were taking advantage of the yard sale weekend to unload the last of their goods before tucking it all away for the season. A sign in their shop encouraged sales by declaring YOUR HUSBAND JUST CALLED AND SAID YOU SHOULD BUY WHAT YOU WANT.

On the way I passed through Stony Creek, a multiple crossroads near the basin of a dry rocky creek where a town used to be and still was, of a hardscrabble, weathered-plank sort, and I took the hill road out of town toward Warrensburg after checking the map and getting reoriented. Finally I hit the west side of town and saw Alden Avenue on my right, to which Viele Pond Road would have taken me if I had stuck with it. Immediately I again saw signs for $5 parking, and even the smallest alley was jammed with cars. My circuitous route had gotten me into town, but it had so abruptly dumped me into the middle of the sale I had no hope of finding a place to park and actually taking part. Instead, I was funneled down the main drag, nowhere to go but straight ahead, the road lined with tents, perched on spaces no bigger than the tables sitting there. People were spilling out onto the street. In fact there was barely room to drive through the fattened curbs full of pedestrians, walking ten abreast around the burgeoning vendors. Drivers maintained a stuttering crawl to keep from clipping them.

A woman stepped out into the middle of the street to stop me so someone could leave an impromptu parking lot and nodded appreciatively when I did. But my hopes for claiming that spot were not redeemed when someone else pulled in the lot while the woman had me stopped. Somehow I was not wholly disappointed, as from my truck I could see only craft booths, T-shirt displays, and new, surplus merchandise sellers in tent after tent, surrounded by food vendors, everything from hot dogs to ribs to corn on the cob. What's more, the people seemed grim, beleaguered by the mere presence of so many like-minded shoppers.

With mere access to the World's Largest Yard Sale so daunting, how could it continue to function? How could you make a large purchase and possibly carry it to your vehicle if you had to park miles away? The World's Largest Yard Sale was out of control. Still I marveled at the force and attraction of used goods. The mob was not here for Harley-Davidson

T-shirts or semi-precious stone jewelry. They were here for junk. The flea marketeers had colonized the event, and the sale offered more trinkets than used treasures. Once spaces were rented to outsiders, and people had exhausted the corners of their closets and the mystery boxes in their attics, it became more profitable to allow the traveling junker and surplus tribe to usurp the sale. However, it would continue only as long as people remained convinced it was truly a yard sale, refulgent with castoffs.

Driving through Warrensburg was claustrophobic, so I inched and squeezed through the bottleneck at the end of town; only then did I pull over at a couple of sales. At one I saw more Currier & Ives–patterned dishes, and a buyer there complained to me about the crowds. "They are backed up for miles on the Northway. Where do they come from?" She was looking at an intriguing golf item, a putting tray marked "Made in the Royal Colony of Hong Kong." Such a colony was now a mere part of history, and such bric-a-brac was one of the few tangible reminders. It was not enough of a curio to tempt me, though. "I thought if I got here at eight o'clock I'd be in the clear," the buyer continued, "but they were already backed up."

I talked to the man running the sale and found out he too was a vendor and had only rented the space. The town had worried about how the event had been growing—and about traffic flow—and had posted his space as off-limits for a sale. "But they don't own it," the vendor said, "those folks over there do." He pointed to a nearby, one-storey house. We were interrupted by a customer. "I'll give you four-fifty for that," she said, gesturing toward an all-terrain vehicle parked near the road, "I'd like it for my granddaughter."

When she pulled out her wallet, her husband caught up with her. "I think that's four *hundred* and fifty *dollars*," he said, and the vendor nodded. I understood the woman's confusion; any price is possible at this level of the used continuum.

I stopped in front of a run-down house, and though a sign laid claim to it being a genuine yard sale, I saw a panel van in the back yard with the rear door open, signifying a flea marketeer was there, too. Still I hoped the goods would be cheaper, that some true yard sale fare would be mixed in. A dozen other shoppers had made the same hunch. Again I was wrong. The curb-appeal iron plows and mowing scythes belonged to the man with the van, and when I saw that nothing bore prices, I was wary. I walked about with the appropriate thoughtfulness, as the seller was hovering nearby, exuding cheerfulness, calling out prices and descriptions whenever someone touched anything. He had a long, white beard and a T-shirt touting the World's Biggest Motorcycle Rally. His clothing was not dirty, exactly, but dingy. I guessed he didn't want to look more prosperous than the run-down cottage behind him, supposedly his home.

I picked up another of those strange wooden barbells I had seen at The Yankee Peddler, and as I did he said, "It's for darning socks. You can put a sock on each end, I guess."

"Really?" I said.

He shrugged. "Long before my day." Yet another explanation for these mystery items. I made another mental note to find out what they were actually used for.

Next I saw a tattered little notepad. It was a bit larger than a checkbook, and its card-stock cover was speckled and rippled in a fashion intended to imitate leather. It was bound with a silk ribbon woven through three holes and had long sat in the sun, because the back cover was a deep jade green, while the front was faded to a dun brown, nearly obliterating the gold embossed script reading "My School Day Autobiography." The words were surrounded by a flourished and curlicued border and accompanied by the image of an inkwell and a quill pen.

Inside the front cover a floral-bedecked slogan asserted:

Schoolday Memories bring back,
Pleasant Thoughts of Happy Hours,
Spent in Work and Play.

The next page had a simple line for the owner to write his name, which "Milburn F. Roberts" had, in fountain pen, with a nice flourish to cross the ending t. Next was a page on which Milburn was supposed to record "My Teachers," with a column for name and grade, but he had left it blank. Next followed five pages for "Names and Addresses of My Class Mates," and here, on the second page, were the signatures of thirteen, without addresses, either all that he had, or those he considered his friends. The list has an odd formality: "Carl O. Randall, Jr., Charles Birch, Arnold B. Chaddick, R. Henry Fuller . . . " It was clear that each of the students had been taught the same style of penmanship, what used to be called the Peterson Method, but there were subtle distinctions in their hands, even between the Blanchard brothers, Floyd and Gordon. Strict regulation of pen stroke had not stripped them of the personal touch of the dipping tail on the final *d*, or a loop at the beginning of the initial *B*.

These dedicated pages were followed by blank pages, about fifty in all. The little notebook was the predecessor of the school yearbook, with its photographs and quotes. It would not have been worth more than a quick perusal, and I would not have bothered to spend the time I had with it, had the blank papers not yielded a couple more entries. On the first one a name and date was drawn in ballooned letters: "John W. Mutton, August 3, 1934." It was topped by a crude drawing of a one-room schoolhouse with a church-style steeple. On the next page I found a poem. All the other pages were blank. The poem was a bit of doggerel:

> I can't send flowers,
>   I can't sent [sic] cake
> Or gum to give you
>   A swell toothache;
> Books or a telegram,
>   Even a card,
> Because the depression
>   Has hit me so hard
>
>   Anonymous

This simple sentiment, with its sonnet-like twist at the end, was clear and reverberent with history. What hardships had Milburn seen to move him to copy these eight lines into his book? Or had a classmate given it to him, in lieu of another gift deserved or expected, hoping the pathetic humor would suffice?

The verse was written in pencil, while the rest of the inscriptions were in ink, still Milburn had not corrected his error. He knew, though, and I did too, reading it almost seventy years later, that it was worth saving, a sign of the times as poignant as the song "Brother, Can You Spare a Dime?"

The verse was even more meaningful for me, as I imagined my father writing it himself as a boy in a one-room schoolhouse during the Depression. He and his parents lived in the remote mountain hamlet of Mahoning, Pennsylvania, where the Mahoning Creek ran into the Allegheny River. Each morning his father rowed a dinghy out to a buoy in the

Allegheny where he boarded a riverboat that took him to work for the railroad, or in the mines, whatever was to be done for a dollar downriver.

When he came home, my father would be waiting, watching out the window of the yellow brick schoolhouse. So eager was my father to see his father, the teacher allowed him to bolt from the classroom when he saw the dinghy heading to shore. He would run to the riverbank to meet his father, and they would then go to Walker's General Store, where his father would buy him a cup of ice cream.

My father's family moved to a larger town when he was in the third grade, and there he went to a school with multiple classes, a frightening experience for a mountain boy who was used to the familiarity of his one-room school. Knowing the boy was frightened, his father showed up at the school building to meet him at the end of the first day. As my father tells it, his third grade class was lined up, ready to be dismissed. However, when my father saw his father walking up the street, he broke ranks and made a dash for the door, astonished when he was met with a severe reprimand from his new teacher. He didn't know any better, though; he was still operating on backcountry rules.

That story ran briskly through me as I flipped the pages, so with the book in hand I approached the seller.

"Five dollars?" he said with a fatal tentative tone. I knew from his rising inflection that he'd deal.

"No," I said with a little laugh. "I'll give you a dollar for it. That's all."

"Everyone picks it up," he said.

"Well, if that makes it worth it to you . . ." I said, not adding the implied, "then you can keep it."

"I could take three," he added quickly, sensing I might walk.

Casually pulling out $3 from my wallet, I realized I could have talked him down to $2 or $2.50, but I didn't see the point. I only knew that I had to have, and preserve, this little artifact of time and circumstance.

I found out the seller was an aspiring antique dealer and had bought this desperate shanty to house his stuff. He actually lived in Boston where he worked as a machinist. "I don't make a living at this," he said. "I hold this sale twice a year. That's all they will allow me to do it," he said with a nervous laugh. "They" were town officials, who didn't want a junker at the gateway to their town. "So I come out here to see if I can make a few bucks."

"How are you doing this year?"

"A little slow. Last year the Northway [I–87] was backed up for miles. I sat here and listened to horns blowing. I even heard gunshots," he said with a raised eyebrow.

Although I had not heard of last year's sale generating road rage violence, I could see how it might happen. The town was riding the proverbial tiger. It had tried to stem the burgeoning number of semi-professional junkers, even declaring some private land not available to rent to them, though the owners ignored the designations. Anyone who wanted to contain the World's Largest Yard Sale was tilting at wind-mills. The critical mass of sellers and buyers for two September days was overwhelming. The sale might have reached its reasonable limit, but the momentum had not; for good or for ill they had become a Mecca for people who loved flea markets, yard sales, and general scavenging.

Chapter Seventeen

❧

The World's Longest

I

T BEGINS IN KENTUCKY, just south of the Ohio border near Cincinnati, and it ends in Alabama. Residents on 459 miles of Route 127 hold a yard sale on the same four days in August every year, billed as the World's Longest Yard Sale. When I attended the sale it was held August 15 to 18. It had been founded in Jamestown, Tennessee, and spread in both directions from there, the brainchild of Fentress County Executive Mike Walker and designed to bring travelers off the major interstates and into the hinterlands. The sale was in its fifteenth year and coordinated by the Fentress County Chamber of Commerce in Jamestown, which remained its central point.

On August 13th I sat in a motel in Clarion, Pennsylvania, within striking distance of Athens, Ohio, where I would pick up traveling partner Mark Hackworth, a veteran of most of my other ill-conceived, seat-of-the-pants road trips. I spent that night studying AAA maps of Kentucky, Tennessee, and Alabama as they were traversed by Route 127. For a federal highway, the road was a corkscrewish affair. The Army Corps of Engineers had to negotiate the pitching and rolling southern Appalachians. They could dam the Colorado, channelize the Mississippi, but the Corps had to tip their caps to the mountains and go around. Even the newer interstates had to sidle around those storied hills and hollows. I looked ahead to some of what we'd see: the state capital of Kentucky, Frankfort, which is off the interstate grid; Danville, Kentucky; and Pall Mall, Tennessee. Lexington, Kentucky, and Knoxville, Tennessee, were fed by big interstates, but old Route 127 went through past glories.

Mark was also a compatriot of castoffs and denizen of Hawk's junk shop. At Mark's house I would be leaving my little car behind, preferring to make the trek in Mark's pickup; in it I'd feel like less of an interloper than in a Cavalier with New York plates. Mark and I planned to get to the beginning of the sale, south of Cincinnati in Kentucky, Mark's ancestral homeland. The pickup would be better for hauling finds, too. Since Mark did not have a cap over the bed, we planned to carry a box of black garbage bags in which to hide purchases. "It'll look like we have a load of garbage," he had said over the phone when we planned the trip. Nonetheless, precious garbage would be taken into our motel room at night. I had a want list provided by friends: a small bookcase, a router, an acoustic guitar. I was looking for that elusive, eye-catching anything. As usual, my agenda was in the moment, not concrete.

Since I was in Clarion, Pennsylvania, my own ancestral mountain home, I decided before nightfall to visit one of my personal monuments of scavenger utility, the garage my grandfather Leslie built with my father on his forty-acre farm. The building was erected entirely of scavenged lumber and nails—materials already a hundred years old—and built on a foundation of scavenged, squared barn stone. It was outside of town, near Scotch Hill.

The farm had changed almost beyond recognition. The house my grandfather built in the 1950s had weathered a number of additions and revisions, and the pine forest he had planted was forty feet tall. In the middle of it all sat the humble garage, not a sag in its roofline, the same plank door on hand-forged strap hinges. The garage had seen new shingles; otherwise it remained unchanged. Surrounded by an enlarged house, and a campground for vacationers to the nearby state park, Cooks Forest, and with an overgrown strip mine across the road, the little building was a last vestige, a minor testament to the fruits of scavenging. I was pleased to see it; one day only I would know its origins.

The next day I made it to Athens, Ohio, and reacquainted myself with the humid basin of air that often gets trapped between the foothills of the Appalachians in the summer; I was starting to doubt the wisdom of heading into the Deep South in August. To escape the heat, Mark and I discussed the trip and its possible travails, over a couple of beers at Tony's, one of the few bars not dominated by students from nearby Ohio University. Besides the fact Mark was an intrepid traveler and always up for an adventure, I wanted to know why he had agreed to accompany me on this trek. It was simple, really. He was going for artistic reasons. As an artist who combines photographs and printmaking, Mark is always on the lookout for images, and in the secondhand world he had found a particular tenor. Given the leftover nature of each item in the network, he expected them to exude a particular sense of loss, of absence and dislocation, so crucial to the images he found meaningful. For him, loss was meaningful, giving the abstract, or material, significance. For him, an overgrown path or a cracked egg shell elicited the same sense of loss; even things that carried some sense of instant loss, as loss over time for him was insignificant or resulted in simple nostalgia. A moment passing could produce the resonance he was seeking. As we pilgrimaged down Route 127, Mark would be looking for those nudges with a camera in hand while I was fulfilling my twin desire for happenstance and cheap thrills. His interior motives for making the long, hot drive made sense, at least after a couple of cold beers at Tony's.

The next day we were on the road, taking the Appalachian Highway across southern Ohio, one of the public works of the infamous James Rhodes, the governor who ordered the National Guard onto the Kent State Campus in 1970. Building the highway had been a nod to developing the most rural part of the state, the home of his most staunch supporters. This road, running south from the mid-state capital of Columbus to Athens, then west to Cincinnati, would have made an excellent route for another extensive yard sale had it actually passed through anywhere. It didn't, though, and so it simply served to bypass the bottom of the state, not promote interest it.

We stopped at one of the few towns within a mile of the highway, Prebles, Ohio, and took lunch at the White Star Restaurant. I ordered a Pub Burger and was surprised when the waitress brought me two sandwiches, one large burger cut in half and put on two buns. Stopping at a neighborhood diner in a town not accustomed to passers-by is a sure-fire way to remind yourself you are not from around there. As long as you don't disrupt the natural order of things—sitting in someone's favorite counter seat, for instance—you can eat without the extended glower of the regulars. So, if you order one sandwich in Shrub Township, so named for the many stands of stunted arctic trees left behind by the retreating glaciers 10,000 years ago, and you get two, it is best not to question the waitress.

This is middle America, where you best eat what you are given and not leave much behind, where towns like Preble are dry, and hosted, in 1957, the World Plowing Competition. Mark and I ate our pile of Pub Burgers, tipped well, and left without causing the locals much real consternation.

Halfway to Cincinnati we swung south on Route 41, called the Zane Trace, a road blazed by pioneers north from the Ohio River into the heart of Ohio territory and south into the rolling hills of western Kentucky. We had time to while away before getting to the head of the longest sale, so we decided to tour horse and whiskey country, beginning with Paris.

The county seat of Bourbon County, Paris, Kentucky, did not quite live up to its namesake, but it had a kind of genteel charm even the most ragged West Kentucky farms evince. A staid, Virginia old-money feel persisted in the town with its Ionic columned courthouse, sitting ever so prim and regal on a slight promontory toward which the main commercial streets were aimed. Those streets were well past their prime, though, just the kind of place where I would expect junkers and other secondhand mavens to be.

We saw several used and antique shops lodged in old storefronts and decided to check for a good used guitar; I had fantasies of a classic Gibson or Martin for a few dollars surfacing in the hills of Appalachia. I stopped at an antique store, and while the dealer did not have any guitars, he directed me to a barbershop on the corner.

"They have guitars in there," he said, as though buying a guitar in a barbershop was the most natural thing in the world.

We walked into what was indeed a barbershop/used musical instrument store. "How ya'll doin'," one of two barbers said as we breached the door. He had a long, iron-gray beard and a customer with a lathered face in front of him, one swath on his chin cleared by a straight razor.

"All right," Mark and I said in unison, and I pointed at the row of guitars hanging from the ceiling of the wall opposite the barber chairs.

"Go ahead and look around," the barber said. We could tell right away their guitars were not very good or appealing, but we spent a respectable amount of time looking at them before bidding the barbers/guitar sellers a good afternoon and leaving.

Next we stopped at a crammed antique store, where an extremely well-dressed, consummately tanned dealer commented on the upcoming long sale. "Lots of that stuff ought to be buried," he said of what we

were going to encounter. "It's the end of the line." I wasn't quite convinced of the accuracy of his point of view, though, as the quality of goods
in his shop, from high Victorian to American primitive, was pretty high.
I assumed it would take a good deal to impress him, and 100 percent
Appalachian Junk, aged on the front porch for a few years, would not do
the trick.

All the best buys were south of Kentucky, he said, disparaging his
native state as only having the worst castoffs for sale. "It goes on forever," he added, calculating if you stopped at every sale you'd only make
fifty miles a day. The last time he attended the sale he went as a seller, not
a buyer. His voice dropped as he confided the best way to make money
was to take a truckload down Route 127 and periodically stop along the
road and unload. Every time you unloaded you started what he called a
feeding frenzy, as people would rush over, figuring what you were taking
off your truck had not been picked through before. However, if you
stayed in that spot very long all the customers would drift away; after that
initial bout of selling, it was best to load up, go down the road, and set
up again. The man said he wasn't going to the sale this year because all
of that loading and unloading was too much hard work.

He also spent some time trying to interest me in his own arcana, including a deed signed by liberty-or-death Patrick Henry, then Governor
of Virginia, ceding land in Lexington, Kentucky, to a Revolutionary War
veteran as payment for his services to the young nation. Kentucky was
claimed by Virginia then, and from the proud jut of the man's jaw I could
tell this splendidly sartorial dealer wished the claim had prevailed.

As I had everywhere in Paris, I asked the man if he had any guitars;
he referred me to the barber shop. "I've already been there," I said, "And
I have to say that's the first barber shop/used guitar shop I have ever
seen, or ever will."

"They just moved in here," the man said, his eyes narrowing.
"They're mountain people. They're different." He fairly oozed conde-
scension, and I could practically hear Mark growling with indignation.
His family was originally "mountain people" from Pikeville in East
Kentucky, Scots-Irish stock, not the Virginia thoroughbreds favored in
Bourbon County.

"I knew there was something about him I didn't like," Mark said as
we left the shop. The class division between East and West Kentucky was

as real as the mountains separating them. The picturesque black barns and rail fences of the horse and tobacco farms lining the road assumed a huffy demeanor as we took the back roads out of Paris.

August 15th was the first day of the sale, and that morning when Mark and I got to Route 127 we found a truck-stop motel there, with no vacancies, of course. Scavengers were just starting to roll out of bed, and a stream of road-weary, disheveled pickers were lugging coffees to trucks and vans. Some flea marketeers had set up in the parking lot, but I gave them only a cursory glance; it was best to be on the road as soon as possible, to get ahead of the hordes.

As the Virginian-wannabe antique dealer had said, the first part of the sale was a little disappointing. The old road had been widened, slicing through limestone hillocks it had otherwise gone around; the Corps had prevailed in part. The sales were being held on bits of the old road, now little detours, that looped beside the straight new byway like a vine around a tree trunk. So the sales were far away and hard to rubberneck, especially since the new road invited higher driving speeds, though Mark was cruising as slowly as other traffic would permit. On the side roads you'd find encampments of sellers, some indigenous, some not. Still, if you were looking for curb appeal to help you choose where to stop, you were out of luck. All I found were signs promising superior finds around every bypassed curve and in every skirted village. Some only had ROUTE 127 spray-painted onto a piece of plywood propped up against a rock or tree. One simply read, 127 RAIN OR SHINE. For four days in August, that three-digit number was shorthand for secondhand.

Route 127 actually narrowed and went through Glencoe, Kentucky, and here Mark and I made our first stop, parking across the street from a junk shop that had burped out its wares street-side. However, we didn't get more than a few yards into browsing the sales lining Glencoe's main street when Mark turned to me and said solemnly, "I locked my keys in the truck."

We ran back to Mark's truck. The keys hung tantalizingly from the ignition, but both doors were locked. At first we circled the truck, yanking on the door handles in an incredulous stupor; we were stuck in the middle of Kentucky, with the closest locksmith probably more than a hundred miles away, and with hundreds of miles of sales ahead to which the other scavengers were beating us.

Right before panic set in, I remembered the junk shop across the street. Surely, in the midden of castoffs on his front porch would lie the appropriate implement of destruction to give us ingress to a Nissan pickup. "I'll be right back," I called to Mark as I bounded across the street, zipping between cars that had stopped in front of the sale.

Inside I found the junk merchant, a sandy-looking fellow wearing a worn cotton dress shirt and green work pants. I explained our plight. First I went for the obvious: a coat hanger. I had once been a master at opening cars with a bent coat hanger, though that was back when cars had door lock *knobs*, not sliding or nubby lock mechanisms. The junk seller led me outside to a rack of children's clothes and helped me pick a hanger stiff enough to hold its shape when fished behind the door seal.

As I suspected, though, the truck was cunningly designed to thwart such amateurish efforts; even the lock on the rear sliding windows of the cab could not be tripped with a mere wire. Back across the street I hunted for more tools, and after several trips back and forth to Mark, who was toiling mightily, I had bought an impressive array of tools with burglar potential. Eventually the yard sale owner stopped charging me for tools. "Just use it," he said. "If it works, bring it back. If it doesn't, bring it back." I was delighted that he wasn't trying to take advantage of our plight; after all, he could have charged outrageous prices for the rusted screwdriver, putty knife, pry bar, and hammer I trotted out to Mark.

After forty-five minutes of sweaty trial and error, Mark finally broke the lock on the rear window by slipping the putty knife through the jamb and pounding on it with a hammer; he then reached through and snatched the keys as I ran back across the street and returned the tools I hadn't purchased, thanking the man profusely and making a quick perusal to see if I could pay him back with a sale. However, I left with no more than gratitude and relief, and Mark and I beat a hasty exit from Glencoe. I concluded, though, that the best place to lock yourself out of your vehicle was in front of a yard sale with lots of tools.

"That right there they sell for $34 at Wal-Mart," I had heard the seller remark about a car jack when I was picking around for tools. "But we ain't Wal-Mart and we ain't doing it like that." Wal-Mart wouldn't be found on Route 127; the big-box stores would be crouching near the interstates where they could efficiently draw traffic. Even if they had plunked down a Super Store on the old road, Wal-Mart would not allow its parking lot to be used by flea marketeers and junk sellers, as did Hudnall's Auto Garage. Hudnall's had a couple thousand feet of road frontage and had lent it out to a dozen junkers. Mark was driving and I was surveying; we had decided to stop at any sale that had good curb appeal, so he had turned off when I called out "guitar!"

The guitar was priced right, at $15, but it was essentially ruined, missing both the bridge and tuning pegs. We made a pass through the other sellers while we were there, though. One of them had a campsite set up next to his wares, a screened canopy over a camouflage pup tent, folding camp chairs, a cook stove, and other gear. Despite what the Paris antique dealer had claimed, they obviously were dug in for the long haul, not setting up repeatedly as they traipsed down the road.

As in town-wide yard sales, people with parking lots or large fields were capitalizing on the big event by renting spaces to vendors. One sign offered them for $25 a day. Instinctively I avoided these sellers, but when such an assemblage in a farmer's field just south of Frankfort presented itself, it was far too enticing to pass by. The owner of the field had organized the sale with elaborate exit and entrance lanes leading to and from an enormous encampment, which Mark called "the Woodstock of Yard Sales."

It did have the aura of a rock concert, with a steady stream of vehicles peeling off Route 127 to join the fray; Mark and I followed a truck into the parking lot that had been singularly outfitted for a scavenging sojourn. The bed had been fitted with wooden sides nearly ten feet tall, serving as a combination camper and mobile storage shed. Gear was tied and bungee-corded to the tops and sides so that it looked like it had been inspired by photographs of dustbowl rigs heading out west. The entire truck was so overloaded, its gear included big wooden wedges to chock the wheels when parked on an incline.

Normally I'd breeze through an organized field of vendors, but we ended up spending much more time than I would have predicted. Almost immediately I saw a dealer of guitars, fiddles, saddles, and riding tackle, all hanging from clotheslines. I approached a guitar, and the vendor, sitting in the doorway of a trailer, more bridles and halters framing him, started to drop the price on it and then on every guitar dangling around me. His eagerness to dicker was unnerving, but I had seen the tactic before; discount something so drastically that people feel compelled to buy out of fear that not buying will be seen as an insult to the quality of the seller's merchandise. It sounds absurd, but it works. If something is lowered to a fraction of the asking price, and you appear to be interested, what's stopping you from buying it?

I didn't want to appear to insult his guitars, which were in fact meager in terms of quality, so I said quickly, "It's not the price as much as the kind of guitar."

"You won't find any Martins or Gibsons around here because us thieves are out getting them first," the man said, a variation on the pitch sellers use to persuade a customer to settle on what is on-hand instead of holding out for something different and better. He then went on to tell me how he sent any classic guitars he found in the used market to a high-end Lexington guitar shop. Great instruments immediately graduated to the upper echelons.

Mark at least got a picture. The seller was sitting solidly on a white plastic lawn chair in the open door of his battered travel trailer, looking a bit glum about not being able to sell one of his ignominious guitars. Beside pictures signifying loss, Mark had also decided to take portraits of sellers, finding their images compelling. Nearly everyone we met was cooperative; one posed with his favorite collectible plastic action figures hanging behind him, while another, wearing a Frankfort American Legion Post Softball tournament T-shirt and a Nordic beard, brandished a brass-barreled percussion pistol across his chest. "Just to show you can find anything at a yard sale," he said proudly. Most sellers sat contentedly in chairs, a cigar box or coffee can for cash sitting nearby on a folding table.

A seller of modern firearms was less pleased when Mark photographed him. He had not set up much of a display; from what I could tell, he had simply backed up a pickup and arranged ten rifles, shotguns, and hand-guns on a blanket draped over the lowered tailgate. Most were standard sporting rifles with telescopic sights; one handgun was a semi-automatic, and one rifle had a long banana-clip for ammunition. Both looking vaguely illegal, though I had been told that there are no laws regulating firearm sales in Kentucky.

The seller was sitting lumpishly on the tailgate, and two hangers-on, lean and ferret-like, stood to his right. I had just walked up to casually in-spect his weaponry, planning to walk by quickly, when Mark popped up behind me and started snapping pictures, without asking permission as he had with other sellers. The reaction from all these men was funereal.

"You ain't federal are you?" one of the standing men drawled, his words dragging like a sack through sand.

"'Cause if you's federal, they gonna find you in the river," said the other, the more rodent-like of the two, who had the ability to chew his lower lip and talk simultaneously. The seated seller made nearly sub-audible growls in agreement.

Mark snapped another picture, this time of the guns lying on the tailgate. The men stepped away from the angle of his camera, exchanging looks, and I stepped away from Mark, wondering if these hill-country gun-runners had noticed that he and I had been wandering about together. Without missing a beat, Mark dropped into his best East Kentucky accent and quipped, "I ain't pretty enough to be federal." If anything, Mark had nerve.

Mark eventually allayed their fears by examining their guns and chatting, though I was not convinced they ever fully let down their guard. When we left, Mark said, "Did you ever see such a guilty-looking bunch of guys? They looked like they had lots to hide."

"Mark, I wouldn't do that again. Next time you want to take pictures of people selling guns out of the back of a truck parked beside the road, tell me first so I can get the hell away from you."

"I just wanted to get a candid shot," he said. Why couldn't he take candid shots of people selling baseball cards? I wondered. I could feel the gun-runners watching us for the rest of the sale, and I checked to see if we were being followed when we got back in Mark's truck and pulled back onto Route 127.

The antique dealer in Paris was right about the sale in one respect: Much of the stuff should have been buried. I saw an overload of imported new stuff, much of it the same; for instance, everyone had Bowie knives made in Pakistan, priced for six or seven dollars, or lampshades painted with pictures of famous people, everyone from Geronimo to Jesus. The gaudy predictability of such things made them worth less than true junk.

Surplus sellers couldn't possibly dominate such an extensive sale, though. "It's like a treasure hunt," a seller said, a tired aphorism passed hand to hand throughout the used network. Mark and I were picking through his boxes of rusted tools and machine parts, seeing precious little treasure.

The seller picked up a palm-sized wooden box with electrical terminals on it. "Take this, for instance. This here is a starter coil from a Model

T Ford." He gave us a toothy look of seriousness. "See how it's dovetailed?" The box was joined with interlaced joints like overlapping fingers,
but it was far from dovetailed. Still, the junker knew dovetailing was a
sign of fine furniture and carpentry, so he wanted to claim that attribute
for his ancient auto part. He pulled out two more to show they all had
similar construction.

"Do you know how to tell if it's genuine?" he said. "It'll say Ford
right here." He pointed at the palmed box as though showing us a signed
baseball. "Can you see it?"

I said that I did, but without my reading glasses, I couldn't make out
any logo. Mark also leaned in to take a look, then exchanged one with me.

The seller fondled the box. "I'd put that on my mantel if I had a
cabin or somewhere else and just look at it. I like old things." Such are the
attractions of yard sale junk; even part of an old car can become what is
commonly called a conversation piece. Later Mark wondered why anyone
would need a mark to prove the parts were originals. "Who'd bother to
make phony Model T starter coils?"

"It sure seemed to matter to him," I said. At the level of high-end
antiques, a maker's mark meant all the difference on the bottom of a
piece of silver, so it made a kind of analogous sense that a Ford mark
would make the difference on an auto part.

Sales thinned out south of Danville, and sellers there were covering
their tables with plastic as a fearsome storm approached from the west,
cracking open the hot and humid day. It struck just as we crossed the
southern border into Tennessee, at a town called Static.

We had been waiting on Static. We had stopped near Danville to find
supplies, hopefully a bottle of gin. A grocery store clerk told me we had
to go "a hundred miles in any direction" in order to find spirits of any
sort. "The closest is south to Static. That's where most folks go." So we
stayed on Route 127 for the next one hundred miles south, past the
scenic Cumberland Reservoir ("Where the Mountains Meet the Water"),
in a pure Bible-belt dry zone, where I swore to Mark the people looked
so clear-eyed and sober they had a Stepford-like spookiness.

At Static, the mountain resort/sanctified county aura withered in
the presence of two prodigious juke joints, one on each side of the road,
ratty cement block warehouses decorated with graffiti and with Alhambra-
like neon lights around the doorways. All hundred miles to the north in

God-fearing Kentucky might be dry, but here were facilities perfectly poised to take advantage of it.

While Route 127 had been improved and straightened in Kentucky, with steep cliffsides along a roadway now bored through the hills, it remained as unchanged as the day it was surveyed in Tennessee. Here the road narrowed, curved, and dipped through the balladized hills, and after the rain abated, the water steamed off the mountainsides like a Hollywood set of foggy Appalachian hollows. In the late afternoon light it was easy to imagine you could hear a high-lonesome song with a forlorn fiddle wafting over the hills. Then the good people of Tennessee along Route 127 reminded you that Appalachia is not just a romantic rural vision of moonshine-swigging primitives in rocking chairs, but an economic entity. Little houses and mobile homes lay clustered in the lowlands and valleys, some looking as though they had slid down from some higher perch, and the stuff in the gravel driveways and tufted yards was so numerous it barely looked like all of it would fit inside of them. Perhaps, I thought, they had simply dragged out all of their possessions in the hope of making some money, any money, and then buying something better, or just using it to keep the wolf from the door. I didn't encounter more mountain poverty in Tennessee than in Kentucky, but on unimproved 127, the houses were much closer to the road so the sale and its vendors were more intimately connected to it. Even the vendors from elsewhere camping in the yards seemed less affluent, with rusted trailers, campers, trucks, and vans on their last legs, made even more dreary that afternoon by the wet tarps shrouding their nearby wares.

The even mix of dire financial straits and the entrepreneurial spirit of the yard sale was unsettling, but perversely optimistic. These people knew money was coming down the road, and everyone had an equal chance at it. We pulled over at a place with sales in front of four houses, and as I approached one, a wan-looking woman with a long flowing skirt asked me cheerily, "Do you want to buy a rock?"

She pointed at a small, flatbed trailer on which she had arranged an assortment of smooth round stones, obviously plucked from a local creek, and a line-up of gnarled roots, washed and polished. "No, and I wouldn't admit it if I did," I said with a wink.

"Lots of people like them. They're just the thing for sidewalks, you know, or to put in a garden." The stones were $5 each. They were shiny and slick, being one of the few things for sale actually enhanced by the rain. The woman looked unapologetic and eager to make a sale, and Mark and I just smiled and shook our heads; I made a few mental calculations about how much it would cost to buy enough stones for a twenty-foot walkway. I couldn't think of a use for the roots.

If you legally could put a price on it, the good people of Route 127 were trying to sell it. Tennesseeans were much more concerned with tourist traffic on their stretch of the road than had been Kentuckians. Before long we passed through Pall Mall, touted in sign after commemorative sign as the birthplace of Sergeant Alvin York. Once a household name, York needs much more context today; even though a movie was once made about his life and exploits, starring Gary Cooper.

I don't remember if the Great War was already underway when York joined up, or whether he merely had plain old bad luck. I could have found out if I had bought a copy of his locally published memoir, available in a junk shop in Pall Mall, but the real details are not so interesting as the legend. They never are. The truth is that York was courageous in that war and came back highly decorated, a national hero. According to legend, and the movie, Alvin York single-handedly captured dozens of German soldiers, using the hunting and stalking skills he had fine-tuned in the pursuit of turkey in the very mountains through which Route 127 now bumped and rolled. Only an actor with the silent strength of Gary Cooper could capture York's cool and fearless nature.

At least that was the angle being worked by the Pall Mall junk shop, once a true general store. Now, in addition to the diary, the owners had etchings and drawings of the hero in uniform, in action—plus the obligatory memo pads, plates, and other incidentals, all emblazoned with "Pall Mall, Tennessee, Birthplace of Sergeant Alvin York." Everything in town, such as it was, was named after York: the park, the school, and the hunting and fishing club. For the citizens of Pall Mall, Alvin York was a modest but real bid for tourism; it was as though they had grown so accustomed to the gothic mountain scenery with its dramatic lurches and swoons, they believed they had to offer travelers other diversions and heroics. What could be more heroic, though, than watching hawks catch the summer thermals and curl endlessly over the tops of mountains puffing morning fog?

Daylight was waning, so Mark and I decided to try for the next largest town in the hopes of finding a place to stay. Everyone we spoke to said that we should head to Jamestown, the origin of the sale and a logical mid-point. Another two hours of mountain careening, and we arrived, Route 127 plunging us into the middle of a downtown Jamestown, where the only hotel looked like it had taken in its last guest years ago. After a couple of passes along the main drag, we finally found a more prosperous suburban sprawl to the west of Route 127, where a full complement of chain hotels presented itself. All of them were full, though, and I silently kicked myself for not foreseeing that the world's longest sale would be so popular that veteran scavengers would have called ahead for rooms

In another thirty-five miles on Route 127 we'd be at Interstate 40, where I was sure the big motels would have a place for us; all of the yard sales would be closed on the way, but we had no choice. I looked with thwarted longing at the gauntlet of covered tables along the way, but everything about the trip prefigured our eventual disappointment with finding a room on the interstate. People were crowded into camper jungles, and the diner where we stopped was crammed, and had run out of most of its specials, including ribs, which I imagined was unimaginable in a southern restaurant. Like at Warrensburg, the popularity of the World's Longest Yard Sale had outstripped the capacity of the locale to host it.

In this case, however, it seemed that the entire state was under the influence of a giant sale of junk. We headed east for a while toward Nashville, and west toward Knoxville, and every time were treated to the same song: no vacancies. At the desk of a Best Western, I saw more of the tired and roomless, a man whose shoulders bespoke a great load of boxes stashed in the back of his van and a woman with hands hipped in helpless outrage asking the clerk to call several exits to the east to check for rooms in their sister motels. The disappointed legions of junkers hit the road again, with Mark and I among their ranks. The longest yard sale and its adherents had locked up every motel within easy reach.

With Tennessee uninhabitable, we headed farther east, and after a two-hour traffic snarl that funneled three lanes of traffic into one for no reason neither Mark nor I could see, we crawled to a former Howard Johnson's over the Kentucky border, renamed "The Hospitality Inn," a gesture of irony since very little was hospitable about it. The phone was broken; the ice machine sounded like it was a space ship in a 1950s

B science fiction film; the light switches didn't work, or at least didn't operate lights in our room; and the bulk of the accommodations were taken
up with the national convention of a college sorority, though I never
learned which Greek letters were involved. The hallways were littered
with young women chatting on cell phones, and Mark and I retreated to
a balcony facing a trash-strewn inner courtyard, where we drank gin and
listened as room after room burst into spontaneous sorority songs.

If I planned to return to the World's Longest Yard Sale, I'd definitely
call and reserve rooms in advance, in Jamestown, for the first night. I'd
also not start running Route 127 until south of Frankfort, as the sales to
the north of the state capital of Kentucky were too sparse. More helpful
hints would be forthcoming, if Mark and I had chosen a more typical year
to make the trek. However, we learned after we returned home that weekend was also the twenty-fifth anniversary of the death of Elvis Presley.
The faithful had snapped up every room that scavengers hadn't. You
couldn't rent a room in a henhouse in all of Tennessee, and the King's
minions were getting their beauty rests in preparation for descending
upon Memphis and Graceland for the festivities.

It was futile to try to get closer so that we could traverse the last
leg of Route 127 into Alabama, and so that part of the World's Longest
remains mythic. If the escalation of the sale from Kentucky to Tennessee
was any indicator, then Alabama was the Eldorado of yard sales, the her-
alded bonanza just-around-the-bend. Somehow it seemed fitting that
the Ghost of Elvis rose up to stop us penetrating into the Deep South,
into the wild and wonderful junk to be had there. Subject of so much
kitsch and collectible junk, Elvis is a fitting patron saint of junk. I wasn't
surprised that the high holy days of the King of Velvet Paintings would
coincide with the longest sale of castoffs and unloved junk in all of
Appalachia, if not the entire world.

Chapter Eighteen

✣

Sales of Distinction and Taste

At times, even in our present urban mode of life with its mass-produced abundance, we may catch sight of the haunted, displaced hunter and gatherer seeking among the bins and aisles his lost tribal self. . . . But of course, this is what people in malls and supermarkets are doing: reading brands and labels in place of animal signs and vegetable seasons.

JOHN HAINES'S OBSERVATION about modern consumers applies more literally to those who haunt yard sales. Unlike those who go to supermarkets and simply scan labels, yard-salers must seek out the sources of what they want by turning down that mystery road, pulling over in a never-visited neighborhood, and marching up a stranger's driveway to the mouth of garage or cavity of a porch, perhaps even by being invited into the house itself if the owners are holding a moving sale. It astonishes me how open such sales can be; try walking up to a random house not holding a sale, ringing the doorbell on a Saturday morning, and asking what they have to sell. You will be lucky if they open the door beyond a crack, and a screen door will remain between you, your request, and the home itself. The American home is a great sanctuary, the least public space in the world.

What a difference a sign makes. That slight invitation turns the American home into a marketplace, using the historic margin between the public and private: the porch or front yard. This is a fair-weather phenomenon because the outdoors is required to bridge this gap between the inner sanctum and the world of secondhand commerce. At this intersection we provide for the needs of others from the plentitude of our leftovers. I have seen sellers plunge into their own possessions to turn up what a buyer has been seeking. Once, when I was looking for hinges for storm windows, a fellow scavenger took me into his garage to poke through his jars and cans of hardware until I had what I needed— for next to nothing. When one person approaches another at home with a simple need, an instinct beyond the one for buying and selling kicks in. Instead, the yard sale can foster the neighborliness oft declared missing in our modern social constructions.

I wouldn't want to put too high a gloss on the enterprise; people are, after all, buying and selling junk here, not engaging in acts of high altruism or charity. Still, this is an arena of high civility where people exchange niceties along with money for goods. Seldom have I attended a yard sale when some comment on the weather and its suitability is not part of the ritual. Only antique dealers and other sharpies have the hubris to be aggressive or boorish in this setting; for the rest of us, attending a yard sale is a civil engagement. In no other commercial setting is it common to hear a buyer wish a seller good luck. When was the last time you wished the merchants at Wal-Mart or Sears a profitable day?

Although the entire used network is noncentralized, the yard sale is its most democratic level. It takes no special equipment to run a sale, nothing beyond a handmade sign. Even location, a primary aspect of other venues, is less important; I have followed signs with arrows down a labyrinth of streets rivaling those of Venice to find a yard sale in the most cloistered of suburban neighborhoods. The sale itself can be held on a lawn, on a porch, in an open garage, in a barn, anywhere that allows the free traffic of visitors. Some might tie balloons to their mailboxes, or go to the expense of running a newspaper advertisement, but really nothing else is required. Anyone, on any day, anywhere, can hold a yard sale. In the space of an hour or two you can become a used goods merchant, setting up shop on a whim. No other business requires less capital investment; even a lemonade stand requires you buy lemons. A yard sale takes no training, no special knowledge, and no skill. No one makes a living at yard sales, so they are the most amateurish and *ad hoc* and maybe the most rewarding, of any corner of the trade.

The queen of the yard sale is the estate sale. Most are not well-advertised, as they are usually run by antique dealers who invite other dealers exclusively to the sale. Estate sales are special because they offer the accumulated goods of a single lifetime, stuff absolutely fresh to the market, though not as choice as what you will find on the auction circuit. I have on rare occasions been on the inside of one of these sales. My next-door neighbor, Gladys Moser, was ninety-six when she died, and by virtue of her longevity, most of her possessions were either antique or collectible, and the executor of her estate called a local dealer I knew to handle the liquidation. I remembered seeing some of her prized possessions, especially a walnut library desk, almost grotesquely carved, which she said had been given to her uncle, an ambassador, by the president of Mexico. Her other household goods, while more modest, were all fetching; I hoped to buy a wicker porch swing that she put out each spring and took in each fall, but which I only saw her sit in once. Gladys had been too feeble to spend much time outside.

I had been talking with the dealer in the backyard when she was hauling out the stuff she wanted for herself. "We'll let people come in tomorrow and take their pick," she told me, but when I mentioned liking the wicker swing she was willing to sell it to me immediately. Then she allowed me to go through the house first, and I picked up several other useful and entertaining finds, such as a solid copper flashlight, one of the first ever made. The Mexican desk was gone—the executor had claimed it—but other fine things, including some eighteenth-century Windsor chairs, remained for the picking. I was satisfied with my wicker though. The dealers who walked through the house the next day could glean the real precious stuff.

Auctioneer John Christman told me estate sales were attractive because the deceased provided provenance. He learned that lesson early from his father, who was also in the used business. John was fifteen and helping his father with a sale, and he decided to test his father's advice about the importance of provenance. He started telling customers elaborate stories about how they had found a shaving mirror at the sale. It was a $60 item, he said, but sold for $145. Like high-end auctions, estate sales are intimately tied to the former owner. Even former Sotheby's employee Colin Stair had an estate sale to help dispense with the lifetime accoutrements of Frederick Hughes. After assessing what would command interest, and a good price, at his fledgling auction, Colin advertised a "tag sale," the New England term for yard or estate sale, to be held in the Elks Lodge.

I took along Michael Sham, the classics scholar, whom I lured there with the promise of Roman era coins for $10, a cheap piece of The Empire. At the Elks hall we were met at the entrance by a man in a suit who opened the door for us. Leave it to Colin to use a doorman at an estate sale, to lend a classy touch even at this low range of the used spectrum.

This "tag sale" was certainly unusual, befitting "A Man of Distinction and Taste" as a sign read near the cash-out table. There too was a photograph of Hughes, looking dapper and bright and staring out at the proceedings. Nearby a table was taken up with Mexican Day of the Dead trinkets, papier-mâché skulls and skeletons (all for $3), and a folk art sculpture depicting the baptism of Jesus by John the Baptist in the Jordan River. Both figures were naked, and one of Colin's staff was joking with a customer about finding their postures pornographic. Some of Hughes's bottom-level leavings were erotic, such as a ceramic figure of a bride with bouquet which, when turned over, revealed a copulating couple beneath her flowing skirt—a wedding cake ornament. A man of distinction, it seems, has many tastes.

More of these many tastes were well represented: A polar bear rug sprawled over a rolling cart, two Prussian eagle candle wall sconces sat beside a birdhouse made of cement and sea shells, and I spotted a Korean chest of drawers with exquisite little compartments, which Colin assured me was genuinely old. Michael examined a table full of silk scarves, printed with the abdication speech of Edward the VII. Larger scarves were priced at $20 and the smaller for $10. Hughes's clothing was eliciting the least interest, a rack of tiny suits and vests, that most twelve-year-olds could not wear.

The place bobbed with dealers and avid collectors who had made Colin's customer list. One woman near the scarves asked Michael a question, which he deflected to me. "He had to have a house somewhere," she whined. "Why is the sale here?"

"Hughes lived on Long Island." I answered.

"So why is the sale here? Is it a better location?" she demanded, and I guessed she had traveled to Hudson from New York City.

I shrugged, not wanting to get into a long explanation about Stair's Sotheby's connection. If Colin was going to appeal to New York City clientele, he'd have to overcome some of their aversion to traveling beyond the five boroughs.

Two hours into the sale, the hall had been depleted of most of its best items, so Colin's staff began consolidating stuff into the center of the room, filling holes and making the browsing more intense, and crowded. Colin said six hundred items had sold in the first hour and a half. "But nobody bought Elvis," Colin said about a three-foot statue of The King, the patron saint of junk. "I even put him in the photo." Colin had advertised the sale with a postcard—an unusual tactic for an estate sale—with a color photograph of a selection of the goods in a poised arrangement: Elvis, a Marilyn Monroe à la Warhol print, and a crystal top hat. The result was a still life of the kind of stuff you could expect. Colin helped with the reorganizing. As Colin was wheeling a cart carrying the polar bear skin up to the front, someone took his picture. He good-naturedly turned his head in the direction of the flash and muttered, "You bastard." The picture was rather absurd—a big man pushing a rolling bearskin.

Hughes was a collector, and Colin's own staff bought most of Hughes collection of auction catalogues, a mother lode of information about pricing that would now inform the entire used network. There were still many boxes of record albums for sale, and audiophiles were flipping through them. It was an odd mixture, though, mostly classical and jazz with a little rock, but nearly always signed, though the signatures were unreadable to my unaccustomed eyes. Hughes had assembled a music collection based upon who he knew or met. Sometimes the albums were in homemade album covers, and the records themselves lacked labels. These I assumed were private pressings. I supposed someone more familiar with the New York jazz scene might know who Hughes had known and which were worth buying, but they were all anonymous to me.

Much of what Hughes's estate had contributed to the sale were equally puzzling, such as a box of Barbie heads, all with a 1960s brunette page-boy cut. The entire box was offered at $50. Why would Hughes want several dozen identical Barbie heads? Why would he keep them until he died? An ornate wooden rack, like a track and field hurdle, sat near the Mexican folk art table. "What was that used for?" I asked Colin.

"I can't figure it out," he admitted.

"Maybe it was used by a dancer for exercises," I guessed.

"Or something Hughes used himself. He had MS," Colin offered. Whatever the piece was, no one had snatched it up during the first couple of hours.

Nothing was too personal to sell. I found Michael going through a plastic bag full of handwritten notes. They included a tally from the dissolution of Andy Warhol's estate, a sale that Hughes had helped supervise as the pop artist's business agent. Also, a reminder that Hughes owed someone $100,000 as a result of the sale. Other slips of paper were from a professional phone answering service. Hughes had dozens of messages on one day in 1973. Elizabeth Montgomery of *Bewitched* fame called, as did Bianca Jagger, who simply reported she was back in London. Hughes was certainly at the center of a swirling social set.

In addition to hosting sales, the Elks hall was also rented for dances. In keeping with the spirit of Hughes's life, Colin turned on the disco reflecting ball and trained a couple of colored lights on it. "Nice touch," I said to Colin.

"I couldn't resist. Fred would have wanted it that way," Colin said with a bit of black humor. "He was a Studio 54 kind of guy."

Michael got his Roman coin, with the profile of Emperor Constantine. Colin gave me a six-inch papier-mâché Mexican skeleton. Pleased with our finds, Michael and I went to a local diner to take stock and reconstruct Hughes's life, which an estate sale invites you to do, if the whole picture is surprising enough to make such speculation entertaining. Hughes was a great socialite and lover, and a collection of postcards revealed he had many admirers. One admirer asked coquettishly, "How about tea, and Sicily?" Another present or former lover reported on having "a glacial steam bath with Mark, a future rock star" in Rome. The semiotics of Hughes's leavings pointed to a full life, but a debilitating end.

Any estate resounds with a former life, and not necessarily one so florid and public. I love going to estate sales in areas where heavy industries thrive, such as General Electric's Schenectady, New York, or Pittsburgh, Pennsylvania. Workers in industry are great collectors of tools, and a lifetime's collection can make for fine pickings, if you like tools, that is. And I like tools, because they allow me to fix the castoffs I find or to adapt them to other uses. That's why I like to go "saling" (as my scavenger compadre Bob Miner calls attending yard sales, enjoying the homonym with the more genteel "sailing") in suburbs built to house General Electric workers. At one sale I hit a bonanza of hand tools owned by a fastidious former engineer. The dealer running the sale had the good sense to leave the tools hanging in the carefully arranged spots in the garage, the outline of each wrench and hammer painted on the wall. "A place for everything and everything in its place," as my father used to say. The teeth of each handsaw were sheathed in a cardboard sleeve, and each chisel was polished, sharp, and oiled.

The house was an unassuming raised ranch in the suburbs, perfect for picking, because people in the suburbs don't understand castoffs, and most likely neither would their heirs. The scavenger tribe was certainly there. People were so eagerly snapping up the old engineer's stuff that a line had formed at the cash table of people with their finds in-hand. I saw an auctioneer/antique dealer with a tackle box. He opened it to show another buyer. "Yeah, I know what I have," he said gleefully. He scooped up a handful of old lures and grinned. He had scored a real find, given the hot collectibles market for fishing tackle. I hope he sold them quickly, as I predict the hundreds now being paid for old lures is as ethereal as the beer can market. As usual, I was content to let the sharpies speculate, as long as I got my bucket of files, pliers, and wooden-handled machinist's screwdrivers.

As in other parts of the used network, even an estate sale is not necessarily what it seems—context is manipulated. Once, when saling north of Schenectady, I saw an estate sale sign pointing to a large barn on top of a hill. Then I spotted a second faded sign: HOPE HILL FURNITURE. At one time the barn had housed one of those huge outlets for unfinished wood furniture. Most of these stores started in the 1970s, at the beginning of the discovery of the appeal of used, solid wood furniture that had been painted in the preceding new-is-better decades and now was being stripped and sold for less than new furniture made of pressboard and plastic. New merchandisers, always trying to respond to a perceived need, scrambled to offer a cheaper alternative. True to form, most of the retail outlets were housed in newer "barns," imitating antique stores. Unfinished furniture also often imitated older styles, and manufacturers churned out warehouses full of pine versions of Golden Oak classics from the turn of the twentieth century. After the public realized the descriptor "solid wood" alone did not guarantee quality, most of these "furniture barns" closed.

I was skeptical. Were furniture barn owners using the "estate sale" sign as a ruse to get shoppers into a clearance sale of new furniture? I drove on, but on a hunch turned around. Maybe the people who had owned the store had died. Cars were parked on the curb, showing others had stopped. Maybe it was a true estate sale. It warranted a look.

I had to park along the road, and I noticed the neighbors had put up NO PARKING signs. They had obviously been through more than one weekend in which these "estate sales" had occurred and did not want people parking on their lawns. Although estate sales have higher prices than the average yard sale, the goods are generally better, because they have been saved by the owner over a lifetime. The dealers who run the sales work on commission but have to sell everything in a few days so the prices have to be reasonable. Likewise the sales are aimed at other dealers who have to resell the items and make a profit, so prices have to recognize this. These factors make estate sales a siphon for bargain hunters. However, if this had been the site of estate sales in the past, I was skeptical; after all, you only get to die once.

I almost decided not to go up to the barn, but since I had already parked, I made the hike up the hill. At the end of the long lane was an old dairy barn with long buildings tacked onto the front, the additions made when the farmstead was converted to selling cheap furniture. Inside was a series of showrooms for furniture, but I immediately perceived they were being put to a far different display use. The first room was full of old toys, mostly what might be associated with a boy's life in the 1930s: leather-working and crafts kits, Erector sets, games, baseball bats, boxing gloves, and some lead soldiers. The second room contained a strange mix of military and police items, even a half-dozen nightsticks, a collection of holsters, gauntlet gloves identified as being from the Spanish-American War, and Delaware and Hudson railroad gloves. I also saw plastic sandwich bags full of knives, a collection of spyglasses, and a purple heart in a case. At a glance I could start to put together a deeply resonant story, as each object was accompanied by a swirl of narratives. This was a genuine estate sale; the presence of such personal mementos confirmed it.

Personal or not, the stuff here was the being assessed for its bargain potential more than its biographical relevance. In the military room I saw a young man dressed in a heavy-metal band T-shirt holding up a silver chain he was thinking of buying for his girlfriend. "Girls go wild for jewelry," he said to an older woman with him who looked to be his mother. "It works every time. Though it would be all over if they knew how little I paid for it." His eyebrows did a sly dance.

"I'm not even going to grace that with a response," his mother said dryly.

Most of the furniture was newer, and the prices were low. In the two rooms of furniture and dishes, I saw a couple haggling over a $1,900, five-piece dining room set. Although I thought they were ignoble pieces of 1960s Colonial furniture, they were solid maple and well made for the times, so they were probably worth the price. From the low prices and humble provenance on the furniture, I deduced this must be a true estate sale, though some of it was probably salted, especially among the toys and knives. (I saw different initials on some of the price tags, suggesting some of the items came from another source.) Antique dealers who run estate sales will bring items from their own stock that coincide with the nature of the goods the deceased had, using the sale as a context. An antique dealer once told me, "If you can get that idea in their minds, that something came out of an old farmhouse, then you get more money for it." He had proved it once in an estate sale in a farmhouse in Vermont. He added some crocks that shouldn't have sold for more than $10, but he "sold them right and left for $40 to $50." However, most of the items here appeared fresh to the market.

I looked about for the sale operator and saw a woman with red hair and a big fanny-pack talking to people, so I went up to speak to her. She was with Estate Resolution, a used merchandizer who specialized in these post-mortem sales. A wall sign advertised a Web site.

The woman said that she preferred to hold estate sales at the home of the deceased, but when their homes were in poor locations she rented the old furniture warehouse. Most of the stuff from this weekend's sale came from a house that now sat on a four-lane freeway. "You'd have been hit and killed," she said about parking for the sale. "I'd have lost customers." She rented the barn a couple of times a year, whenever she needed to move stuff out of a house immediately. "Sometimes someone will just want stuff out of the dead person's house," she said, because they had sold it, or because an heir is moving in.

The woman then provided the provenance the rented setting could not. The estate had belonged to a man who had reached one hundred years old before he died. He had been a railroad bull—a security officer—for the Delaware and Hudson (hence the nightsticks, holsters, and gloves). His father's possessions were being sold, too. The father had been a veteran of the Spanish-American War and was represented by the gauntlet gloves and medal. As I had guessed, other stuff was mixed, such as two newer chests of drawers, nicer than the other furniture as it was made of fine walnut. The woman said two sons had been fighting over them during the dissolution of an estate so a judge had ordered her to sell them, and the brothers to buy them if they really wanted them, the other getting the money, minus her commission. It was telling that they remained unsold; the brothers were only fiercely covetous when the furniture was free. "There's a story behind everything here," she said.

As the woman spoke her eyes never made direct contact with me. She was constantly surveying the sale. She turned her attention to a woman who approached her and asked her about handling her mother's estate.

"Did the dead person have cats?" she asked.

"No, why?" the customer asked.

"Allergies. That's the only stuff I can't handle."

The customer gave her a puzzled look. I wondered, perhaps as the customer was, how you could specialize in estate sales and rule out the leavings of cat owners? I also shuddered at her strangely callous reference to "the dead person."

The seller smiled brightly and quipped. "I hear they're developing an allergy-free cat. Have you heard that?" And with that they began making arrangements.

Estate sales might bear the shadow of the vulture branch of the scavenger family, but they are a necessary part and bring much fresh merchandise into the market. However, yard sales in general are a more joyous affair. Instead of items that have been hoarded for a lifetime, people hold yard sales to get rid of unwanted items. It is the level at which the professionals are stymied, most of the time, from making the most of life's leavings. All of the operating principles are suspended, or at least muted. Free of the ballet of the auction and the theater of the antique store, used goods sold in yard sales are solo acts. Something featured at a yard sale is either precious, or just plain junk.

Chapter Nineteen

✿

The Rank and File

STOPPING AT A STEWART'S CONVENIENCE STORE FOR GAS, I saw a flyer on the community bulletin board for a "30 Family Yard Sale" in a condominium complex on Carr Road, a locale I didn't know, but which I could locate in my Gazetteer. I made a mental note of the 10:00 A.M. Friday starting time. Yard sales are always held on weekends, of course, but most traditionally start during the workday on Friday, and I've never quite understood why. It only gives antique dealers, and bargain hunters like me, a jump on the general buying public. The diminished competition is a bit offset by the seller's general reluctance to dicker, anticipating the larger crowds on the next day, but you have first crack at most of the merchandise, and at the best buys. At least, that's how it should work.

Early birds do everything they can to undermine even the most dedicated Friday saler. These antique dealers and junkers arrive even before the tables have been set up and ask sellers whether they can go through the boxes being carried out of the garage. Sometimes they don't even ask; you might be setting up in the morning and find people already sidewinding up the driveway. They even harangue sellers to ferret out other things in their houses for sale. Because of this behavior, I've seen newspaper advertisements for sales that declare "early birds 10 percent more," meaning those arriving before the official opening have to pay a premium for the privilege. However, the hunger for first dibs on used goods is so intense even this extra fee will scarcely dampen a junker's ardor. I call this passion "junger."

I alerted Bob Miner, the yeoman of yard sales, and we arranged to make the Carr Road sale sometime on Friday morning. We had no overweening needs, so we had the luxury of letting early birds have their crack at the best. We needed only garden-variety junk. When I got to the wooded hilltop where Bob and his family live, I saw an old Greyhound bus parked there. Another Bob had arrived from his constant wandering. Bus Bob, as I knew him, had outfitted his rolling home with computers, and a Landsat satellite tracking device. The bus had been his home for fifteen years, since he quit his practice as a neurologist; he sold everything and hit the road. Bus Bob was a consummate scavenger. Among other nomadic sources of subsistence, Bus Bob lived entirely on castoffs.

I was always delighted to see Bus Bob whenever he chose to make an appearance; this time he seemed leaner and older. It had been a couple of years. However, Bus Bob had returned to the hilltop outside of rural Middle Grove, New York, for an auspicious event. Bob Miner was turning sixty years old. What better way to celebrate than a saling expedition?

Bus Bob and Bob Miner were eager to get to the sales. Then Carolyn, Bob's neighbor, saw we were about to embark. "To heck with the day," she said as she climbed into Bob's van with us, unable to resist houses worth of junk, "shanghaied again."

Carr Road was near MacGregor Mountain, site of a New York State penitentiary and Grant's Cottage, a historic site where Ulysses S. Grant retired to write his memoirs before succumbing to throat cancer. The houses on Carr Road were neither historic nor cottages; they were new retirement condominiums. Builders were still putting up more units (new houses are always "units"), eating up a giant patch of forest. The double houses were in the middle of an exclusive golf course. Signs along the road warned drivers to WATCH OUT FOR GOLFERS.

"If you buy a condo here, you are guaranteed twenty-four-hour golf," Bus Bob said with a sneer. He had retired to the open road instead, and even found gathering places for others of the Winnebago set, such as Quartzite, Arizona, a bit too genteel. On Carr Road each condo was the same shade of GI green, ostensibly to seem eco-friendly, though any sign of nature that wasn't a rock too big to move had been stripped and replaced with farmed sod and nursery maple, cedar, and azalea.

Neighborhood yard sales have their pros and cons. Each house would not have as much to offer, but since the sales were closer together you could reach several quickly on foot. Thirty families would offer as much as a half dozen good, full yard sales, and some surprises, especially among those to whom it would never occur to hold a yard sale but who decided to set out a few items, perhaps real treasures, on the day the others held theirs.

The first sale was a bad portent, and laughable. A dour woman was sitting in her garage with a large cardboard box full of purses—each $50 or more. Carolyn picked one up, then dropped it when she saw the price, which the woman noticed. "They cost $200 new," she countered with a scowl, and I guessed she had seen other customers balk.

"Absolutely irrelevant," Carolyn said to me as we walked away, and she was absolutely right. We had just landed at the sale of someone who had spent no time buying used and was clueless about how disconnected a price for something new was from its value secondhand. Such inexperience with the prevailing prices of used goods has two results in yard sales: either the prices are based on the new merchandise trade and therefore much higher; or conversely, the sellers have the money to buy everything they want new and don't value their excess goods, nor are they really trying to make money, so they practically give stuff away. We saw both at the Carr Road sale; next door to the purse merchant was a woman selling common discount department store stuff, such as stainless-steel picture frames and ceramic trivets, all for $5 apiece. She was as unpleasantly disappointed as her neighbor.

As soon as we had started at the sales, Bus Bob wandered away like a bird-dog on point, but making a wide survey. That is one probable path to a quick good deal, to pluck the best buy. Bob Miner adopted the converse approach, dawdling over each table, each rack of clothes— nearly everything he wore came from these sales, so he was careful not to miss any tidbit. Carolyn and I took the middle way. We checked the sales quickly but fully, buying hesitantly. Even though most items were suitably cheap, they were also not applicable to our needs. The retired folks in the Land of Golf had already downsized before moving into condos; I found myself wishing I'd attended their moving sales then. There was certainly no children's clothing or no-longer-loved toys. These sellers had been through with children years ago.

As usual, though, the most interesting sale contained goods outside of what we'd expect. A frail, barely audible man was sitting in a lawn chair against the far wall of his garage, and his driveway was lined with brass and copper pots, pails, and other vessels. The man had bought them many years ago in Pakistan, he whispered, in a shop where they sold hand-forged and smelted items "by the pound." Now with infirmity plaguing the man's last years, he was divesting himself of his collection.

The prices were higher than you'd expect at a yard sale, as much as $15 for a pot, but they were easily worth three times that much. I bought two brass canisters for $10 each, and Bob, a lover of hammered copper and brass from his days growing up in Istanbul, bought a brass hip flask. Probably corroded inside, the flask would be difficult to clean so couldn't be used for liquor, but it touched some chord in Bob. The sale was a perfect example of how you bought what you found where you found it, and for needs you had not acknowledged.

When many sales are advertised together, the variety and quality of stuff to be found can be offset by the competition of other alerted buyers. Such was the case in the Ballston Spa town-wide yard sale. Originally a resort town, Ballston Spa, then Ballston Springs, was a destination of the rich and famous in the early 1800s. The town's main drag, Front Street, once studded with grand hotels, now had few retail businesses: a drugstore, variety store, restaurant, and a bank. However, with a town's worth of building collateral, alternative businesses had bloomed, such as a reject clothing store and junk shops or antique stores.

On the town-wide sale weekend, simply called "Family Days," the main street was closed to all but pedestrians who, when they had finished skimming the local castoffs in the surrounding neighborhoods, spent a few minutes among the tented vendors who rented space from the village. They mostly offered the kind of surplus stuff I had seen at flea markets: jewelry, T-shirts, ceramics, sports memorabilia and flamfleur, belts and wallets, dinner plates, videotapes and CDs, Chinese textiles and tools, marijuana pipes, and wind chimes. They took up four blocks—the extent of the business district—and at the end formed a pool of sellers in a park circling a cupola housing the source of the "restorative" water on which the town's old resort status had rested, the Old Iron Spring.

The status of these marketeers relied on a comparison with the price of their cheap goods on the new retail grid. MACY'S PRICE, $62.00 PER SET read a sign on the tent post of the seller of dinnerware: YOUR CHOICE,

$10.00. For that reason they are simply an appendage to the used goods market, not a true part of it. One of the primary reasons they had migrated to Ballston Spa on this one weekend was the traffic generated by those selling castoffs. The town had increased the space rental to $75, a local antique dealer told me, which had discouraged some of them. However, as long as the sale was popular, they would come. If the downtown stretch got too expensive, these marketeers would rent private yards.

I approached from a side road and passed up some scattered sales bearing the hallmarks of enterprising kids: items on the ground instead of on tables and plenty of things with amorphous shapes and bright primary colors indicating toys. Those signs seen from the road were enough to make me drive by; I also passed up sales where I spied collections of cheap furniture, marked by the tell-tale blond finish on composite wood and the bright glare of chrome and plate glass of shelves and tables bought in big-box department stores. When you have lots of sales from which to choose, either because it's a town-wide sale or the listing in the newspaper want ads is two feet long, it's best to have some way to be discriminating.

The first sale at which I stopped was a benefit for the local Girl Scout troop. Benefit sales are often quite good because you have a choice selection of goods from many houses. Donors usually contribute one or two things that they think will sell in order to help the cause—not simply any unwanted items they have on hand. One other customer was there: a man with a long, thin black overcoat, thick blond-gray hair, and a chiseled sandpapery face. The man moved in an automatic, dispassionate way, eyes flitting over the sale for only the best items. He was a picker, I decided, on the hunt.

Two sleepy dogs staggered to their feet and nosed me as I approached. I immediately saw something interesting, a white crock with a lid fastened with a screw-down clamp, the kind used for preserving food before the Ball brothers invented the glass canning jar in 1884. It was made by Akron Stoneware in Ohio. I wondered how the picker had missed it; it was either not the kind of stuff he was used to selling, or my eye had simply come to rest where his had not. It cost fifty cents.

As I pulled out a dollar, the black dog sniffed my hand. "He has to check you out to see if your money is okay," his owner said.

"So *that's* his job?" I answered, and we swapped pleasantries about the weather, about the startlingly high blue sky topping a day in the mid-seventies, picture-perfect for yard sales. The picker eyed me as I tucked the crock under my arm. I'm no mind reader, but I knew that he knew I had snatched up a real deal. I'd have to move quickly to get ahead of him, if I was to find another. Since we were both practiced yard sale gleaners, our orbits would overlap as we were likely to stop at the same sales for the same curb-appeal reasons.

The roads had not quite started to fill with slow-moving, sale-gawking customers, so I still had the luxury of driving quickly; soon I'd simply have to park. I went down Chapman Street, which I knew from experience always turned out lots of sales. At the end sat a lacy Victorian house on a double corner lot whose owners always rented space to several junkers with good prices. Immediately I saw a domino pile of old windows and doors on the curb with a sign saying FREE. Though I was driving my pickup, I resisted scooping them up. I didn't need them, and the trash-pickers were out in force as well, so they wouldn't last long, though the real picking wouldn't start until the afternoon of the last day. I also spied a sale with lots of good power drills and saws, but I didn't need them either. Still, anyone could easily fill out a workshop by shopping on Chapman Street alone.

I poked along, with one eye on the man in black dogging my tail, until I reached the junkers at the corner Victorian. The usual enticing bazaar was set up, and I overheard a seller trying to unload a bench vise. As the customers cranked and uncranked its jaws, the seller fell back on eBay. "You look it up on the Internet, he said. "That's a good price." He wanted $20, which was a bit high for a yard sale, but once again the on-line market was used as validation for real-world prices.

I picked up a strange crescent-shaped African carving in ebony, faces on either tip looking at each other, thinking of Bob and his collection of primitive wooden masks, totems, and Middle Eastern copper and brass. He'd love the little carving.

I approached a pair of dealers to see what they knew about it. They were ending a conversation about someone who had gotten a deal on a valuable item. "So we got taken?" the red-haired man asked the other, talking with his hands in puppet-like movements.

His companion nodded slowly as I interrupted. "Yours?" I said, holding the carving.

"That's Joe's," the red-haired man said, pivoting off to fetch him.

Joe arrived at our side, a gnomish man with a single eyebrow from temple to temple. "I'm putting $20 on that, because I don't know what it is."

I set the carving down.

"It might be a sleeper. You never know," he blurted, trying to keep my interest fanned. A "sleeper" is a term generally reserved for an item that was undervalued at a high-end auction, but genuinely worth more.

I shook my head.

"I don't know. It came out of the right house, and I'm not just saying that to sell it," he said, looking at me, but I was being careful to register no reaction.

"Okay, everyone says that," he said quickly. "It comes from a house where a doctor lived. He died, and his widow sells me things a little at a time."

"I see," I said, "thanks anyway." The price was still too dear, and nothing he had said made any difference. As the man dithered and trotted out rationale and hazy bits of provenance, I was certain he could tell I'd heard it all before. I had become marked by experience, and often was mistaken for a junk seller or antique dealer, a full-fledged member of the tribe. Now I could dicker without saying a word. As I drove away I could see the archetypical three-toned pickup of the picker, stacked with furniture, rounding the corner.

I stopped at another sale simply because I liked the sign: AIR CONDITIONED YARD SALE UNTIL THE AIR CONDITIONER SELLS. The price tags contained other good-humored touches: "If you don't have an axe to grind, here's one for you—$10; and "Steal me for $60" said a desk. A woman was buying a horse harness, which was tagged "For the Horse You Rode In On." "Everybody's in the car waiting on me," she said, pointing to a car full of children at the curb. "I just said, 'Wait on me while I look at these saddles.'" As she paid she asked hopefully, "You sell your horses?"

"Never had horses. Only saddles," the seller said with a grin. "We just sat on them and pretended."

At that sale, the children living in the house, an old Italianate mansion topped with a wrought-iron cupola, were trying to make some side money selling lemonade. People often use yard sales as an opportunity to teach children some pointed lessons about the value of money, and allow them to sell some of their old toys or engage in this venerable bit of juvenile capitalism. I nearly always buy some lemonade when a stand has been established at a sale; as savvy as I try to be in my used merchandising, I'm a sucker in some ways. At this one, a boy who looked to be in the first grade took my quarter when I offered it for a cup and then sat complacently. His father coached, "You're not finished yet. Now you have to serve the customer." The boy did, with much ceremony and spillage.

"Thank you," I said to complete the exchange as I took the cup from his hand, trying not to grimace when I sipped the product and realized too much sugar had gone into the recipe. I knew by the end of the day my bladder would be bursting, but I simply can't pass up a stand, and always find room for another cup when my approaching charges a child's bored eyes with a little hope.

The next sale looked very promising, as it was at a house with a carriage barn—always a good sign. A portly seller was hovering over tables made from sawhorses and sheets of plywood. I picked up a metal box the size of a half dollar; when I twisted off the top I found two clear lenses inside—neither convex nor concave, so they had no magnifying properties.

"I found that digging in the garden," the man said.

The box was monogrammed and engraved, and it so intrigued me I gave him a quarter for it. I have no idea what it is to this day, but someday I'll find out. However, I could see the picker in black eyeing me from across the street, before he headed my way. I also spied an old ice pick, a promotional item from Consolidated Ice Company of Huntington, New York, which offered "Hygeia Ice," reminiscent of the germ scare spawned by the polio outbreak in the 1920s and 1930s. I also noticed the phone number: 83. I rushed backward, imagining a time when Huntington was that small, or the telephone was that new.

I had to pay a dollar for the ice pick, but it had curiosity collateral. As I handed over the dollar, the picker was at my elbow. "Damn," he said, "I was sure I had seen all of it," he groused. The ice pick would fetch $7 to $12 at an antique store.

"I'll let you have it for $5," I said quickly and held it out. If I could magnify or multiply the glower he gave me, it would qualify as a weapon of mass destruction.

I left the general circuit, deciding to break my pattern and get out of the picker's hair, to visit Paul Ferrara, the show dealer, who lived in Ballston Spa. Paul would be holding a sale in the carriage house behind his home, with a sign saying "Barn Sale," knowing full-well the magnetic power of those two words. When I got there Paul's wife, Millie, was running the sale; I gathered that Paul was out saling himself. They were selling odds and ends—stuff I knew Paul either didn't want to fix or wasn't worth fixing. Paul used "Family Days" to clear out unwanted inventory. What he didn't sell, he'd take to an auction. Anything in his barn not for sale he covered with an old sheet. Millie was covering a mahogany cabinet, a confessional from a Catholic church; it had sold, and she wanted to keep other people from making an offer while she waited for the buyers to return with a truck.

I wandered next door, where a young couple was selling a phalanx of pole lamps, an old computer, and a pile of jewelry—the latter was marked FREE, so I poked through it. It consisted of single earrings, French cufflinks, and cheap, gold-ish chains. The guy told me he had bought a pile of shirts at a church rummage sale in New Hampshire, but when he got them home he found they all needed cufflinks. So next he had to scavenge cufflinks to go with them, but he kept losing them. Now the shirts were gone and all that was left was the solo cufflinks he was giving away. Perhaps wearing mismatched cufflinks would become a fashion statement. How else would he ever get rid of them, even for free?

Oh, me-of-little-faith. Everything has a buyer. The guy told me Paul had come over to see what they had and had donated a broken wagon wheel he had found in the weeds behind their house. "'Put it out and put two dollars on it. People will want it to put in their gardens,'" he said Paul had promised. "We could have sold it three times," the man added, shaking his head. The wheel had sold immediately, and though they had put it aside for the buyer to pick up later, people repeatedly asked about it.

Just then, as though to further prove the point, a woman stopped at the sale. She asked if they had any Avon perfume containers, and to show what she meant, pulled one out of her bag, a bottle in the shape of a Heidi figurine. "I see them as art," she said. "I'm going to arrange them in my bathroom." Then she commented ruefully, "This one is missing her pigtail." She fingered the stub. "Oh well, I have three of them."

*

The last day of a yard sale can be just as good as the first, but for different reasons. On the Sunday of Ballston Spa Family Days weekend, I took
off for the hinter-sales. The first was at the end of a dead-end road, part
of what used to be the main road to Saratoga Springs. It had become
truncated when nearby railroad tracks became a four-lane highway. Signs
at the end of the road announced GARAGE SALE and PLANTS.

Nothing would have induced me to go down this dead-end road
besides a yard sale, so I never would have known about the exquisite old
farmhouse down there, with a stunning view of the Kayaderroseras Creek
bottom and the hills rising away from it. The sale was across the road from
the house in what had been a machine shed, an ancient post-and-beam
structure with a new metal roof. We were far enough from the main road
that traffic noise was eclipsed by the rushing creek.

The shanty was such a perfect setting for a yard sale I wondered
whether it was a permanent one. However, here the goods were too disorganized, and cheap. Price signs were drawn on the sides of paper-covered
clothes hangers, the kind used at a dry cleaners. They separated the shanty
into price zones in which stuff was offered for $2, $1, fifty cents, and free.

Near the shanty door a woman was demonstrating a lawn chair to a
prospective new owner. "It's supposed to fold up," she said, struggling
with the frame. She stood up, exasperated, the chair still unbent. "Oh
well," she chuckled, "it'll fold up when you sit in it."

The customer gave her a dollar for the chair, then handed her a real
estate business card. "I go to yard sales to find listings," she told me. "It
gives me an opportunity to look over an attractive house, and I figure if
someone is selling stuff, they might be thinking of moving." That was
certainly an after-effect of attending yard sales I'd never considered, but
it made sense; however, this time the owner of this quaint farmhouse
wasn't going anywhere.

I slipped through the shanty and found three wooden boxes built
like those the Shakers made. They sat on a table beneath a hanger sign
declaring everything was free. I carried them to where the woman was
sitting. "Are you really giving these away?"

"If that's where my daughter put them," she said. "It's her sale." I
had seen a ten-year-old orbiting. "She said next year she's not going to

have a sale. She said I've been making all of the money." The mother was selling houseplants. The daughter had originally marked the boxes at $1.50, then scratched that off and wrote fifty cents. Now she was giving them away. She certainly wasn't going to make any money that way, but that was one of the advantages of the end of a sale—bargains and give-aways. I gladly took the boxes with me.

I wound back into the village, and on the outskirts saw a sale in a Chinese restaurant parking lot. I parked nearby, and a sunburnt man with a cigarette launching from his lower lip watched as I approached. "Every price you see is lower. This is the last of my father's estate, and we don't want to box it up and take it away."

I looked at a glistening snow blower parked nearby on which his son, about eight years old, was monkeying around on the handlebars. "Yeah, $50 for that," the man said even though I had yet to check the price. "He bought it last year and used it three times. Why'd he have to go and do that? He was eighty-nine years old, and he buys a new snow blower." Why not? I thought. The son was being far too pragmatic. Few people have the presence of mind to anticipate their deaths when considering the needs of the moment.

Death. One of the "Three Ds," the others being debt and divorce, was still a major factor even at this level, the same as at a high-end, celebrity auction or a sale in a parking lot. Next I went looking for John Christman, auctioneer from Talk of the Town. I found him on the sidewalk in front of his house. Our talk was interrupted by his calling out to pedestrians, "Everything in the boxes is twenty-five cents—six for a dollar," even though a sign announced the same.

We had barely said hello when an elderly man with a WWII veteran cap with some military pins approached John. "You don't know me?"

John looked at him hard.

"You've been out to my house," the old man said before realizing he was mistaking John for another dealer to whom he had sold stuff. He named him, but I didn't catch it.

"I know him," John said, but added quickly, "Do you have anything else for sale? He's a friend of mine, but I pay more." John was always ready to make a purchase.

The old guy described his military pin collection, hundreds of items—he sold them a few at a time. The other dealer had given him $75 for two

Nazi pins. He seemed pleased with the price, but John only murmured noncommittally.

When the guy left, John turned to me and said, "He got taken. Two Nazi pins for only 75 bucks!"

John bought things in yard sales and resold them either in his store or at the Talk of the Town Auction. His wife, Heidi, told me what it was like prowling on Thursday evening before sales began, hunting with the other early birds. John would offer sellers 10 percent more than what they wanted if he could get a look before the others. "Some will order you off their property" when you approached them. It was a ticklish business trying to beat the others to a deal, but junger will drive people to all kinds of shenanigans.

Once, Heidi said, John was walking up a driveway when another dealer was walking down. When John got to the sale he saw three Victorian chairs, but the woman running the sale said, "They're already sold. The guy has to come back for them."

"Pretty soon," John said, "everyone's there," meaning at the sale, "I couldn't compete with all those guys."

And every dealer cruising the sales had seen those chairs. John saw the dealer who had bought the chairs driving around. He pulled up alongside John's van. "Do you remember which house is the one where I bought those chairs? I can't find them."

John smirked. "I'll tell you, but you got to cut me in," he said, glad to have the cagey dealer on the defensive.

"I'll find them if I have to walk up every driveway here," he said defiantly. When early-birding, John often saw other dealers. "When we pass, we are all smiles, but we're saying to ourselves, 'That son of a bitch probably beat me to the good stuff.'"

Heidi claimed dealers were under some unwritten code of ethics, if not with other dealers, among whom even the honor of thieves was dying from disuse. She liked to deal in jewelry, and once found a woman at a yard sale selling her deceased mother's. The woman had it priced for pennies, and some of it was made of highly collectible Bakelite. "To the woman it was all just plastic," Heidi said. She had picked out some pieces and "told her to sell them separately, on eBay. It was the right thing to do." Heidi could have bought the three pieces for seventy-five cents, and made a real killing. "If she had been asking $15 or $20 for each, I could have said, "Will you take $40?" Her conscience kept her from nearly stealing the valuable baubles. My estimation of the Christmans' virtuous trafficking in used goods and antiques rose with the story, but my over-all impression of the general climate of others in the trade did not.

Sellers can be equally as deceptive. They can subvert the system, such as those who run what I call permanent yard sales. Usually these are on well-traveled roads. Perhaps they began as genuine temporary sales, but because of the choice location, they had made so much money over the course of one weekend they soon held another. Perhaps they raided their attics and basements one more time, this time being more heartless about what they could send out into the world of junk; perhaps they even began gathering used stuff, scavenging from the curb or going to other yard sales. Another sale, maybe a month later, and they become hooked on the uncanny ability of junk to attract adherents. Before long they put out a sign every weekend, and experience price-creep; things no longer need to be sold in a couple of days and could be priced to sit rather than sell. These sellers have made the evolutionary leap from yard sellers to junkers.

As a result, they are my least favorite sales, but they are an undeniable part of the landscape. I wonder how long such faux-impromptu sales remain open before officials notice and demand that they charge and report sales tax. As a junker once told me, "The seven-percenters [meaning those who enforced the local 7 percent sales tax], are worse than the IRS. They'll close your doors for seven cents." For that reason I won't reveal the exact location of the permanent sales I have found, although most have probably pulled up their signs and folded.

One was on a well-traveled cut-off between two main north–south roads in upstate New York, a perfect setting for a continuous sale. A white van had already pulled over, and a couple had disembarked. If I had not already determined this was a permanent yard sale, I'd have thought the van was driven by pickers, but surely expert gleaners would see the same signifiers I had. The sign was painted too neatly on a piece of hinged plywood, like a sandwich board, something easily set up. Very little of their merchandise was on the lawn in front of the garage. Even from the car I could tell the sale was entirely too neat, too organized—with merchandise on *shelves*. The garage had been adapted over time to a sale, rather than serving *ad hoc*. To me, the difference was visually stark.

What was on the lawn had been chosen for curb appeal and served as both advertisement and as an evocation of a true yard sale. Sadly, their curb goods were unappealing: a snow blower; a bicycle; a pole lamp. It would have helped their cause to offer at least one piece of wooden furniture, anything to intimate that antiques might be lurking there. The sale was on the line between a conscious and random arrangement.

Inside were more signs of a continuing sale. A glass-doored cabinet housed ceramic dogs, ashtrays, and frog-shaped iron trivets, among other smalls. The cabinet was not for sale, only employed for display. Likewise, the sale sported a bank of built-in shelves for more merchandise. The second sign of permanence was that everything was dreadfully overpriced, twice or three times what you'd expect at a genuine yard sale. I wouldn't be buying unless something really called my name. My full name.

The shelves held inventory from a closed restaurant: dishes and glassware, even "reserved" signs for tables. I deduced that either the sellers had once owned an eatery, or they had simply bought out the contents of one in their search for more stuff to sell. In a permanent yard sale it's difficult to determine. A woman was diving into a box and said to the man with her, "You don't see these anymore," pointing to an industrial-sized vegetable strainer. He sniffed in reply. When the woman left, though, she left without it; instead she had some sort of appliance in a box under her arm. The bored way the couple running the sale took her money, sans cheery greetings, cinched my impression of the sale.

I don't avoid permanent sales, but I don't like being manipulated into thinking they are their more bargain-laden doppelgangers. When traveling on another main road I saw Day-Glo green signs promising MOVING SALE—EVERYTHING MUST GO. Moving sales are among the best. They have some of the lowest prices because if the sellers don't get rid of their stuff, they either have to move it or throw it away. Common sense would prescribe that a low price is better than no price.

I turned down the road, and when I found a sale it looked unpromising; all I saw were baby carriages and other outmoded children's equipment, almost as hard to unload as exercise machines because safety guidelines upgrade almost yearly, making them truly obsolete. I pulled over anyway. It surely wasn't the moving sale, but probably one spontaneously set up to take advantage of the advertising of the bigger sale farther down the road. Nothing interested me immediately, I decided quickly, though

I scanned some clothing draped over the rungs of ladder; I was still thinking of the big moving sale down the road. As I turned to leave, I saw a box of old hay hooks, handles with hand-forged hooks for moving bales of hay. A sign on the box read: 8 DOLLARS EACH. ANTIQUE.

The hooks bore prices from the day before—it was Saturday—$12 and even $18. The hooks were still there, after all of the pickers and dealers had been through, attesting to their being overpriced. The sellers were trying to get top dollar for what they knew was old and had at least modest collector appeal, but they were hampered by the wrong context, living as they were in a house in suburbia. They might have had better luck if they had been living in a farmhouse or old center-hall Colonial, and if someone had been standing vigil, ready to tell stories about the days of yore, of grandfathers pitching hay for a dollar a day.

I drove farther down the road to find the moving sale, but I never saw it, nor more of the bright signs. When I drove back to the one that had sent me on the chase, I saw the address listed was the house with the hay hooks. I suspected they were using the term moving sale very loosely; someone was moving, somewhere, probably. They understood this common sign rhetoric would increase traffic. I suspected they might be repeat sellers, if not permanent, when I saw their weathered, wooden sign, itself perhaps soon antique.

Ah, the magic of the term "antique." I once bought a coffee table at a permanent yard sale, a sale I believed had formed out of sere economic conditions. A woman was living in a banged-up house trailer on a busy road and had gathered about her as much junk finery as could be had cheaply. It was a fine day for saling, and lots of people had pulled over. The woman was obviously quite overwhelmed by the numbers, both gleeful and energized as she crowed about the value of this thing and savored someone's interest in that. She was going to make some money this day, I knew, hook or crook.

I spied a coffee table that matched a 1920s living room set to which I had been adding lamp stands and bookcases for a couple of years. It wasn't from the 1920s—they didn't make coffee tables then—but it was in a pre–Art Deco style and would match the rest.

As I turned over the table, the woman rushed over, cackling, "That there is an antique," she said, her tongue finding no front teeth to make a convincing middle t. The table bottom showed pressboard corner braces. It was clearly from the 1970s. What's more, the top had been ruined by rain, and the veneer would have to be stripped. However, I could tell from experience that the poplar wood underneath would actually refinish nicely and would stain to match the mahogany of the rest of my furniture.

The woman wanted an amazing $45 for it, for a piece of clearly half-ruined, trash-picked furniture. "There's nothing antique about it," I responded stiffly, wanting to cut to the chase and not maintain the fiction of its inflated value. The woman scowled, and I got it for $10. While I was glad she was having a good day, I'd been around too long to be taken for a rube.

In fact, if you insist something you are selling at a yard sale is an antique and stick to what you think is an appropriate price, you are likely to keep it. In a sale in the suburbs, amidst plastic wading pools and a collection of flotation devices, I saw an old crosscut saw sitting on a blanket, tagged for $50. It would sit there all weekend, and if not lowered, would go back into the corner of the two-car attached garage. I can imagine the conversation the sellers had when arranging their goods: "Here," the husband said, "let's put out that old saw that belonged to my grandfather. It's an *antique*." His emphasis would betray he had just thought of that angle on selling it. Until the notion of it being antique occurred to him, it was merely something to jettison. Now the man added, "We'll put fifty bucks on it. You see people hang them on walls. We can get real money for something like that."

Unfortunately for the owner, real money wasn't coming anywhere near that saw. If the man asked for a best offer, he would likely get $5 from a picker who would then sell it to an antique dealer for $10—who'd pay it reluctantly and put a price of about $40 on it and hang it on the wall. The dealer would know the saw was going to hang there a long time, but if the shop was in a barn, it would provide a little ambience while it waited for a buyer. The saw would have to pass through the ranks and levels at appropriate prices before it could find someone who would love it at the price the yard seller seemed to think it would command.

The two-way traffic of used goods, finding the appropriate level at which it had value, was at its most viscous at yard sales. A sale outside of West Stockbridge, Massachusetts, had several aisles of stuff; one table full of tools and fishing tackle boxes drew me. A cluster of men were nimbly picking through the latter, holding up lures to the light as though appraising jewelry piled in treasure chests.

I thumbed through dozens of screwdrivers and pliers in cardboard trays, all mildly oily, dulling the sound they made as I picked them up and tossed them down. I looked up to survey the rest of the sale: two more tables sat in the backyard with household stuff, such as sets of three, five, and seven glasses or cups, and wire racks once sold as cupboard organizers, but that took up too much room. A greasy winch with a hunk of frayed cable sticking out one pulley lay underneath in the grass.

I should have known that this was not a pure yard sale when I saw a set of white wicker porch furniture, protected by sheets of cardboard and shrink-wrapped, obviously new. As I drifted away from the tools, I saw items on other tables with printed price tags. This was a flea marketeer, or another species of vendor. Then I noticed, as though it was formerly invisible, a panel truck with its doors open behind the house. When I had stopped at the sale, I had seen a barn with open doors behind a yard full of junk, like the spilled contents of a great, ancient storehouse. That visual rhetoric had sufficed to bring me in.

A man approached the seller, who was sitting on a warm October day with a straw hat, a hank of gray hair restrained in a puffy tie behind. The man showed him a handful of pliers. "How about fifty cents apiece," the seller replied.

The customer reached in his pocket and said something I didn't catch, but the seller's answer suggested it. "I buy the contents of storage units, then sell it around. Sometimes I keep things out to research. Like this," he said, picking up a set of snips sitting beside him. It looked like something a surgeon might use. "That says Klause on it. Now, I don't know what it is, but I know Klause only makes the best, so I'm going to wait until I find out."

"So you buy stuff from self-storage places?"

"Yeah, people put stuff into storage, and don't pay the rent, so the storage unit owners sell it to get something back. Usually I go to flea markets. I have a place I set up every Saturday and Sunday. There wasn't a market today, so I told my friend here," he made a backward nod at the house, "'Hey, you know that yard sale you want to have? Let's have it this weekend.' He brought out what he wants rid of, and I brought in some stuff to see what I can get for it. I'm doing it as a favor to him."

The man was doing himself a favor, too. October is near the end of the flea market season in the Northeast, so the seller was dumping what hadn't sold during the long spring and summer selling season for anything he could get. Still, forfeited storage units were a source of used goods that I had not before considered. What had caused that flow of defaulted junk? Death? Debt? Divorce? What troubles could have been so severe as to get between someone and his fishing tackle?

I asked the seller about a table full of restaurant equipment, such as fryers, coffee makers, and boxes of plain dishware. "A friend of mine sold out his diner. He sold the big stuff, and I'm getting rid of the small stuff." Then the seller noticed me putting a hand on the deep-fryer. "I could sell the fryer easy if I drove to Mayfair," he said. Mayfair, I learned, is a big Massachusetts flea market. "But I don't want to drive to Mayfair," he added smugly. The seller leaned back in his chair. He was a confident, practiced junker, who knew how to get money out of whatever passed through his fingers. He was simply a conduit.

All of the first principles of used buying and selling were in full force in yard sales, perhaps with even more vagaries and marginal effects. Weather even mattered; I once saw a guy trying at first to sell, and then give away, a NordicTrack on a sweltering July day, not a day for contemplating fitness regime. Personal significances, that near-nostalgic nudge that fuels some purchases, also remained. At a rummage sale at a Methodist church, the clerical equivalent of the yard sale, I ran headlong into relics of my past with tremendous resonance.

The rummage sale was staffed by two older women and a bored teenaged boy who eyed me with studied disinterest as I entered their compound of junk in the parking lot. I had arrived late on a Saturday afternoon, and everything had been picked over. I had stopped to kill time, on a whim. Within a moment, though, I was ambushed by a box of books, specifically by a book on top with a familiar cover. It was one volume of an illustrated atlas I had read as a child, a volume on each of the continents. I had forgotten the book, and when I opened it I did not remember many of the pictures, but the cover was perfectly imprinted in my memory.

Beneath the volume rested a stack of really resonant books, though: a full set of children's encyclopedias. Those I recalled intimately. My mother had gotten them as bonuses when buying groceries at the A&P.

The editions at the sale were in nearly new condition. Ours had to be taped together because I had read them to pieces. I opened up the first volume, and every brightly colored picture was for me an icon, a mental representative of the concept it was meant to illustrate. These pictures had become buried images, and when I saw them they were brilliantly familiar. Almost without thinking I pulled out Volume Seven, G to H, or as it said on the cover: Ghosts to History. It had been my favorite, because it contained so many marvels. I never tired of reading the first entry on ghosts with its pictures of transparent people descending staircases trailing chains and bunches of keys. It was followed by "Giants," which depicted the Cyclops menacing Odysseus' ship, a drawing of a "circus giant and circus midget," for an exaggerated comparison, and something called "a Storybook Giant," who was laughing and holding what looked to be a mouse-sized swan in his hands. He was a jolly giant, not one of the fe-fi-fo-fum variety.

Next came "Gold," with its nuggets and the death mask of Agamemnon, and then "History" itself, laid in several pages of illustrated panels, depicting "great events," ending when history ended then, in 1958, with a rocket going into space. In the very next panel, though, crouched a nearly naked man drawing in the dirt with a stick, accompanied by the caption: "While we explore space, some people are still living in the Stone Age."

The circular nature of this illustration, supposedly demonstrating that time and progress are twinned for some and not for others, was so blatantly racist, so thoroughly biased toward what were colonial European powers, that I slammed the book shut, and stood up, instantly dismayed over how I had been trained to think, even by such unexpected, and benign, agents. I looked around and noticed the teenager was looking at me incredulously. What had so absorbed me for nearly half an hour? I imagined him thinking. What could I have found so engrossing in a box of old children's encyclopedias?

I couldn't tell the boy that inside those books, latent bigotry aside, lay my first stirrings of curiosity, my first glimpse of the knowable world. Those books had provided me with mysteries, legends, lost worlds, wars, and heroes. So why didn't I buy them, the whole box full, and spend two days re-igniting an adult-muted wonder? I'm unsure. Perhaps the last illustration had alerted me. I was beyond those books and their interpretations. The older, more critical me no longer could believe in their simple world, one both tainted and pure. I wanted to preserve what I had loved about those encyclopedias, untouched, unrecovered. I belonged to those books, and they already belonged to me. For five bucks I could have taken home the entire boxful, but I didn't. I had used them too well already, and at some recessed level I had them memorized. What child will browse the Internet decades later and experience the same shock of recognition, a similar sweet sadness at the irretrievable past?

While the phenomena of junk shops and antique stores arise in towns where other forms of commerce have fled, yard sales lend themselves to rural settings for the quantity of stuff available in the barns and sheds of fallow farms. Greenfield, New York, is the perfect prospecting ground for a day of saling. On any late spring, summer, or languid fall day, the country roads sprouted signs for sales, although the controversy over PCB contamination of the Hudson and General Electric's culpability had added CLEAN THE HUDSON and WE OPPOSE DREDGING signs to the eye clutter. Mix in real estate for sale signs—property was a hot commodity in Saratoga County since the September 11 tragedy—and you really had to slow down to locate yard sale notices.

I slid by a few sales without stopping, relying on curb appeal, and then stopped at a place called Bittersweet Farm, realizing I had stopped there at a sale a year before. I had bought a hammer there for a friend of mine, John Bowler, who ran a charity volleyball tournament on Million Dollar Beach in Lake George each year. John wanted a specific tool to help with driving tent stakes—a twelve-pound sledge on a short handle. John had the kind of physique that would make such a hammer powerfully persuasive, though most people would be unable to wield one. I found a hammer head for John at the sale for fifty cents and a broken handle I cut down for his use. On this day I saw show dealers had set up in the barn and yard, so I did not expect many bargains. They had rows of furniture in varying stages of repair or refinishing and put low prices on them—low for antiques, but too high for what was supposed to be a yard sale. If I were a dealer, or out for antiques, I'd have been pleased, but I left the lineup of broken-backed hall trees and hobbled rockers to another, bittersweet fate.

The next place was also a small farm, but better seas, at least from a saler's perspective. Six cars and trucks had pulled over, and I had trouble finding a spot to park off the country road. I headed toward the back porch where the seller sat, an old, creaky fellow with a long, gray beard that he wore to great effect with a bespangled, Uncle Sam stovepipe hat. He was clearly enjoying his sale, yukking it up with customers.

I gathered from overheard snatches of conversation that he was planning to release the junk that long had been locked up in his fragile barn, what had once served a dairy farm. Thus far he had liberated lots of old tools and bits of iron hardware, some of it hand-forged and weather-worn. Milk pails and bottles were scattered throughout.

A man approached him and asked, "Do you have any milking stools?"

"Two of them," he answered. "They're made of steel, not wood, and they're about this high." He slowly bent down with his palm, like he was petting a large dog. I sensed he wasn't sure if he wanted to show them to the man, or ready to part with them.

"I used to hunt raccoons on your property when you grew corn," the buyer said. I sensed he was trying to soften the man's resistance.

"That brings them in. They'll eat anything, but they like corn," the old man replied.

"I must have taken 125 here."

"There's no end to them."

"Rabies has thinned them out some."

"That's the only thing that can," the old man said and with that he picked up his two canes and hobbled toward the barn, opening it to reveal his hidden cache.

Yard sales, more than most of the other levels of used merchandising, have a genuine communal facet; that was why the buyer who wanted milking stools had to establish a connection, a history with the old man. A customer at Jack's Outback told me a story that further underscores this, and the generosity of spirit that sometimes accompanies a sale: "I saw an ad in the newspaper, 'Old couple breaking up household,' so I went, and I saw some nice flannel sheets. My wife likes flannel sheets, and I asked the old woman how much she wanted. She said $2, and I bought them. Then I said how I would be getting a big kiss when I got home, and she laughed and told me about their new littler house. Now, whenever I sleep in those sheets, I think of that nice old couple. It's a connection.

A yard sale is a way of saying, 'Don't make me throw this away. Take it and use it.'"

Fair prices, at least among occasional rather than permanent yard salers, is pretty much a standard; greed happens at all parts of human commerce, of course, but so little money is involved at this level of the used network the truly avaricious go elsewhere. Therefore the prices at another sale in Greenfield were satisfactory. The couple had a gorgeous hodge-podge of old tools, furniture, dishware, buckets of bolts and other hardware, and old wooden cheese boxes, all priced to go, nothing deemed too precious and smaller stuff for a dollar or less. It was a fine example of the "take-this-and-use-it" philosophy.

However, they were less conversant with dickering. A boy was whining at his mother to wait while he thumbed through a box of comic books, finding it hard to choose those worth a quarter. "How much do you want for the whole box?" his mother asked.

"Count them up, and we'll give you a price," the woman seller said. She obviously hadn't noticed the woman's impatience, because her offer forced the boy to sit in the driveway and continue to go through the box, counting. The seller should have given the buyer a figure off the top of her head and been done with it.

Yard sales are far too decentralized to be bound by rules, yet some unwritten precepts seem always in effect. Although weather is always a factor, the dedicated yard saler will still troll. One stormy spring Friday I went out in search of what had been advertised as a "Five-Family" sale. When I got there at 8:30 it was mobbed, cars parked in all directions for blocks. The sale didn't formally start until 9:00.

The sale was held in a garage that had been closed off into a den of sorts, with sliding glass doors; the weather wouldn't shut down this sale. I was attracted to a row of old shovels leaning against the outside wall, only protected from the elements by an eave. I hefted one and admired the patina on the carved wooden handles, the smooth way the handle fit the steel shaft—the tactile pleasure of the unity of metal and wood extending even to a modest garden tool. I already owned three of them and wasn't interesting in making a collection of shovels.

Inside, the sparse offerings spoke of the ferocity of the early-morning mob. The woman running the sale was sitting on a folding metal chair—the others were for sale—crocheting and watching a portable television.

Not looking for great bargains, I nevertheless snatched up a good, light winter coat, marked "new," though that was hardly the appeal, for $2. A couple knelt below the clothes rack and sifted through a box of vinyl records. They stood up with several records under their arms, but the crocheting woman wouldn't sell them individually, the opposite of the people with the comic books. "I have about seventy-six of them, and want to sell them all," she said. At least she had a bulk price ready.

Just then a woman came into the garage. "What's the price on the shovels?"

"Four dollars," the crocheter said, without missing a stitch.

"Four dollars for each?"

"That's right."

"Would you take two for one of them?"

She dropped her sewing into her lap. "I'll dicker. What about three?"

The customer nodded and went outside to pick one out. She came back inside and handed the woman $3 just as I was paying for my coat. We stepped outside together. "Those are nice shovels," I said as we passed the ones she had left behind.

"I've been trying to get my husband to spade up a garden," she explained. "But he keeps balking, saying, 'I'd have to borrow the neighbor's flat shovel.'"

I noticed the shovel she had picked out was scoop-shaped, the kind you'd use for shoveling gravel. I picked up a flat spade, the one with a silken worn handle. "This is the one you want," I said, pointing out the flat, sod-cutting edge, reluctant immediately to hand it over, the patina was so exquisite.

"Thanks! I see what you mean," she said brightly, setting down the scoop, grabbing the spade, and heading toward her car. "Thanks again," she called as she put the shovel in her back seat of her Lexus.

I thought about her dicker. She was probably the kind of woman who would squander any amount of money in a mall, but at a yard sale she felt driven to dicker, to save one dollar, even when she was unsure which shovel would suit her reluctant husband's chore. Like any other yard saler, she probably was not out on the prowl for a shovel; but when she saw the stack of tools leaning against the garage wall she likely recalled her frustration over her husband's procrastination and saw a way to motivate him, or at least remove one of the obstacles he had thrown up. The woman was willing to take a chance, for a couple of bucks, that the shovel would do the trick, and because I was there, she had the shovel best adapted to the job. The vagaries of the yard sale had combined to give her what she needed.

Some communities have begun asking people holding sales to apply for permits; their rationale is that this would discourage permanent, weekly sales. Those proposing permits claim sales are a traffic hazard, a nuisance to neighbors, etc., but they really want to exercise control for control's sake. It is futile, however, as the yard sale is a weedy enterprise, and its adherents are indomitable. Junger will prevail.

Chapter Twenty

❧

On the Curb, or,
The End Is the Beginning

W HEN THE MOVING SALE at which I sold my chest of drawers was over, a small mound of unsold stuff was left. I certainly hadn't overpriced anything—I wanted rid of *my* junk—but some things simply don't find their next owners easily. For instance, I had a blender I had priced at twenty-five cents, and a woman had stopped to look at it. She had bluish gray hair and had undergone so many face lifts she could clean her ears by brushing her back molars. The woman picked up the blender with two fingers. "Does this run?" she asked with a whine.

It once had worked, but I hadn't used it in years. "It's only a quarter. Take a chance," I answered.

The blender remained, along with two glass light fixture globes, a print of a red-tailed hawk, and a manual typewriter. I put them in a row on the curb with a sign reading FREE.

Within minutes of closing my sale, a long white sedan rumbled up to the curb, and a man leaned out the door to inspect what I'd deposited there. He picked up the globes, handed them to someone in the passenger seat next to him, and roared away. By morning the scavengers had gleaned every last item from my curb—except my typewriter.

It should be abundantly clear by now I don't usually throw things away, but the typewriter was the exception that proves the rule. I had used it all throughout college, cranking out paper after paper, without so much as a correction ribbon. The machine, a Royal Five, represented so many hours of pure toil, that rather than take it apart to save the screws and springs and other goodies, I gleefully took it down to the county recycling center. There I stood over a white metal bin, the recycling category for old appliances, typewriter in my arms. As I raised it over my head to hurl it into the pile of dented filing cabinets and scarred avocado refrigerators, I let out a little cry of catharsis. I doubt throwing anything away has ever given me such pleasure, or will again.

If a scavenger had picked up the typewriter, I would have as cheerfully forgone the pleasure of its ignominious end. This is the final arena of used trafficking, and it is wholly free. On any Sunday you can find scavengers on the slow cruise, eyeballing the tailings of that weekend's yard sales. Some indiscriminate gatherers will show up in the afternoon and offer yard sellers a blanket price for everything leftover, but the pure scavenger will wait until the end of the day and simply trash-pick. While you might hesitate over spending even a quarter for something, when something is free it's easy to decide if it might be useful.

Thomas Edison said that to be an inventor, all you need is a good imagination and a pile of junk. The same is true if you want to be a successful scavenger. You can find what you need, if you are able to look at something and "see the bones," as they say in the real estate business about a fixer-upper. You have to extinguish desire and need and simply accept what you find. Trash-picking is a Zen Buddhist enterprise. For instance, nearly every piece of furniture I own has been acquired from the curb; I had only to recognize the inner value, the repairable core.

One of my first trash-picking stories is about a modest acquisition, an end table of no certain ancestry someone had painted a dusty lime. I had been refinishing the woodwork on a house—for $5 an hour—and now could look beyond what time and taste had wrought on a painted castoff. I had refinished furniture before, but only good country oak pieces given me by my grandmother, things guaranteed to reward reworking. This piece had unknown qualities, but it was obviously solid wood. What's more, I had learned more techniques—being a good scavenger demands that you acquire volumes of otherwise useless knowledge—and I knew the latex paint could be removed with a sharp knife. I would not need the noxious chemical strippers I had been using on the job that my employer joked turned me a shade of green not unlike the paint on the end table.

Rescuing castoffs from the trash requires leisure and a complacency born of a lack of desire. The end table did not warrant the work I put into it: It was neither a valuable nor a rare antique. Likewise, the method

I chose for banishing its green paint was inefficient, but nearly as cathartic as smashing my old Royal Five. I spent any number of peaceful evenings sitting on my side porch, knife, sharpening stone, and strop at my side, scraping paint off each lathed leg with the care of a museum curator, discovering the straight grain of rock maple, undecorative but stout and clean, when exposing the top. The work was not hard, but it called for a close attention to detail and the willingness to imagine its final state of repair. I was inventing a new life for the table.

I've never met anyone in the used merchandise world who didn't trash-pick. Even the headiest antique dealer will rubberneck a pile of garbage for the sign of choice debris, and most have yarns about some fabulous find. Why would people discard things with so much utility, even value, left in them? Because they do not have junker vision, the ability to see those remaining qualities. It is also a matter of context, the same factor that makes a barn a better site for an antique store or yard sale. Once something is on the curb, it is, in the minds of mainstream consumers, tainted. When something is in the revealing light of the sun, no longer surrounded by walls, it looks forlorn, even tawdry. Scavengers are conscious of that trick of the light, and they can filter it to find the thing itself.

So when I saw an older couple carrying a lamp stand to the curb of a residential street in Saratoga Springs, I stomped my brakes. They had already deposited an oak library table with massive turned legs and a quarter-sawn oak top, wood cut at a 45-percent angle to the grain in order to reveal broad contrasts in dark and light—a wasteful but dramatic way to cut wood.

"Are you throwing these out?" I asked.

"Yeah. Why, do you want them?" the old man asked.

"Sure, I could use them," I said. "But I'll have to get my truck."

"My wife and I had these tables since we were married. They've been sitting in the basement, but they're good and sturdy. Let's just set them behind the hedge here so no one else decides to pick them up," he said, as though he was selling them to me and didn't want me to change my mind. He and I carried the tables behind the bushes. I noticed he was missing a hand and carried his end with the table balanced on his wrist stump, and I took off to get my truck. The tables were still technically on the curb and so fair game for any scavenger who came by. When I got back, with a friend to help, the couple had done a little more house-cleaning. An old wire wastebasket sat on the library table, and inside were two plastic grocery bags full of clothing. At first I was puzzled, but then I realized the couple assumed anyone grabbing furniture off the curb was poor and probably could use some decent clothing to wear as well.

I took the clothing, though the work shirts and trousers didn't fit me and eventually made it into my rag bag, because I didn't want to openly eschew the couple's misdirected generosity. The tables were the real gift. Both could be refinished with a knife. The veneer on the edges of the library tabletop had to be reglued and clamped, but besides that they were perfectly sound pieces of furniture, as the man had claimed, and the oak shimmered after several coats of tung oil. I considered pho-tographing both tables to show the old couple, but thought better of it. They believed they had bestowed some useful trash on someone who could not afford "real" furniture, so I didn't want them to see just how beautiful the tables had become. Likewise, I had seen a similar lamp stand, with a clover-shaped top, in an antique store for $400. I didn't want them to think they had made a mistake or that I had taken advantage of them. I planned to use the tables, not sell them, and in fact still do, and I wouldn't want to deter them from discarding other bits of choice junk, or tarnish their generosity with a modicum of cynicism.

Scavengers need people like that old couple to keep a steady stream of junk for the picking. College students are another excellent source of good junk, and, to paraphrase one of my scavenger colleagues, if you live in a college town, you simply must become a trash-picker. It would be foolhardy to resist. At the end of each school year, students empty apart-ments and rooms of their accumulated possessions. With limited storage space in their parents' homes, students jettison some really functional stuff; I even found a great Sony stereo, abandoned because the wires had jiggled loose inside the speakers. A couple of drops of solder, and the stereo was good as new. Even better, because it was free. When I lived in Oxford, Ohio, home of Miami University, an entire subculture of trash-trawlers materialized on the street on the morning after the last day of final examinations, a brother- and sisterhood of bandaged trucks, rattle-trap vans, and ancient sedans with trunks the size of front-end loader buckets. Ah, but the picking was sweet, with furniture, clothing, school supplies, books, and electronic gear. You name it, and the nearly fifteen thousand students retreating to their home turfs had abandoned it. It was the ultimate moving sale.

All people on the move, whether students or not, are fruitful sources for the bottom-feeding secondhand consumer. If you live in even a modest-sized town with a population of renters, the first and last of any month is prime picking time. And, as Bob says, if you can wait long enough, you will find not only what you want but what you need. For instance, lately Bob had been making the shift from vinyl to compact discs, maintaining his turntable so he could still play records scavenged for pennies or less. Soon after I turned up a portable CD player in an apartment house Dumpster. Likewise, when Bob's wife, Elaine, expressed an interest in taking up painting, I made another corollary find.

I was eating dinner at a corner sandwich shop when I saw someone carrying boxes to the curb across the street. I watched with interest as the pile grew higher, and I lingered over a coffee while the man finished the task. Then I paid my bill and walked over. It was a pile of art supplies, among other goodies.

All I needed to say to Bob over the phone was, "Scavenging alert: trash pile on Spring Street," and he soon met me at the site. From what I could tell from the nature of what he was discarding, the man worked as an artist/graphic designer for the local newspaper and was leaving behind supplies related to artistic media he no longer practiced or enjoyed. Among these were tubes of good acrylic paints, as well as brushes, T-squares, and other supplies. These we scooped up and loaded into the back of Bob's van. His wife wanted art supplies, and now she had them. There was plenty of other stuff to be picked, such as household goods like dishes, but we only took what we immediately needed, leaving the rest of the leavings to others. If you are an indiscriminate hoarder, you are doomed.

Sometimes, though, you just have to grab what you can when you see it. A news anchor from the local television station lived in the same apartment building as me while she was waiting for a luxury condominium to be built. When she moved, I noticed the Dumpster was overflowing, with more bags sitting nearby. It was Monday, and I knew the trash-hauling company would be there later that day, so I went Dumpster diving.

The broadcaster had unwittingly aided my scavenging by packaging all of her castoffs in clear garbage bags, so I could tell at a glance whether one was worth opening. This was a quick salvage operation, so I switched off my filter and took anything that might be useful or that I guessed one of my friends might want. In total, my partner Susan and I snatched a wire plant stand; a handmade wool afghan; a day pack containing a bonanza of pens, notebooks, and even a stash of quarters for downtown parking; decorative wicker baskets; new clothing with price tags attached; a video-tape player; leg weights; pewter decanter labels; a telescope on a tripod; and candlesticks and candles. How much escaped my rescue efforts I'll never know. Within a couple of days I found owners or users for nearly everything; everything, that is, except the leg weights. Exercise equipment remains the lowliest of castoffs, especially when in comes in electric pink. I had to throw them away again.

Raw material is among the best candidates for scavenging, and construction site Dumpsters are some of my favorite places to dive. In Oxford, Ohio, a local farmer and part-time preacher had given up raising corn for raising duplexes to rent to local faculty and graduate students at Miami University, a complex he called Calico Acres. When I rented one, the duplex was at the end of a dead-end lane, with nothing but fallow fields outside. Its semi-isolation was one of the reasons I had rented the place.

One morning, heavy earthmoving equipment moved in, and gangs of construction workers began erecting identical duplexes behind and beyond mine. While my precious isolation was gone, another benefit had replaced it: construction debris. At the end of every day, I noticed the workers started little fires and realized they were burning odds and ends. Construction workers waste tons of good lumber because it is time-efficient to do so. Because the duplexes were of two types, one- or two-storey, materials were ordered in bulk to the specifications of only two sets of blueprints. So when a twelve-foot 1x10 for soffits was too warped to be easily used, it was tossed aside and another put in its place. Like-wise, nothing less than five feet long was saved, so shortening a board left some very usable waste. These lay jackstrawed about the construction site and were readily picked and redeemed.

I used most of the wood to make sturdy storage boxes. I would never make wooden crates out of expensive new lumber, but scavenged lumber actually has more uses. The wood is free, so you are free to imagine, as Edison said, and complete whatever project strikes your fancy. When I had made enough boxes, I started making bookshelves. Then, because the flow of scrap cedar was copious, I made boxes and shelves for friends.

Still the workmen continued to toss board after board. When I moved, I gave a big pile of lumber to a fellow woodworker and scavenger.

I've made kitchen cabinets, workbenches, jewelry boxes, and garden trellises—everything you might think of out of lumber originally used as pallets, forms for pouring cement, and scaffolding. I have scavenged plate glass from closing retail stores for plant stands, replaced more than ninety broken windows with glass cut from windows left for the garbage truck after a house renovation. Renovations provided me with nearly all of the construction material I needed to fix up a fourteen-room Victorian house. When I replaced the crisscrossed lattice under the wraparound porch, I made every inch of it myself—3,000 feet of lath—out of scavenged wood cut on a table saw. What's more, I made it to the original 1900 specifications, so the porch retained its antique look. Renovation is the ruination of a classic old house.

Tools for turning raw materials into useful stuff also can be had on the curb, or wherever discards can be found. I used to work at a recycling center at Miami University, the proceeds of which benefited a day care center for the children of older students, almost exclusively women. In Ohio, without a bottle bill, recycling was lucrative, and most of our money was made on aluminum cans. However, we recycled plastic, glass, and steel as well. I got lots of windows through this source. One time an old man in a clunky old car, obviously a retired cab, pulled up. I walked over to help him with his recyclables, but before I could get there he stepped out, opened his trunk, and pulled out what looked like a doctor's bag.

"Here," he said, "see what you can get for this in scrap."

I took the bag from him—it was actually a metal toolbox—and nearly dropped it. The frail old man, dressed in a plain brown suit, had gingerly handed me fifty pounds of mechanic's tools. Socket sets have replaced the straight wrenches in most mechanic's tool kits, and the old man had tossed in several bunches of those, including some with Ford stamped on them, wrenches that used to come free with the Model T, helping to spawn its nickname "Fix Or Repair Daily." The old man also had adjustable wrenches, pliers, screwdrivers, and Allen wrenches—enough tools to fix most small machines. I cleaned and oiled the tools and painted the old box, saving them from the scrapper, and still use them now, fifteen years later.

An appliance salesman once told me every Electrolux vacuum cleaner has three lives: new, hand-me-down, and scavenged off the street, repaired, and used again. In fact, those who marketed them took this into account in the same way newspaper managers count the probable times the same newspaper will be read in a diner or barber shop when determining circulation. As with any level of the used continuum, though, successful trash-picking requires you make yourself available to the flow of goods, at any time. So, while Bob Miner, his daughter Allison, and I—all scavenger black-belts—weren't focused on junk the day we found the Hudson River Trading Company, there it was. We were delighted, once we crossed the Erie Canal into Mechanicville, to find out it was "big trash day."

Next to moving, big trash day is a scavenger's greatest bonanza. In most towns, one or two days a year are designated on which people can discard whatever is too large for their weekly trash hauler. Many people take this opportunity to unburden themselves of broken refrigerators and stoves and overstuffed furniture of the kind only Trink would love; others would look about their homes and ask themselves that heart-rending question, but one crucial to the junk-picker's quest: "What could I live without?" Those are the junk sutlers, the providers for the clan, and we were fortunate in Mechanicville. Every house was accompanied by a suitable pile near the street.

Assuredly this bounty had been already picked over by early-morning scavengers, but one joy of junk is that no two people agree on what is worth carting away. Ten junkers can sail by a mound of discards, and each will prospect it for something different than the last, that is, unless one of them is a doomed, indiscriminate gatherer and wants to hoard it all. A junk pile is less like a warehouse than a mine. In Mechanicville, each pile only hinted at its possibilities through what could be seen on the surface. With three fully committed scavengers eying the debris, we were sure to turn up many treasures.

We were driving my pickup, so we could afford to pick freely, yet prudence, and lack of storage space, demanded Allison stay her hand in picking up a wonderful—and not badly dented—metal double-door cabinet. She succumbed to an old typewriter stand, though, which we learned was only a *little* bent. When we picked it, the owner came out of his house to help us untangle it from other junk and to demonstrate some of its wobbly properties so we might better remedy them. I got a beautiful six-foot, four-panel door—obviously ripped from the ribs of an old Colonial house, because the board between the panels was sixteen inches wide. The door was made of pine and had been painted, but would easily refinish, so into the back of the truck it went. We could have picked all day, but we kept ourselves to these two finds. That day Bob abstained entirely, and I still marvel at his self-control.

Sometimes you can swap what you find for what you need, but first you must be integrated into the trash-picking tribe. For these connections I always rely on Bob. Once I found a chain saw when I was driving around scavenging for firewood for after a windstorm. When a thunderstorm takes down trees in towns, people will usually cut them into stove lengths and put them on the curb, knowing someone will stop to get them and help clean up debris. I pulled over in a posh neighborhood in Saratoga Springs to toss a dozen maple logs into my truck when a nearby garbage can revealed a Homelite chain saw, one with an all-cast-aluminum body. It was clearly from the 1970s, when saws, and heating with wood, became popular during the Middle East oil embargo. I imagined the saw had repeatedly stalled for its owner, and because it had been in service for more than thirty years, the exasperated sawyer had thrown it away. It still might work, or be fixed, so in the truck it went with the logs.

I took it to Eddie. Son of a salvage yard owner, Eddie lived at the bottom of the hill where Bob lived and had proved a valued member of the neighborhood because of his ability to fix anything; his garage was always abuzz with activity, a scavenger's command post. When I got there Eddie and Bob were digging an old boat trailer out from under mounds of other castoffs behind Eddie's house. Eddie used a forklift on the front of a tractor to move the stuff; when Eddie had work to do in his own accumulated pile of junk he didn't fool around.

Eddie immediately admired the chain saw, wanting to know where I'd found it. "You got there before we did," said a friend standing nearby who had been helping Eddie direct his forklift. These guys were veteran curb-shoppers and knew a good pick when they saw it. Eddie showed me the starter rope had stretched from repeated pulling and only needed shortening. It then started easily, especially if you understand "the gravity start." The Adirondack lumberman's way of starting a chain saw involved holding the cord in one hand and saw in the other, and, while pulling the cord, allowing the saw to fall away while being held in the other hand. This provided a kind of double-pull and would help start the most recalcitrant saw; I would have placed the saw on the ground, held it down with one foot on the housing, and pulled the cord—the safer, less effective way.

Eddie said these particular Homelites were great. They never wore out, "so they quit making them," he said with a knowing look. Eddie already had two of them stashed in a shack in the back with other fabulous, legendary engines, such as Johnson outboard motors. He had one boat motor that Bob coveted especially, so I gave Bob my newly picked chain saw, hoping at some time he could bundle it with something else and trade Eddie for the Johnson. It was all he needed. He had a great boat that someone had practically given him, and now a boat trailer, and I had managed to find other things for him to use, including several lengths of mooring rope someone had piled on the curb and a boat jack. Finding the jack was an adventure in itself.

I was patrolling on the last day of a town-wide yard sale when I stumbled onto a porch weighed down with new, made-in-China anvils, vises, and wrenches. "Let me know what you're looking for, and maybe I have it," said a man with a cigar-holder for a face.

"I just stopped on a hunch you might have a boat jack," I said. "A buddy of mine needs one."

"I got just what you're looking for," the man said, leaving his porch and leading me to an overstuffed garage with an equally endowed lean-to. On the floor lay old tools and machine parts, partially covered by leaves that had blown in around the sagging, wooden door. The man lifted up a sheet of damp, flaccid cardboard and picked up a pneumatic boat trailer tongue jack—the formal name for the gizmo. "If this one doesn't work, come back. I have a couple others that might do it. I used to sell trailers." The man wouldn't take a dime for it.

I triumphantly delivered the jack to Bob, cockles warmed by the notion that the scavenger tribe had once again joined forces to supply one of its number. The jack needed adapting and could only be mounted by rigging a series of clamps, etc., but it would do the job.

*

Jack Metzger, invaluable ally in my quest for all aspects of the second-hand world, first introduced me to Karen Koziol, or at least to her art, in a gallery in Cambridge, New York. Jack thought I should meet Karen because she made art out of discards, and not just any discards, out of pure, hard-to-redeem junk. Karen made usefulness by making art.

I met Karen for coffee and immediately knew she was a fully involved member of the tribe. Her eyes took on a sheen when I mentioned my interest in junk, and what followed was a spirited dissertation on its joys and qualities. Karen's art consisted of three-dimensional collages or assemblages, junk in communication with other junk. Entire pieces looked like a hybrid of knickknack shelf, Cornell box, Rube Goldberg contraption, and the random pattern of castoffs you might find inhabiting the corner of an attic. Most of the pieces had a lost quality, as though something was missing or misplaced, and we were looking at only part of the whole. Together the found objects created a narrative, micro-stories about something forlorn or forgotten. I realized Karen's work had the tone Mark Hackworth had been trying to photograph when we were traversing the World's Longest Yard Sale.

"I just like how some stuff looks," Karen said as she pushed a stack of pictures of her art across the table. The look she found appealing had a natural finish or patina accrued over time. Being thrown away was part of the process her materials went through on the way to becoming art. Anything after years of weathering outside had earned the physical properties giving it meaning. Wood with only traces of a finish, with the appropriate scars and weathering, also made good media. "And rust is good," Karen said. Her customers were usually people who also liked antiques, so they embraced her work because the pieces looked old. She never stabilized the pieces, slathering polyurethane over chipped paint, for instance, because she felt it changed the impact, making the assemblage look static.

In the snapshots I recognized porch posts, chair pieces, a carburetor from a lawnmower engine, wooden clothes hangers, coat hooks, pieces of old toys and games, and springs from beds or upholstered chairs, all united through Karen's eye. "Bicycle wheels are a favorite," she said. Karen chose by looking at stuff and imagining "what it could be part of."

She was particularly fond of doll parts, and friends who visited her in her studio found her boxes of arms and legs a bit gruesome. "I see doll parts as a way of humanizing a piece," she remarked, their faux humanness counteracting the mechanical nature of much of what she used in conjunction with them. Karen was not immune to original sources of the castoffs she appropriated, and she often wondered about them. "Everything has a history. It's like the pink and blue shoe forms I have. I have a bunch of them, and sometimes I wonder why someone would have so many." For the most part, though, Karen had to adapt the pieces to new contexts, inventing new ways to see them.

Karen and her husband, an architect, lived in a Colonial-era farmhouse in the hills near Greenwich, New York. "We like places with old worn treads on the stairs," she said. It was the second house they had fixed up, largely using scavenged building materials. They loved Gerry's junk shop, actually run by a junker named Harry Karp, Karen explained. The Gerry sign was left over from his son's half-hearted attempt at establishing an antique store. "He had really poor antiques, cheap veneered stuff," Karen laughed. When he gave up, his father took over the barns and became a junker. Karen remarked that he was a no-nonsense kind of guy, but I already knew that. "He's the door and window man," she added, though, with a glint of admiration. "We love that place."

Gerry's didn't yield the kind of castoffs Karen needed for her work; for that, only pedigreed junk would do. She went to yard sales for her stuff, but she complained, "you have to go through too much" to find what would work. She would also drive around town on what she called "Spring Cleaning Day," looking for good stuff on the curb. People familiar with Karen's art even helped by giving her things they found and thought she would like. Castoffs from all levels of the used network entered her assemblages. I even gave her the six-inch papier-mâché skeleton, a souvenir from the Mexican Day of the Dead ceremony, I had gotten from Colin Stair's tag sale for the Frederick Hughes estate. However, Karen loved it so much she claimed she would never use it in her art; she would hang it in her studio instead.

Much of what Karen used came from her own personal source, a pile of junk even Einstein might have envied. She had a dump. Behind their house, beyond a stone wall and down a ravine, people had discarded stuff for probably two centuries. "It's heaven back there," she sighed. It was so chock-full of junk she recalled working on a piece and remarking to her husband, "I need a bicycle wheel." He simply went to the dump and fetched her one. With such a wide selection, Karen was free to imagine anything.

Karen's need for junk was never far from her mind. No matter where she and her husband went, scavenging figured into the plans. So, prior to a trip to Great Barrington, Massachusetts, for a wedding anniversary, they checked the local papers for sales of used stuff. They spotted a notice that a junk shop was going out of business and having a one-day liquidation sale. That was not to be missed.

They nearly did, though. They got there fifteen minutes before the sale was over for the day, and the junker's treasure house "was all picked through, and only broken stuff was left," Karen said. That couldn't deter Karen, of course; she loved the broken as much as the weathered and aged. Seeing Karen and her husband eager to trash-pick, the junker gave them five minutes to gather what they could. For a dollar, he said, they could fill their station wagon.

They laid hands on an old shopping cart and started to run through the warehouse. "I told my husband it was like being in a game show," she said. A one point they found a tattered American flag, and they stuck it in their cart where it flapped victoriously as they careened about the place, gathering with an exhilarating urgency.

Karen even saw another artist she knew there, from Canaan, Connecticut, whom she described as making things out of junk "because he had to," a sentiment I was growing to understand. Annie Dillard once reported that a painter told her he painted because he liked the smell of paint; in order to make art out of junk, you had to love junk. So it didn't surprise me that she had stuff she didn't use because she couldn't part with it. For instance, she had found a clock face in her dump, with no hands but with a root growing through the center hole. "It would have been perfect for lots of pieces, but I just can't part with it," she said. Junk can be as ironic as Shelley's poem about the statue of Ozymandias. The imperfections bestowed by time corrupted its initial purpose but gave it new properties.

It was not unlike Wabi-sabi, a Zen concept that embraces the paradox that beauty can only be achieved through imperfection, impermanence, and incompletion. This concept pops up everywhere, in both humble and majestic renderings. In Gothic architecture, irregularities produce sublime effects in great European cathedrals, while in making Middle and Near Eastern rugs, weavers deliberately incorporated an error, believing any attempt at perfection would be an affront to Allah. For Karen, imperfection has been accomplished by time and by the fact that her materials are discards. The flawed nature of castoffs is a kind of liberation, Karen said, giving her permission to let something not be perfect. Even so, in each of her pieces, I sensed another incompletion suggested, like the open possibilities of a fine poem.

We left the coffeehouse, and I followed Karen to her house in the country. The old Colonial was striking in its severe, saltbox lines, with eight-over-eight windows symmetrically arranged in a distinctively non-Wabi-sabi way. Still, the age of the house, with its patina of paint layers, presented subtle imperfections to ensure its suitability for Karen's aesthetic. The nearby barn was more clearly apt for a scavenger. It was gone, burned long ago, and the rubbled stone foundation now sheltered a wildflower and perennial garden. As they dug the garden beds, more castoffs came to light; I saw some sitting on the wall, an iron splitting wedge and an axe head that had surfaced that spring. The barn was elegantly preserved in its new, ghostly, floral form.

Behind the flower bed was a bicycle perched on top of a lopped-off tree trunk, eight feet in the air. Karen smiled impishly when I looked from it to her with amused puzzlement. "That's my mother's bicycle," she said.

"What does your mother think of you putting it up there?"

"I think she's touched," she said and then told me that when her mother gave her the bike, she immediately thought to display it there. Her husband had warned her not to try to carry the clunky bike up there, "but you know, don't tell me I can't do something." She carried the heavy steel bike up a ladder and stuck the teeth of the pedal gear in a groove in the top of the log, where it stoically remained, like a highwire walker perpetually in the middle of an act.

Karen took me through the house, pointing out ancient, wide plank floors they had uncovered and saved. Her studio was in the back, part of an old pantry, and was long and narrow, perhaps 9 x 20 feet. It was lined with boxes of items, in categories, such as wheels or doll parts. Karen's workbench sat at one edge, protected by two "guardian angels," female figurines to which wings cut from soup cans had been added. The clock face with a root growing through the center hole hung nearby. Saws and other woodworking equipment sat at the other end.

Karen pulled other cherished items from her storage boxes and shelves; I was struck by the molars and incisors mounted on index cards, and though Karen didn't know what had been their original use, I speculated they were samples for a false teeth maker. She had lots of other items she hadn't used because she couldn't part with them, such as doll eyeballs with interior weights so they would open and close, and game boards painted by Portuguese immigrants on Cape Cod. The latter she considered art all by themselves.

Karen had very little artwork on hand to show me. It always sold well, and she had been cleaned out in her last show, when more than two dozen pieces had sold. Works-in-progress still lived in her studio, though, such as a wheel mounted on the end of a push mower handle—"I don't know where to go with that one," she said when I stooped to examine it. Another reason she had nothing at hand: Her art was now featured on Sothebys.com, the on-line version of the venerable in-house auction. So the used hierarchy came full circle.

Back outside, Karen pointed to a treehouse she and her husband had made for their children, entirely out of used, scavenged lumber, of course. Set in a tree on the edge of the yard, the treehouse marked the edge of the part of their property on which the children could play; beyond that, in the wood lot behind, was the dump, full of glass and rusty metal and a danger to small hands and feet, made more treacherous by being overgrown with brush.

Such a junk minefield was no obstacle for Karen. She had grown up on a farm and spent her idle summer days digging in old dumps on the property with her sister, earning a passion for junk early on. Karen had a few well-worn paths into the dump, and she led me through a briar patch and into the junk moraine. I began to scan the ground, and beneath the leaves and undergrowth lay hundreds of enticing bits; once more I remembered my days as a child scavenging in dumps for bottles and crocks to sell to Tara Antiques.

Karen picked up a ball at our feet and said, "See?" It was an old-fashioned hard rubber ball, and years in the dump had endowed it with fascinating fissures and textures. Then Karen took a few strides ahead of me, stopped abruptly, reached down at her feet with a shriek of joy and giant bloom of a smile. In her hand rested a doll covered in mud; she was on her way to replenishing her store of artwork. "You just never know what you are going to find!" she called out. It was a fine trash-picker's credo.

Conclusion

❧

Back Where It Belongs

A T THE END, used culture is outside of economics, even beyond money. Things take on attributes that have little to do with their original designs or intentions, finding new uses, new meanings. Even the vaunted law of supply and demand has been skewed; everything, after all, is unique at the secondhand stage. Nothing can accrue the same history, patina, or provenance as something else. Pride of ownership takes on strange and idiosyncratic features, because such pride has not been charmed into responding to advertisements. Mainstream retail is so available, consciously patterned, and abundant, you have to make a special effort to live on castoffs. Tapping into all levels of the network, pure scavengers must have a passion bordering on mania. It also requires a flexibility of mind that would astonish the best thinkers of the Renaissance. You have to enjoy resurrecting the forsaken.

Bob Miner told me I could see a genuine, full-throttle scavenger at work in Hadley, New York, in the Adirondacks, minutes from fashionable Lake George. Rodge lived on a mountainside, and from there gathered, fixed and lived the scavenging life to the full.

Bob and I made the expedition to Rodge's in the morning after what they call a "spring snow" in the North Country, as though you should *expect* snow in the spring, too. I was worried all of Rodge's stuff would be hidden under the new snow like the sandy mounds covering ancient cities in the Middle East, but I had no idea just how massive Rodge's collection would be.

Hadley and Stony Creek are in forgotten country, not full of tourists like Lake George or blessed with the heart-fluttering mountains of the High Peaks Region. This is just the woods, remote and pristine with a woodsy/impoverished population living in shanties and house trailers. Stony Creek has a population of about six hundred, but at least three thriving taverns. These mountain-top communities have remained sheltered from the kind of progress most of us take for granted. Some are nearly tribal; Allentown, for instance, is comprised mostly of people who have the last name of Allen—on both sides of their family.

At the foot of Hadley Hill, a dirt road made a steep ascent, carrying me, my pickup, and Bob as sidekick and guide. Bob had me slow down whenever we saw a lane running into the woods; Rodge's house was not well marked. People in these woods seldom bother with signs; if you don't know where people live, what business do you have visiting them? Bob had been to see Rodge, of course, but never often enough to have memorized the approach to his house. Several lanes, some perhaps only timbering roads, led over Hadley Hill.

Finally we saw a hand-lettered sign at the head of a lane that simply read GUNS in red paint. Rodge was much more than a scavenger of firearms—he was also a capable gunsmith. I turned onto the lane, then stopped; it was impassable, blocked by an armada of boats, as though a diluvian force had deposited them all on the mountainside. I backed out and immediately saw another lane fifty feet farther up Hadley Hill. It, too, led to Rodge's place. Bob said it hadn't been there the last time he had visited. Rather than clear the old lane, Rodge had simply bulldozed open another.

No gravel had been applied to the new lane, and it had the consistency of fresh pie dough, so I put the truck into four-wheel-drive and slipped and sloshed through the ascent, passing hollowed-out cars, upturned trucks, abandoned camp trailers. The lane to Rodge's looked for all the world like the bombed road out of Kuwait taken by the retreating Iraqis, without the grizzly "collateral damage." My truck sashayed wildly in the mud between these destroyed hulks, and each one loomed wickedly, first near my door, then Bob's. Above the lane I saw battalions of other vehicles and flotillas of boats, taking advantage of any level notch in Rodge's portion of Hadley Hill.

As the lane leveled off and we stopped fighting the sucking mud, my truck was met by a mass of migrating chickens, animals living in some of the vehicles and camp trailers. The chickens were as many-hued as their number, but they barely outnumbered the cats that also made Rodge's junk their home. Some of the cats attempted to run away, skittish as sparrows, and in a kind of feral panic. In attempting to climb off the top of a truck camper, two kittens slid down, face first, with the grace of someone falling off a fence. I saw motion inside the camper and a wisp of smoke from a narrow stovepipe, and I realized someone was living inside. My back rippled as I wondered how many unseen eyes had been watching us come up Rodge's lane.

Closer to the building, a many-additioned structure covered in waferboard, a mammoth black dog began barking frothily. Bob had told me Rodge's dogs were definitely not friendly, but this one was testing geometry by straining at a leash that seemed to get longer as we approached. The dog's snapping head was the size of a restaurant-grade microwave oven, and the cur's eyes glistened with alarm and fury, surrounded by Neanderthal brow ridges. We sidled through the mud, trying to keep a ruined truck between us and the beast, as we walked around the house or shop or barn or shed—it was hard to give it a name—to the side with a door. A large, unfinished barn, like an open machine shed, sat nearby and shielded even more vehicles and machines.

Rodge greeted Bob heartily at the door and shook both of our hands; he was an open, easy-smiling man with hands the size of a bunch of bananas, wearing tight red sweat pants, a sweatshirt, and, as a nod to the recent snow, an insulated vest. "That's one enormous dog you have out there," I said.

"He'd probably lick you to death if he got loose," Rodge said. He locked the dog inside the building whenever he left; combination burglar alarm and booby trap. Despite Rodge's disclaimer, I pitied anyone who chanced to pry open a window and climb into the dog's waiting jaws.

While part of the building contained broken guns and boxes of ammunition, Rodge essentially had a machine shop with metal lathes, drill presses, and grinders. His workbench sat in front of a large picture window. From there he could fix anything. What he couldn't fix, his wife Betty could. She was known as a first-class outboard motor mechanic.

According to Rodge, he had no real skill, no mastery of an individual trade. He had a knack. A knack is a propensity for fixing things, and as a concept differs greatly from simply being handy, or being a jack-of-all-trades. Rodge was neither. Both required too much direct, applicable knowledge and logic. Rodge explained the knack was more intuitive. He might be presented with something to fix—an engine, refrigerator, or firearm—and though he had never seen one like it, or knew exactly what was wrong, he could simply find his way into the solution. I imagined the knack as a parallel skill to what I call the scavenger's eye. In the same way that I can look at a pile of discards and see one piece that needs rescuing or can be used, Rodge could see the inner workings of a broken machine, conjure out the relationship of the parts, and figure out how to make it whole again.

"I don't have any money," Rodge said through a guffaw. Obviously a knack was not necessarily lucrative; in fact, Bob had told me Rodge and his wife had been down to their last $35 the winter before. I was looking at an old musket with silver inlay hanging on the wall. It had a cracked stock and had a pleasing old repair with brass and tightly wound wire. Rodge saw me fingering the patch and immediately offered to seriously discount it.

I wasn't interested, but as I shook my head I let him know I didn't mind that the gun was damaged. I didn't want to insult him. "Wire was the duct tape of the nineteenth century," I replied, repeating a Jack Metzger original.

Rodge beamed, and I sensed that he was making a mental filing. He'd use that line in the future. I soon learned Rodge had a bulging storage of facts rivaling his crowded acres. He was looking at a German Mauser and began commenting, "People say there's always been a Germany, but there was no Germany until 1870. Before that it was all a bunch of duchys and principalities. Bismarck was probably history's greatest diplomat. . . . " Information and opinions streamed out of Rodge continually, associative strings of notions, confirming for me that scavengers are often petty savants. The quality of mind that produces those with a knack must also sharpen the intellectual or remove the filters so random facts drift in.

While we were there, people drifted in, packing and pulling in a steady stream of stuff for Rodge to buy or fix, or with lists of stuff they wanted. Rodge sat at his long, blackened workbench receiving them all. He had found his place in this mountain community, an identity carved out of the needs of others and out of the volume of used merchandise upon which such needs fed. Rodge went to auctions, estate sales, and anywhere else in the continuum that might provide him with sustenance. Dragging it all to his mountaintop refuge, Rodge then became a hub of junk, and those in the know relied upon his reservoir of castoffs for their own scavenging livelihood.

For some of us, the modular identities so readily available never fit, and our lives are not easily retailed. Like Rodge, or nearly any of the people I'd met in the used trade, mainstream culture cannot provide all of the components they need for fulfilled, if not prosperous, lives. Living among the throwaways of mainstream culture, and choosing not to participate in first-level commerce, is a declarative stance.

Bob Miner was once again my entrée when I went in search of the consummate scavenger. Actually, I didn't have to look far. I had already gazed from afar at his collected castoffs on King Road in Middle Grove, New York. Hugo had a virtual farm of junk. Bob had done business with Hugo, relying on his stores for parts and for other choice items. Lately I'd been admiring a metal sled Bob got from Hugo, the kind you'd expect to see behind a dog team. Bob planned to use it when clearing ski trails in the woods, pulling it during the winter behind an all-terrain vehicle. That was exactly the thing only Hugo might provide.

Not everyone celebrated Hugo as much as Bob and me; I had long ago dubbed him "The Reverend Hugo," in deference to his whole-hearted devotion to scavenging, the kind of purity that is rare these days in any arena. Hugo's fifty-acre castoff ranch had been the subject of many articles in the local paper, and not a few court injunctions and appearances. True inhabitants of the area knew and loved Hugo for who he was, if not, as in my case, for what he represented. Those who had arrived in recent years, buying five-acre plots and plopping McMansions on them, turning the countryside outside of Saratoga Springs into an exurban wasteland—and I guess my sentiments are apparent here—had been trying to force Hugo to clean up his property. What they were asking was impossible, though. Hugo's property was clean, cluttered surely, but organized and clean. "Clean up," in this instance, was a euphemism. They wanted Hugo to do away entirely with his vast collection of junk.

They wanted Hugo to stop being Hugo and be instead a less affluent version of themselves.

There might be a dark side to scavenging, as there is to every endeavor that becomes a compulsion. As with indiscriminate trash-pickers, those who become seduced by the sheer availability of castoffs can lose themselves to it. Especially if you have a native organizing knack—as essential in collecting junk as a knack for fixing something—and you can efficiently gather, store, and retrieve stuff when called for, you appear to have no reason to be reasonable. What is the harm in gathering whatever you want, whatever gravity sends your way, if you have room? The material world, for those who can be available to it, is a generous place.

Those who are not organized, however, are in real peril, and for them perhaps such gleaning can turn sinister. People whose houses turn into surreal composts of decades' worth of newspapers, bills, worn-out shoes, tea bags, and slightly used paper towels have a genuine affliction, though I am loath to call it such. What harm is done, either to the collector or to the world, by someone who cannot discard anything, knowing that everything can be reused, reclaimed, and therefore should be saved? Defending those who have mounds of castoffs might seem strident, but I find myself strident in the defense of virtue. In a larger culture in which making something disposable is a marketing *goal*, it seems natural to lay plaudits at the feet of those who resist the urge to comply.

Hugo's homestead sat on both sides of the road and stretched for more than a thousand feet. His house, what is called an eyebrow Colonial, sat on one side, and a clearing where once a barn must have stood sat on the other. Quaint name aside, the house was a patched-together affair, as Hugo had obviously used whatever leftover siding, tar paper, waferboard, and sheet metal he had rustled to keep it intact. If the house had been a dog, you'd be calling a vet. The once hilly land on which the house stood had been judiciously leveled by a backhoe to better store Hugo's great treasures, and, given the absence of a barn, he had gone to great lengths to house and protect them. Welded angle-iron racks held rows of windows and sheets of metal, and both an old school bus and a panel van had been pressed into service as sheds. Hugo's collection included a head-high pile of metal lawn chair frames, a rack garlanded with lengths of chain, pallets full of truck tire rims and engines, makeshift shelves protecting lumpish machine parts, and more, stretching for many acres into the recesses of the woods. Hugoland was especially welcoming to huddled masses of tractors. He had several in varying degrees of repair stationed on his acreage, some sinking with resignation and exhaustion and adding to the overall curb appeal, at least for inveterate scavengers like me.

The day Bob introduced me to Hugo, he was inspecting the cargo on the back of his big flat-bed truck parked in front of his house. Hugo smiled broadly when he saw us, and as I got closer I could see the writing on his purple T-shirt: "Don't Like My Attitude? Call 1–800–WHO-CARES." Hugo was a big man who didn't have a beer belly, as I at first thought. He was actually built solidly, muscles primed from tossing about the carcasses of machines. As chief scavenger in the lower Adirondacks, Hugo got quite a workout. "I'll take a piece of junk the size of a pony if it has one little screw I need," he laughed.

Hugo's collection had appeared a bit more deliberately arranged than I would expect from an all-purpose scavenger, and I was right. People had been showing up and taking photographs, Hugo reported, and he suspected some of them were trying to put him out of business, so he was trying to keep things *looking* neat, at least. He knew he was being watched. Others had been more appreciative. Art students from the local liberal arts college, Skidmore, regularly visited, asking for permission to take photographs of his assemblages, recognizing the deliberate quality of his surroundings and finding that quality, coupled with the patina of weathered iron and wood, compelling. I shared Hugo's drive for making order out of chaos and understood how he, and the art students, might admire the sheer physical presence of his junk.

Hugo is not just a collector and arranger, though. Junk is his livelihood. He told a story that illustrated the way junk found its way to him and then to the next owner. Another nearby scavenger had died, one who had succumbed to pressure and kept most of his wares behind a high privacy fence. His son was liquidating the father's collection. To the last scavenger standing go all the goodies. Hugo attended the estate sale.

The son had used four carbon dioxide gas canisters as legs for a makeshift table on which he was displaying wares for sale. Hugo spied the canisters and had a hunch he might be able to use or sell them. At first he offered the son a dollar apiece for them; he was led behind the fence into the field and saw the old man had collected many more.

"How much do you need if I take all of them?" Hugo asked.

"I suppose there are two hundred," the son said.

"I'll give you fifty cents apiece, but there are more like three hundred," Hugo said. The more canisters, the better the price should be on each one. Buying bulk still operated, even at the level of absolute junk.

The deceased scavenger had been charging people to haul the empty canisters away, removing the brass valves to sell for scrap, and then stashing the rest in the acres behind his privacy fence, hoping someone would want them someday, probably never expecting to die first. Hugo was the scavenger for the job, though, and he and the son piled them onto his flatbed. Hugo was then the proud owner of a minor mountain of gas containers.

Hugo then did some research on how to find a use for his new collection. He didn't use the computer, claiming to have no use for it, but instead relied on the word-of-mouth information that circulates among scavengers at all levels. Eventually he found a man in Ohio who, though he couldn't use the style of canister (with a rubber ring on the bottom), referred him to someone else. This guy sent out a semitruck for them; Hugo spent all day loading it. He sold the canisters for $9 apiece.

Making money is not really the point for Hugo, though. Acquiring is his profession, passion, and central drive. Hugo led Bob and me to the side of his house to show us some anvils, for instance, pronouncing that they were worth about a dollar a pound, just in case we might be moved to secure one for ourselves. All of these anvils were special: they were broken. Anvils have two ends. The square end is called the heel, and the pointed end is the nose. Hugo had found one anvil with the heel broken off. When Hugo failed to sell it, he put it aside, and in short order took in two more, also without heels.

So there they were, perched on black locust stumps Hugo had saved from some firewood cutting job. He now had a collection of them and appeared delighted that each of them was damaged in the same way. It takes a lot of effort to crack off a substantial chunk of an iron anvil. Bob, Hugo, and I speculated on who had done the deed, and why, but mostly basked in the marvel of it all, at the great fortune which had brought all three together under Hugo's aegis. Likewise, Hugo had just brought home a half dozen cable pulleys from overhead cranes that he had bought at an auction for $10 when no one else would bid on them. Hugo planned to make them into winches; never mind that he already had two winches. "The mice are nesting in them," he laughed. The more the better.

Hugo simply couldn't stand to see things wasted and had stepped in when many things were about to be discarded. His property was an expanse of potential, and he kept his materials stashed in groupings in order to emphasize their former and future usefulness. The pile of aluminum lawn chairs was a monument of sorts to the usefulness of aluminum pipe framing, while the alikeness of gas barbecue grills spawned the clearing full of them he had in the woods that Hugo blithely called "Grill City." Everything that needed a shelter had one; even overturned buckets protected engine parts from the elements. To the uninitiated, Hugo's acres of junk appeared to be random, even an eyesore. I was sure, however, of the usefulness of most of it and that the good Reverend knew where everything was stored.

Whether buying a grouping of fine china from the Frederick Hughes estate at Colin Stair's heady auctions or picking up hundreds of used industrial canisters after another scavenger has died, buying used is a self-declarative act. It announces that you have a category of knowledge to back up such acquisitions. You know how valuable or useful they are. It also declares you have settled on a relationship with the physical world. You have discovered some symbiosis, so that great *objets* or a plentitude of junk must come home with you in order to continue on its journey, on the great *hadji* all used merchandise must undertake in order to be established in the world of useful things. The act of buying used requires the faith that such a journey will eventually be completed.

Living within and on the used network is also an act of self-definition. Hugo and Rodge are viewed as outlandish, even outlaws, but only because they have placed themselves outside the boundaries of first-level consumerism. Everything they or anyone gathered, from the doodad collector to the hoarder of rusted machines, was a part of who they know themselves to be. This might be a surface realization, so someone with a wonderful collection of country primitives also might enjoy a simpler life. However, the definition is more apt to involve the intangibles, the personal tentacles that reach out from someplace deep and crucial and enfold that rusted kettle, battered blanket chest, or extraordinary silver candelabra. Scavengers are also salvagers, and part of what they save is often some intrinsic part of themselves. Perhaps once you have opened up the door to those full and solid connections with the world of castoffs, nothing you find on the shelves of a department store will ever fulfill you again. However, thousands of auctioneers, antique dealers, junkers, and yard salers are available to appease even the most ardent scavenger heart.

Works Cited

Interview with Bob Hebler, WAMC 90.3, Albany, New York, May 10, 2002.

Brecka, Shawn. *The Beanie Family Album and Collector's Guide.* Norfolk, VA: Landmark, 1998.

Haines, John. *Fables and Distances: New and Selected Essays.* St. Paul, MN: Graywolf Press, 1996.

Kaiser, Laura Fisher, and Michael Kaiser. *The Official eBay Guide to Buying, Selling and Collecting Just About Anything.* New York: Simon and Schuster, 1999.

Kunstler, James Howard. *The Geography of Nowhere.* New York: Simon and Schuster, 1994.

Roberts, Ralph. *Auction Action: A Survival Companion for Any Auction Goer.* Blue Ridge Summit, PA: Tab Books, 1986.